COSTA RICA
RICA
ALIVE!

Bruce Morris

HUNTER

HUNTER PUBLISHING, INC.
130 Campus Drive, Edison, NJ 08818
☎ 732-225-1900; ☎ 800-255-0343; Fax 732-417-1744
www.hunterpublishing.com
comments@hunterpublishing.com

Ulysses Travel Publications
4176 Saint-Denis
Montréal, Québec, Canada
☎ 514-843-9447

Windsor Books
The Boundary, Wheatley Road, Garsington
Oxford, OX44 9EJ England
☎ 01865-361122; Fax 01865-361133

ISBN 1-58843-323-4

*This and other Hunter travel guides are also
available as e-books in a variety of digital formats
through our online partners, including
Amazon.com, BarnesandNoble.com and NetLibrary.com.*

Cover photo: Buddy Mays/Travel Stock Photography
All other images © Bruce Morris
Maps by Kim Foley MacKinnon & Kim André,
© 2002 Hunter Publishing, Inc.
Index by Nancy Wolff

2   3   4

www.hunterpublishing.com

You can view Hunter's extensive range of travel guides online at our website. Now you can read excerpts from books that interest you and view the table of contents *before* you buy! We also post comments from other readers and reviewers, allowing you to get a real feel for each book. All transactions are processed through our secure server.

We have guidebooks for every type of traveler, no matter the budget, lifestyle or idea of fun, from dive guides and hiking books to volumes that inspire romantic weekend escapes!

Top-selling guides in our **ALIVE!** series include: *St. Martin & St. Barts; Martinique & Guadeloupe; Dominica & St. Lucia; Miami & the Florida Keys* and *Aruba, Bonaire & Curaçao.* Click on "Alive Guides" on the website and you'll see all the other exciting destinations covered in this series.

Active travelers should be sure to check out our ***Adventure Guides***, a series aimed at the independent traveler with a focus on outdoor activities. Adventures can be as mild as beachcombing on a deserted shore or hiking a rugged hill, or as wild as parasailing, hot-air ballooning or diving among shipwrecks. All books in this signature series offer solid travel information, including where to stay and eat, transportation, sightseeing, attractions, culture, history and more.

Log on to www.hunterpublishing.com to learn about our other series – *Landmark Visitors Guides, Romantic Weekends, Nelles Guidebooks* and *Travel Packs* and more.

About the Alive Guides

The **ALIVE!** series was started by Arnold and Harriet Greenberg, who also serve as series editors. The Greenbergs founded the world-famous bookstore, The Complete Traveller, in New York City.

Arnold has co-authored *South America on $40 A Day*, as well as *Alive!* guides to St. Martin & St. Barts; Aruba, Bonaire & Curaçao and Buenos Aires & the Best of Argentina.

Harriet has co-authored *Alive!* guides to the US Virgin Islands and St. Martin & St. Barts.

We Love to Get Mail

This book has been carefully researched to bring you current, accurate information. But no place is unchanging. We welcome your comments for future editions. Please contact us at:

Costa Rica Alive!
c/o Hunter Publishing
130 Campus Drive
Edison, NJ 08818
comments@hunterpublishing.com

About the Author

Bruce Morris has traveled and lived in the US, Europe, Asia and Central America sampling the food, fishing, diving music and good life. He received a B.A. in Journalism from College of the Potomac, where he worked as photographer and designer at the rock magazine *Third Ear*. He has written for a wide variety of magazines and newspapers and wrote *HTML in Action* published in 1996 by Microsoft Press. He founded *The Web Developer's Journal,* started and managed the Internet department at computer manufacturer Gateway 2000, served as Director of Technology at Carlton Online in London and COO of Europe Online. He is an avid diver and angler. He lives with his wife, cats, dogs, horses, ducks, several guitars and other creatures at their farm in East Tennessee.

Acknowledgements

No author can do his job without the support of family and friends. I could not have written *Costa Rica Alive!* without the enormous tolerance of my wife and the editing skills of my mother. Dr. Paul Kanciruk tried to keep me from committing scientific and editorial faux pas. At Hunter, Kim André and Kim Foley MacKinnon have been much more patient than they should have been. In Costa Rica, I want to thank Felix for his tremendous help. Alfonso Martino at Hotel Martino Resort & Spa allowed me to use his wonderful hotel as a base for my San José activities, taught me new things about cooking and eating, and entertained me long into the night over Italian wine. Shawn Feliciano and all the staff at Silver King Lodge provided some of the most exciting fishing I've ever done and fed me well at the end of the day with by far the best food I've had in Costa Rica. Natalie Ewing and Michael Kaye at Costa Rica Expeditions provided me with vital tour information, hospitality and an Internet connection (no small thing, this). Bradd Johnson and Pedro Garro made sure I experienced the beauty of the sea and forest around Drake Bay. The Bug Lady and Carlos opened my eyes to what can be seen in the forest at night if you know how to look. Lauren and Toby Cleaver welcomed me into their warm home and tolerated my rusty guitar playing. Captain Mike in Matapalo, Diana and Milton Lieberman, Glenn Jampol, Captain Tom in Herradura, Judy Heidt, Marco Montoyo in particular and many, many others gave me hospitality and friendship. Thanks to you all.

Contents

OSA PENINSULA & GOLFO DULCE

SOUTH CARIBBEAN

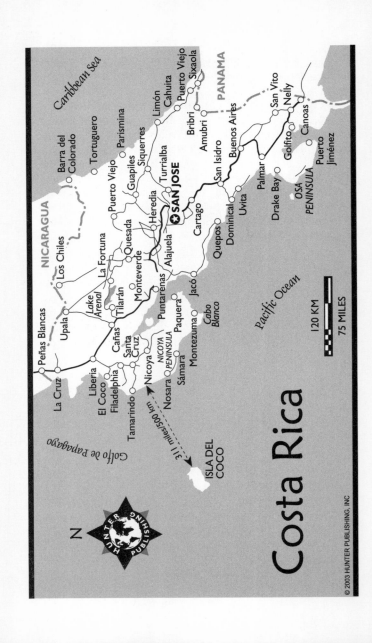

Costa Rica

© 2003 HUNTER PUBLISHING, INC

Introduction

More times than I can count, I have pulled up in front of a lodge in Costa Rica, gotten out of my car and said to myself, "What a lovely, tranquil spot. Look at those flowers, look at those trees, listen to the birds, hear the surf, smell that air!" There are hundreds of stunningly natural, serene places to stay and visit in Costa Rica. Plus, the country is friendly and comfortable for visitors. But Costa Rica is much more than nature, wildlife and serene settings. Costa Rica has the lure of the tropics in one of the most pristine settings left on earth, and is home to a natural, peaceful culture of interested, friendly and outgoing people. It is a small and compact country with the best environmental protection laws and public awareness in Latin America. It's easy to travel around, and has great lodges, beaches, volcanoes, surfing, fishing, diving, rafting and food. You can drink the water.

I've traveled extensively around the world and have found only one or two places that I love as much as Costa Rica. And I'm not the only one who feels this way. Thousands of immigrants from all over the world – North and South America, Europe, Asia – have decided to make Costa Rica their home.

Costa Rica is known as the Switzerland of Central America. It has no army, a thriving economy based on established democratic traditions, and a well-educated and healthy populace. The country is rich in agricultural and natural resources and has preserved more of its territory in national parks and nature preserves than any other country in the world. This has attracted visitors from all over the planet and has built the tourist industry into a well-developed and justly famous success. Development officials from leading and Third World countries come to Costa Rica to see how it has been done and to try to understand ways to transplant Costa Rica's success to their own countries.

Still, Costa Rica does have problems. There is poverty, crime and corruption; greedy people with short-term interests rape the land as they do everywhere. It rains a lot. But the success and good feeling of Costa Rica far outweigh any drawbacks and make it one of the best places to explore in the world. The Costa Rican people (***Ticos***, as they are fondly called) welcome visitors and offer their unique brand of friendliness and charm.

A trip to Costa Rica is an unforgettable experience to one of the last places on earth where tropical rainforests teem with wildlife, volcanoes erupt, the surf crashes against pristine beaches and the seas are healthy and full of fish. The warmth of the people and the wonderful climate are unparalleled.

I am not paid to say these things about Costa Rica; my job is only to describe it. I love the country and want to share the good feelings and rich experiences it has given me. Skip Disney World; skip Las Vegas. Even if you have only a week off, come to Costa Rica.

A Brief History

Costa Rica is different from its neighbors. It's more prosperous, better-developed, its people are better educated and healthier, and the country is free from war and insurrection. A long tradition of democracy ensures peaceful transfers of political power through well-organized and fair elections. The traditions of the country, the personality of the

Costa Rican people themselves and the country they have built have been profoundly influenced by the history of the region.

First Inhabitants

In the early 16th century, at the time of the first European visits to Costa Rica, three distinct indigenous groups populated the region: the **Chorotegas**, the **Bruncas** and the **Térrabas**. Since Costa Rica is smack-dab in the middle of the land bridge between North and South America, a long procession of migrants had moved through the area, leaving behind traces of their cultures and genes. Some groups settled in the area. Over several thousand years, newer arrivals presumably competed or assimilated with the populations they found. The Chorotegas were refugees from oppression in Mexico and were probably the last immigrants before the arrival of the Europeans, who continued the tradition of competition and assimilation. Currently, only about 2% of the population is of indigenous origin.

Indigenous Cultures

As a result of colonial conquest and imported disease, Costa Rica has a much smaller indigenous population than other Latin countries. Most of those remaining are clinging to mountain farms far from population centers. In southern Costa Rica, **Bribri**, **Boruca** and **Cabecar Indians** have almost homogenous reserves. Some **Chorotegas** can be found in Guanacaste. Lack of health care and social services continues to contribute to a low standard of living, and high rates of alcoholism. Borucas continue to speak their traditional language and maintain some traditional cultural practices. In San Vito and

Ciudad Neily, Indians wearing traditional dress may be seen.

Columbus Arrives

On his fourth voyage to what the Europeans called "The New World," on September 11, 1502, Italian explorer Christopher Columbus landed at what is now known as Limón and claimed the area for his sponsor, the Queen of Spain. The indigenous population reportedly welcomed the party, even though the Spaniards shot them, seemingly for sport, and in other ways treated them abominably. A subsequent explorer, Gil Gonzalez Davila, observed indigenous tribal chiefs wearing gold ornaments (probably brought to the area from South America and Mexico and handed down over generations) and named the area Costa Rica or, as it translates, **"Rich Coast."** Later immigrants moved into the area as migrating Indian groups had for centuries, assimilated, and found little need to compete with the locals. They found no gold to speak of.

Spanish Settlers

Costa Rica has a very homogenous population. Almost all the population is of direct Spanish descent. Unlike neighboring Central American countries, there are almost no ethnic minorities. The first conquistadors brought diseases, such as smallpox and syphilis, to which the local inhabitants had no natural immunity and, as a result, the native population was decimated. The few who survived these new diseases fled to the mountains, leaving an empty, fertile land for the mostly Spanish settlers who moved in with their cattle, corn, sugar cane and later, coffee and bananas. Indigenous resistance to Spanish oc-

Introduction

cupation of their lands continued into the early 19th century. Only very small numbers of Africans and Asians were brought to the country for slave or cheap labor. The descendants of these groups continue to provide local color in the Caribbean coastal areas, as well as delicious fried rice concoctions you'll see on menus.

Since 16th-century explorers found no gold, mainstream empire builders mostly ignored the area for the next few hundred years. The Spanish settlers who found their way to Costa Rica were left to fend for themselves. Those who survived built a tradition of self-sufficiency and independence.

Independence

Initially, Costa Rica was part of Guatemala Province, which gained independence from Spain in 1821. A month or so later, the news filtered down to Costa Rica. In 1838, benevolent dictator Braulio Carrillo declared Costa Rica to be an independent country, earning himself a place in history as the "father" of Costa Rica. A few years of political and military conflicts ensued. This period also saw the introduction coffee as a cash crop and the rise of the great coffee barons.

In the 1850s, the interesting and colorful American freebooter, William Walker, organized a mercenary army and effectively took over Nicaragua and attempted to invade and take over Costa Rica. This led to the spontaneous creation of a Costa Rican "Peoples' Army," which marched on Walker's positions in the north of what is now Guanacaste Province and tossed him out. Walker continued an interesting career as a would-be dictator until his unpleasant demise. He was shot in the head by Honduran police.

In 1889, the government attempted to impose a presidential candidate. This action led to a revolt by the population, who demanded a direct, general election. The success of this revolt resulted in the long tradition of peaceful Costa Rican democracy. A contested election in 1948 (the building where the ballots were stored mysteriously burned down) led to a short war between government forces and poor loser candidate Dr. Rafael Angel Calderon, followed by an interim government led by a former exile Jose Maria "Don Pepe" Figueres Ferrer. He banned communism, set up extensive social programs, established a constitution, eliminated apartheid laws, legalized women's right to vote, nationalized all banks and insurance companies, set up presidential term limits, disbanded the army, proclaimed the international neutrality of Costa Rica and then, if all this was not enough, handed the government over to the rightfully elected candidate and moved out of the way. These great deeds earned him the gratitude of the population, who subsequently elected him to two separate terms as president.

Since then the electoral process has been so peaceful and honest that schoolchildren are used to keep order at polling stations. Sons of both Calderon and Figueres have been elected president as candidates of the National Liberation Party (PLN) and the Social Christian Unity Party (PUSC). These two parties have traded power on and off peacefully during a long period of stability. Even so, both parties have generated complaints of nepotism, corruption and economic stagnation. See the section on *Government & Economy*, page 10, for a description of the current political climate and the recent interesting presidential election runoff.

Costa Rica Today

Tico Culture

The people of Costa Rica are memorable for their friendliness. Ticos have a unique and wonderful character. They are mild-mannered, humble yet proud, non-violent, open-minded and progressive.

★ **DID YOU KNOW?**

Costa Ricans have earned the affectionate name "Tico" from their tendency to overuse the Spanish diminutive "-ico" or "-ito," transforming words like taco (taco) into *taquito* (little taco) or *postre* (dessert) into *postrecito* (little bitty dessert).

Pura vida (pure life) is the most useful expression you can learn. It has many uses, and can mean Hello, Goodbye, Okay, Thanks, Great, and even Cool.

Costa Ricans strive to leave a good impression and not seem to be boastful, crude or unhelpful. ***Quedar bien***, which roughly translates as "to remain well," is used to describe this trait. Rudeness, even to thoughtless gringo tourists, is almost unheard of. Ticos want to like you and want to be liked. It is exceedingly difficult to pick a fight with a Tico, and it is a rare Tico who won't casually return a smile.

As you drive through the countryside, it's polite to wave at people you pass on the road. If they don't wave back, it is probably because they simply didn't see you. There is almost no animosity toward North Americans and other gringos. Costa Ricans don't feel they are inferior or superior. They are genuinely curious about visitors and like to practice their English with a bit of casual conversation. They are comfortable striking up conversations with strangers on buses, in lines or simply walking down the street.

The word buenas *all by itself is used to express "good morning, good afternoon, good evening."*

As a show of respect, it is very important to learn a few unique Costa Rican phrases. At the very least, learn to say, "Good morning, how are you?" This effort shows that you are interested in their culture and is rewarded with broad smiles and friendliness. ¿***Como amaneció***? means, "How did you wake up?"

and is a nice way to greet someone you know (even casually) in the morning.

Few of the Latin immigrants and illegal workers in the US are from Costa Rica. Costa Ricans like their country and the life they lead, and few are willing to spend more than short periods living in the US.

"Tico Time"

Tico time (*hora Tica*) is different from the frenetic pace of North American business time (*hora Americana*). However, it is not as casual as Mexico's "*mañana* time" Jamaica's "soon come," both of which leave tourists wondering if punctuality is in the local vocabulary.

So relax; you're on vacation. This is the tropics and you'll overheat if you get too excited. Do build some time for unexpected delays into your plans though. Ticos are sometimes late for appointments or seem to "forget" them. Scheduling numerous business meetings in one day is impractical. Getting anything done in a bank, including changing money, takes a long time.

Ticos rarely correct mistakes I make when conversing in their language, but they don't laugh at them either.

It is perfectly polite to refer to Costa Ricans as "Ticos" and "Ticas." Likewise, Ticos politely refer to North Americans and Europeans as "gringos" & "gringas."

Religion

Most Costa Ricans are at least nominally **Catholic**, but evangelical denominations have made definite inroads. Immigrants from Europe brought **Quakerism** in the mid-18th century and many of their followers settled around Monteverde, where they maintain a close-knit society. Quakers are famous for cheese-making. On the Caribbean side, especially south of Limón, **Rastafarians** peacefully smoke the holy herb and wear their trademark "dreads" relatively undisturbed. In most cases, churches welcome visitors.

Education

With a 95% literacy rate, Costa Rica is one of the best-educated country in Central America. School attendance is mandatory up to the ninth grade, and children wear uniforms supplied by the government. The sizable middle class has a high percentage of college-educated people.

The Costa Rican government spends almost 30% of the national budget on education, but many schools are lacking in basic teaching materials.

A vigorous free press and access to international television stations ensure awareness of the outside world and international issues. Ecological topics are stressed in school and the average Costa Rican is more aware of humanity's negative effect on the earth and what we can do about it than does the average North American. As you drive through the countryside, small villages and local schools seem to be everywhere. English is taught beginning in primary school, but computers are nonexistent in most schools.

Government & Economy

Government

Costa Rica has enjoyed a stable, democratic government for over 100 years. It is very similar to the US government, with an **executive branch** consisting of a president, two vice presidents and their cabinet; the **legislative assembly** consisting of 57 individually elected representatives (*Diputados*); and the **judiciary**, which is made up of civil, criminal and constitutional courts. The president is elected for a single, four-year term. *Diputados* and vice presidents are also elected for four years.

Unfortunately, corruption in high places is a problem in Costa Rica, but not to the extent of some other Latin American countries. It is tolerated by many who see it as a way of getting things done efficiently (?) and as a way of evening the balance between the average guy and the upper class. Newspapers allege that many development projects are slow and poorly run due to *chorizos* (literally, "sausages") or bribes.

Political Parties

ML	Liberation Movement
PLN	Party of National Liberation
PAC	Citizens' Action Party
PUSC	Social Christian Unity Party

Current Political Climate

A new president, television personality and psychiatrist **Abel Pacheco**, was elected in 2002 after a spirited and well-run election. One of the candidates, **Rolando Araya**, hired discredited US political strategist Dick Morris to advise his campaign. The election was so close that a runoff was necessary to determine the winner. In the recent national elections, women won 19 of the 57 seats in the legislative assembly, an unusually high percentage for Latin America.

The top political issues are poverty as well as underdevelopment of infrastructure.

Green issues are on everyone's mind. The average person is well aware that the unique ecological richness of Costa Rica is the main draw for tourists who contribute enormously to the economy. Development issues, such as building dams for hydroelectric plants and drilling for oil off the Caribbean coast, are in contention.

The country is remarkably stable, with no guerrilla groups lurking in remote areas kidnapping tourists and shooting up military convoys. And there is no military whatsoever. Perhaps the lack of a huge military budget is one of the reasons Costa Rica is better developed and more peaceful than almost any other Latin American country.

Although poverty is probably the biggest problem facing the country, there is a large, well-educated middle class that seems to lead a vibrant, satisfying life. An upper class group of families leftover from the days of the coffee barons is accused of being richly high above the rest of the people and hogging the best business opportunities for themselves and their cronies.

Attitudes

Machismo & Women

Most Latin men may find incomprehensible any objection to their macho flirting and casual politically incorrect comments to females. Many consider it their duty to flirt and make flattering (they think) comments to almost any female they encounter. Non-Latin females may find this uncomfortable, but try to remember that you are not in your own country and things are simply done differently in Latin America. Objections to the macho attitude may be received with puzzlement and resentment. That said, Costa Rican men do not tend to be as chauvinistic as stereotyped, and many Costa Rican women may feel insulted if they don't receive a few *piropos* (flirtatious comments) when walking down the

Marianismo *is the female equivalent of machismo.*

street dressed to kill. Women strive to be reliable, quiet and supporting of the family, no matter what the men may be up to. This type of behavior is considered to be the highest, most admirable female quality.

Gays & Lesbians

Macho Costa Rican men are not tolerant of gays and lesbians. In fact, many Costa Rican men do not believe that lesbians exist – they simply can't imagine that any woman could not be completely bowled over by their macho, manly qualities. Although there is a gay culture in San José and other towns, most gays and lesbians remain firmly in the closet and do not flaunt their lifestyles. Once again, as a guest in a foreign country, discretion is a good idea.

Some gay- and lesbian-friendly clubs and bars are listed in the After Dark *sections.*

Retirees

Costa Rica has many North American and European retirees who came looking for an economical and healthy place to live. For the most part, the government and people welcome them. Bureaucratically, it can be an effort to secure permanent resident status. Many people live permanently in Costa Rica, even though they are required to leave for two days every three months in order to renew their visa.

Costa Rica is by far the most prosperous and healthy country in Central America. The infrastructure, while not completely up to North American or European standards, is well developed and reliable. The water is safe to drink, there is electricity and telephone service in almost all parts of the country and health care is sophisticated and economical. The climate is superb. What is amazing is that even more retirees haven't filled the country to the bursting point like what has happened in Florida.

Many North American and European men, and more than a few women, find Costa Rican mates and start new lives.

It is interesting to note that the US has a large number of legal and illegal immigrants from Central and South American developing countries looking for jobs – accepting even the most menial positions. But few Costa Ricans are among that group. Costa Ricans generally have a good life and future prospects at home and don't need to leave to seek their fortune. Amazingly, I have seen the police in Tamarindo and Dominical mount raids rounding up young illegal gringo immigrant restaurant workers to be shipped back to the countries they came from: the US, Canada and England!

Music

Besides the ever-present brain-dead US pop music, most of what you will encounter musically in Costa Rica is the Latin sound, which breaks down into a few common categories: **salsa** is usually fast and danceable (the term is often mistakenly used to cover a bunch of lesser-known musical styles); **merengue**, Dominican in origin, is also fast and danceable but without the many variations of salsa. Most people would be hard-pressed to tell them apart. You may also hear some *trova* and *nueva trova*, which is Cuban pop, usually a bit on the bubblegum side, but some of the old stuff is great. *Punta* is Latin rap apparently stomached by aficionados. **Reggae** certainly isn't Latin but is very popular on the southern Pacific coast and in surfer bars. Popular bands include **Cantoamerica** and **Editus** (instrumental jazz).

Check the Tico Times for live music listings.

Art

Most of the galleries in Costa Rica are in San José, with a few notable exceptions such as Monteverde. Look in the regional chapters for listings for local galleries. Some Costa Rican artists create moving and valuable works. **Barry Biesanz** has his studio in Escazú and is well-known wood for sculptures. A few Costa Rican artists, such as Sara Morales re known for oil and watercolors. The best collectable artwork is usually old ceramic or woodcarvings. There is some "new" Costa Rican art seen in some upscale hotel lobbies.

Language

Costa Ricans speak Spanish in a very personal and unique style. They are particularly fond of using diminutives, such as changing *pequeño* (small) to *pequeñito* (cutely small), or *niña* (little girl) to *niñita* (cute little girl). See the list of local slang and **Ticoisms** in the *Appendix*.

Anyone living in North, Central or South America is an "American." If you are from the States or Canada, you should refer to yourself as a Norteamericano, Estadounidense *or* Canadiense.

Be sure to insert the delightful Tico expression **pura vida** into your vocabulary. *Pura vida* (literally translated as "pure life") is a very useful expression roughly meaning "thanks, sure, OK, hello, see you later" and other things.

Don't worry about speaking proper Castilian Spanish in Costa Rica. Forget the fancy lisping you were taught in high school and just go for it.

No matter how badly you mangle the language, the Ticos won't laugh at you.

Ticos will be glad that you are at least trying. The main problem will be Ticos will almost never correct your mistakes and, if you utter even three or four words in Spanish, off they will go in colloquial Spanish, leaving you puzzled in their linguistic wake. Try saying, *Habla despacio, por favor,* and they may slow down for a few moments.

Food

Tico meals almost always include meat, poultry or fish. Meats are usually fried or grilled. The most common cooking oil is lard. Low-fat cooking is not something that happens in Costa Rica. Salads are popular and almost every meal comes with some form of rice and beans. Corn on the cob (*elote*), and baked or fried yucca frequently accompany meals. A grilled chicken with rice and beans Tico-style can be quite good.

The most typical Costa Rican meal is a *casado* ("married"), which consists of a piece of fish, chicken, pork or beef married with a wide variety of side dishes including yucca, potatoes, rice, beans, pickled vegetables, bread, cabbage and tomato salad, plantain, avocado – usually all of them. A *casado* is always a filling and economical meal. Funky-looking roadside restaurants usually serve a fantastic *casado*.

Hotels and lodges offer spectacular breakfast buffets that usually include the local favorite *gallo pinto* (spotted rooster), which is basically cooked rice quickly stirred into black beans with some garlic and onions. Served with locally produced *Lizano* sauce, *gallo pinto* quickly becomes addictive and is one of the first things I miss when I get back to the US after a trip to Costa Rica. Costa Ricans typically eat fried eggs with tortillas, a slice of cheese and fruit along with their *gallo pinto* for breakfast. You can wolf down such a meal at roadside stands for under $2 in most places along with strong, sweet coffee.

Stomach upsets from eating local food are almost unheard of; you can enjoy the interesting local specialties without fear.

Fruit

One of the very best things about a trip to the tropics is the chance to eat fresh, exotic tropical fruits. Papayas; pineapples; mangoes; star fruit; tiny, sweet bananas and unusual citrus fruits, ar for me, the stars. Tourists and locals eat piles of fruit at breakfast and it is common to be offered fruit for dessert at lunch or dinner.

Papayas come in both yellow and red varieties with the less common red ones usually being sweeter. Pineapples are the white variety and, although delicious, are usually not as sweet and juicy as the ones served up in Hawaii. Bananas like you find in grocery stores in North America are everywhere, but

You'll see plenty of pineapples and bananas on your travels. Costa Rica exports huge quantities of both.

try to find some of the tiny ones, as they are especially sweet and flavorful. Melons are common and are an everyday item on the breakfast buffet. From time to time you are likely to be offered weird fruits you've never heard of before – absolutely give them a try!

Seafood

With both Caribbean and Pacific coastlines and a thriving fishing industry, great seafood is one of the outstanding menu items in Costa Rica. **Dorado** (Mahi-Mahi), **tuna** and **snapper** seem to be served in every restaurant and are almost always fresh and delicious. Shrimp, lobster tails and other crustaceans are also common, although lobster is usually overpriced by North American standards. Farm-raised *tilapia* is another fish you'll be offered and has a sweet flavor and flaky texture. I gorge myself on fish when I visit the country and now find most fish back in the US to be uninteresting and not so fresh.

For a small fee most hotels and many restaurants will cook your catch.

While staying near Puerto Jiménez one December, my brother caught an enormous dorado (60 lbs., 25 kilos), some of which we cooked outside over a wood fire that night making for one of the most memorable fish dinners I've had anywhere. We gave huge chunks away to neighbors and ate more ourselves the next night.

Keep your eye open for ***Pargo Entero*** (whole red snapper) on restaurant menus. Fried or grilled and usually served whole with the head still on, this is one of the best-eating fish in the sea. Visit the restaurant Banco de los Mariscos just outside San José in Santa Barbara de Heredia (see page 153) for a reasonably priced seafood feast.

Wine, Beer, Local Drinks

Costa Rican wines are, uh, interesting, but local beers are good. There is one brewing company that puts out several tasty brews. *Imperial*, *Bavaria Negra* (darker stuff) are not bad at all and locally brewed **Heineken** is very similar to the light, hoppy brew found in the US. **Kaiser**, sometimes referred to as *"esposa"* or "wife," is a non-alcoholic "beer" you will see on menus sometimes. It is best avoided. Bavaria comes in light, regular, and dark (*negra*), my favorite, and is a bit more flavorful than the other local brands. *"Una cerveza, por favor"* will get you a beer. *"Bavaria por favor, una negra sí tenga"* will you get you the best beer in the land.

Local eateries almost always offer delicious *refrescos*, fruit smoothies made with either milk or water and fresh fruit. Blackberry, banana, papaya and watermelon are common choices. *Refrescos* should not be missed! Drink lots of wonderful Costa Rican **coffee**.

Guaro is the local firewater and should be sampled carefully. Chilean wines such as *Concha y Toro* are reasonably priced, available in most restaurants and can be quite good. *Casillero del Diablo* is one of the better choices. It would be a good idea to try a few at home before you go. Wines can be quite high-priced in Costa Rica since there are heavy import duties from most countries. Chile and Spain seem to be favored in the Customs shed and are usually better priced than French or California wines.

*The best rum is **Centenario**. I find the ever-present Nicaraguan **Flor de Caño** usually leads to early exuberance, followed by headaches and, possibly, regret.*

The Land

Volcanoes

On clear days, puffs of smoke and refrigerator-size chunks of lava hint at internal indigestion.

The plates of the earth's crust grind together in a long line that snakes down through Central America from Canada to Tierra del Fuego, which makes for lively volcanic action in Costa Rica. A series of volcanoes that are dormant, active, or thinking about it run right through the middle of the country. Several of them are easily accessible and of interest to visitors. **Arenal**, with its perfect cone shape and almost daily puffs of smoke and nightly displays of red hot lava flying through the sky, is one of the best volcanoes for viewing anywhere in the world. **Poás** and **Irazú** are an easy full-day or half-day trip from San José. **Rincón de La Vieja** looms over the northwest of the country and features hot springs and bubbling pools of mud.

Arenal

Arenal can be reached by car from San José in about four hours.

One problem with volcanic sightseeing is clouds. Arenal is almost always socked in, and many tourists spend their time there hiking through the rainforest or bird-watching hoping for a break in the cloud cover. I've spent six days there over three separate trips and never seen more than the base of the cone and hundreds of monkeys and birds. The volcano emits frequent ominous rumbles that sound kind of like a jet plane taking off, providing tourists with a consolation prize if the cone is hidden.

At night, pieces of flying hot lava and red pyroclastic ejections stream down the sides of the cone, providing spectacular views. Many area lodges are arranged so guests can watch the volcanic fun with their chin on the edge of the pool or from the restaurant. The best rooms allow you to watch the action without getting out of bed. It is too dangerous to hike anywhere near the crater itself. Another major eruption could come at any time. The last one occurred in 1968, killing hundreds of people and thousands of cattle. It covered hundreds of square miles with choking volcanic dust. Years later the dust has helped make the area one of the most fertile ranch lands in Central America.

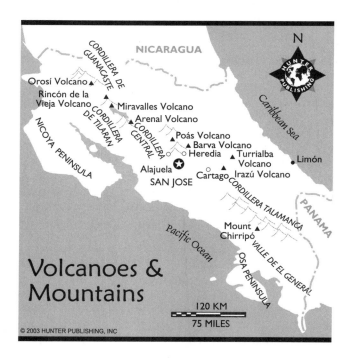

Volcanoes & Mountains

120 KM
75 MILES

© 2003 HUNTER PUBLISHING, INC

Introduction

There are no accommodations in the area that can be called "luxurious," although most are comfortable. **Arenal Observatory Lodge** (see page 174) is closest to the action. **Tabacon Hot Springs** is a great place to soak your bones and, although at first glance it appears to be just another cheesy roadside attraction, it is definitely worth a visit. The nearby **Tabacon Lodge** is one of the better lodges in the area (see page 177). Both the hot springs resort and the lodge have been built directly over debris left from the last ruinous eruption. Volcanologists predict that the next eruption will likely send a deadly pyroclastic flow of lava down the same route, incinerating everything in its path. How quickly we forget!

Poás

One of the best national park headquarters buildings in the country is about a five-minute walk away from the Poás crater and has a gift shop and restaurant. Poás is an easy drive from San José, but be sure to get there very early, as clouds usually cover up the view by mid-morning. The park and shop are open from 8 am-3:30 pm. Be sure to try the tamales and the excellent coffee.

The main crater at Poás is awe-inspiring, but the short walk uphill to the small crater lake is barely worth the effort.

To get to Poás, you go right through coffee country and near the headquarters for both Duka and Café Britt plantations. Combine a trip to the volcano (go there first) with a coffee tour. The main crater is worth a look, but clouds can obscure the view completely.

Irazú

Irazú is also close to San José and is an easy daytrip. In 1963, it blew muddy ash all over San José and the surrounding area, ruining the coffee crop but enriching soil for subsequent years of great coffee. It continued this unpleasantness for almost 20 years but is now laying low. Visitors can view five craters. The landscape surrounding the craters is so desolate it resembles the moon, according to astronaut Neil Armstrong. Theoretically, it is possible to see both the Pacific and Caribbean coasts from the peak, but, rarely happens due to cloud cover. The contiguous national park includes a small portion of protected cloud forest.

Rincón de La Vieja

In the far north, in Guanacaste Province, Rincón de La Vieja offers spectacular views of northern Costa Rica and Nicaragua. It blew in 1995 and is still considered active. There is a wide variety of smoking, bubbling craters and a hot springs in which visitors who feel like being parboiled can soak. Clouds usually cover the peak. Anyone driving around Liberia toward the Nicoya Peninsula will see the massive mountain hulking in the distance.

Flora

Because of Costa Rica's varied terrain – mountains, lowlands, beaches and estuaries – a wide variety of habitats exists, promoting growth of more plant species than almost any other country. Truly tropical rainforests, high-altitude cloud forests, dry forests and estuarine mangroves swamps exist within a short drive of each other. It would easily be possible to visit all these types of vegetation in the same day. Due to this richness in environments, Costa Rica is well-known for its plant life, particularly orchids, bromeliads and other spectacular flowering species.

*Orchids, brome-
liads & bego-
nias bloom by
the side of the
road.*

Unlike forests in North America, which tend to be
mostly pine or hardwoods, tropical forest feature
huge variety with hundreds of plant species crowd-
ing into a single acre. This wide variety of plants
supports many species of bird, animal and insect life.

Fauna

Wildlife in Costa Rica, even within Costa Rica's
national parks, is diverse, unusual and, for the
most part, hidden. The first wildlife most visitors become aware of are usually insects. Flies, mosquitoes
and no-see-ums annoy; butterflies, ants and beetles
delight. As you might expect in such a heavily forested region, the wildlife is camouflaged by the trees
and dense vegetation, so you'll need a guide if you
expect to see much. Tropical forests are home to
iguanas, caimans, crocodiles, howler monkeys, spider monkeys, capuchin monkeys, squirrel monkeys,
toucans, brown-throated three-toed sloths, Hoffmann's two-toed sloths, anteaters, otters, bats and
over 100 species of reptiles.

*Other wildlife
includes cats
and tapirs, but
these are seen
by only a select
few travelers.*

Don't expect to see ocelots and cougars lolling
around under trees for the benefit of whirring tourist lenses. Poison-arrow frogs are easily observed,
along with an amazing array of over 60 species of
strange and stranger frog and toad cousins.

Bird-Watching Bonanza

Costa Rica is directly in the main path of migratory
birds escaping North American winters heading for
the warm south. Every schoolchild learns that birds
fly south in the winter. Most of them pass through
Costa Rica or make it their final southern destination. The skies are peppered with birds. If you focus

your binoculars directly up into a seemingly birdless Costa Rican sky, you are likely to see hundreds of birds, from thousands of feet to miles up, milling about or passing through. Kettles of hawks almost invisible to the naked eye move through on bird free-ways. At any place in the country or in towns, the sounds of birds fill the air night or day. Little brown birds and large spectacularly colored birds seem to be everywhere. The number of identified bird species in Costa Rica changes constantly, with the most recent number said to be about 900.

Costa Rica is indeed a bird-watcher's paradise, one of the top birding destinations anywhere. From the resplendent quetzal and the scarlet macaw to reticulated pygmy owls and a stunning variety of trogons, beautiful and fascinating birds are a major attraction, even for visitors who have never expressed more than a casual interest in birds at home. The number and beauty of the birds casually seen anywhere in the country is astounding.

Be sure to get a copy of The Birds of Costa Rica, *by F. Gary Stiles & Alexander F. Skutch, before you go.*

Hard-core birders are pleased with the variety of birds they see in any part of the country, but favorite birding areas include **Corcovado** in the Osa Peninsula for macaws and toucans; the cloud forests of **Monteverde** for quetzals and hummingbirds; and the **Caribbean lowlands** for yellow-throated vireos and scarlet-rumped tanagers.

Binoculars are a "must-have" item for any visitor to Costa Rica.

Cats

Many kinds of interesting "big" cats inhabit Costa Rica. For the most part they are endangered, because they require quite a bit of space and farming, ranching and urban development are constantly eroding their natural habitat. They are rarely seen by residents, so don't expect to be taking pictures of cute spotted kitties lying about in trees. These cats are shy and very rare, and when they are seen, it is usually for only the briefest of moments. Widespread development usually keeps them way back in the hills. They avoid humans.

Costa Rica's Cats

Jaguar (*tigre*) – the king of cats, jaguars are rarely seen. They're endangered and keep to the remote areas of the largest preserves. They are occasionally seen in or near Corcovado and Tortuguero National Parks. Usually yellow with black spots, but pure black "panthers" have also been reported. They can get quite big, weighing as much as 330 lbs. (150 kilos) – as much as a pony.

Puma – similar to the large North American mountain lion, pumas are generally light brown with no spots.

Ocelot (*manigordo*) – ocelots are seen more frequently than most of the other cats, are beautifully spotted and grow to be as big as a German shepherd.

Margay (*tigrillo* or *caucel*) – spotted and about the size of a house cat, with a white chest.

Oncilla – the smallest of Costa Rican cats; it is difficult to distinguish from the margay, being spotted with a white chest.

Jaguarundi (*león breñero*) – the size of a small dog, they are light brown, with no spots, and have short legs.

I have been lucky enough to encounter two of the big cats in Costa Rica. I saw both in my headlights crossing a remote dirt road just after sundown outside Puerto Jiménez in the Osa Peninsula. The sightings lasted about five seconds each. One was almost certainly an ocelot – it was about the size of a large dog and had the classic spots associated with the large cat. My most vivid memory of the second sighting is the small, very round ears – not at all like the pointed ears of a common tabby. This one was much smaller – about the size of a beagle – and was also spotted. My guess is it was a margay or very young jaguar. One of my friends reports seeing a large black cat (about the size of a German shepherd) crossing a field outside his dining room window in the same area. Fishing guides in the Tortuguero area tell me of seeing jaguars swimming across the river. If you are lucky enough to see one, even very briefly, the excitement will keep your heart racing for quite some time.

Insects

If you look at it in the right way, Costa Rica has a wealth of insects. Thousands of species have been identified and more are being discovered all the time. Giant beetles, butterflies, weird spiders and unusual scorpions abound.

Surprisingly, mosquitoes are not as big of a problem as you might expect; huge swarms seem ready to devour you in some parts of the country but, for the most part, they are so terrible.

Tracie, "The Bug Lady" (see *Tours*, page 334), provides some wonderful information about Costa Rica's tiny (and some not so tiny) insect population.

INTERESTING INSECT FACTS

(Provided by Tracie Stice)

Sexual cannibalism before, during, or after copulation is not a given for all spiders. In fact, some species of male spiders are dedicated house husbands. They do housework such as web repair, and even take out the trash; that is, they remove bits of leaves or debris that may have fallen into the web. Such domestic situations are eagerly sought and are the subject of fierce fighting between rival males. For other species, such as pallid garden spiders, the "kamikaze" male is only able to mate once positioned in the female's fangs – and always dies in her embrace.

The most conspicuous of all **cricket songs** is the so-called "calling song," used by males to attract a mate. Some are audible for over a mile. After the female arrives, the male then begins the courtship or love song, a quiet serenade that induces her to mate. Remarkably, after mating, males of some species call out the "triumphal song." This last song may reinforce the mating bond and stop the female from searching out another mate before she lays at least a few eggs.

On their nuptial flight, **queen leafcutter ants** typically mate with seven different males in one evening, each of which die shortly after mating. After this one wild night she will never mate again, but will use the sperm she received from all seven males to fertilize her eggs one by one. The sperm, some 250 million, will be kept alive as free-living cells in her spermatheca and will be parceled out as needed over her 15-to-20-year life span. She will produce an egg every two minutes.

Once mating has been accomplished, females of many insects produce **antiaphrodisiacs** to discourage the advances of additional suitors. One female ground beetle sprays a chemical "mace" that, within 10 seconds of contact causes the hapless Romeo to enter a deathlike coma for up to three hours.

Many male insects equip their mate with a sort of **chastity belt** to ensure fidelity. Male heliconian butterflies attach a "stink club" that not only blocks the female's genital openings, it smells so repulsive that other males immediately turn around and fly in the opposite direction.

Mosquito Repellent

The most effective mosquito and no-see-um repellents contain DEET as the main active ingredient. You can check the label of the different brands before you buy to make sure you get one with plenty of oomph. You'll need insect repellent with plenty of oomph. The strong brands get as high as 90%. That's the kind you want. Beware of local mixes with very low percentages of DEET. I'm not sure of the personal health consequences of spraying the stuff all over you for weeks at a time, but I can assure you it does keep the bugs away. There have been times when I would have happily drenched myself from head to toe in diesel fuel or other, even more noxious substances just to get away from mosquitoes. Take more than you think you will need. It's cheaper to buy mosquito repellent in the US, Canada or Europe, so stock up before you leave. If anyone knows a more pleasant repellent that works under heavy-duty mangrove swamp conditions, I would like to hear about it.

Monkeys

There are four types of monkeys in Costa Rica: **spider**, **capuchin** (white-faced), **squirrel** (*Titi*) and **howler**. You will certainly at least hear the howlers. They make one of the loudest noises of any animal. The first time I heard them in the distance I thought it was a bunch of big dogs barking but quickly realized the sound was not quite right for dogs. Monkeys are still hunted for food in some areas, but in many places they are not terribly shy of humans and often come within a few yards. Monkeys can be a problem for farmers and suburban homeowners, who wish they would stay out of their gardens as they tend to raid papaya and banana trees. Some lodges have problems with monkeys helping themselves to the breakfast buffet if the dining room is left unattended.

In some areas it is a good idea to close the doors and windows, since monkeys or coatis (related to the raccoon) may come inside and rummage in your luggage.

Sloths

Sloths move incredibly slowly and can spend days without moving perceptibly at all.

Costa Rica is home to two- and three-toed sloths. Both are relatively rare, but sharp-eyed visitors to rainforests may encounter these lethargic creatures. Because they are interestingly lazy, sloths are often high on visitors' "must-see" list but can prove to be a disappointment when seen. The reason for this is precisely because of the character trait that makes them interesting in the first place – their sloth-like nature.

When you see a sloth it will often simply appear as a barely discernable blob of fur high in a distant tree. I once watched a sloth from a canopy platform in the Osa National Wildlife Refuge for a bit over four hours and, as far as I could tell, it never moved so much as an inch. It simply existed as a ball of dirty fur wrapped around a distant branch. I'm glad I saw it and was pleased it was hanging around while I observed birds and other wildlife but, in the end, it was a bit like watching grass grow.

Life in the Sea

Coral Reefs

Although known as a scuba diving and snorkeling destination, Costa Rica is lean on true coral reefs. The Pacific coast has interesting volcanic formations with a few pieces of coral scattered around, but there are no proper reefs. The Caribbean coast has quite good ones especially off Manzanillo and farther south. Diving and snorkeling can be spectacular there when the sea is calm enough to get out.

There has been some damage to the reefs from agricultural runoff and earthquakes around Puerto Viejo, but the reefs to the south are extensive, reasonably healthy and definitely worth a look.

Crocodiles

Gigantic (and dangerous) **crocodiles**, a few **North American alligators**, and the occasional **caiman** (a type of croc) make things interesting in the rivers and swamps. The rivers on the Caribbean side and mangrove swamps on the Pacific are where most people see them. Once in a while a croc will be seen off the beach near Manuel Antonio.

The Tárcoles river bridge on the main road from San José to Jacó is a good spot to get a safe, close-up view of huge crocs.

Dolphins

Pantropical spotted, **spinner**, **bottlenose** and **common dolphins** frequent Costa Rican waters and often cavort about for the benefit of tourists. Few sea creatures are as entertaining and enjoyable. They jump, play, and perform gymnastics around the bows of passing boats, seemingly for our pleasure as much as for theirs.

Dolphins are so common that it is likely you will see some on almost any boat ride you take.

Pods of dolphins numbering in the thousands are sometimes seen offshore along the Pacific coast. I encountered an enormous pod about 41 km (25 miles) off Drake Bay. When we first spotted the dolphins I thought there were maybe 10 or 20 of them jumping in front of the boat. Then a few more appeared behind us, and a few more behind those. Within minutes the sea around us was busy with thousands of dolphins jumping and rolling almost to the horizon. The pod was moving slowly to the north following a school of small tuna and many of them took time out to visit our boat and check us out. We stopped and watched the magnificent sight as they swam by. When we jumped in the water with our snorkeling gear on, they didn't really play with us and kept a certain distance but they definitely came around to have a look to see what we were up to. None came close enough to touch but hundreds swam by and seemed to say "hello" before going on about their business.

Manatees

West Indian manatees are herbivorous aquatic mammals, long hunted for food and for hide so tough it has been used for industrial belting. The species is teetering on the edge of extinction and is truly endangered. Although once common throughout the Caribbean, there are only small pockets of them left in Florida, Cuba, Costa Rica and a few other countries. Cuba probably has the largest population. Their decline is, of course, tied to loss of habitat. A few are killed every year in Costa Rica by being run over by boats or by poachers for food. Other causes for their demise may include pollution from agricultural runoff, entanglement in fishing nets and shrimping trawls, and in the blue plastic bags used to protect bananas in the enormous banana plantations. Thousands of these discarded blue bags are seen all over Costa Rica and many find their way down streams to manatee habitats.

It is estimated there are only a few hundred manatees remaining in Costa Rica and most of those hide themselves in back corners of rarely visited swamps and lagoons northwest of Barra del Colorado. They are rarely seen, but if you think you saw something that looked like a huge, ugly seal, it was probably a manatee. There are no seals or sea lions in Costa Rica. There are otters but they are quite small. Manatees grow up to 600 kg (1,300 lbs) and can be as much as three meters (10 feet) long.

Looking like cows of the sea, manatees suffer from monumental flatulence brought on by eating 100 pounds or more a day of water hyacinths or any other water vegetation. They also eat plants near the edge of the water and occasionally small fish. You can locate them by their bubbles – and smell.

Turtles

Costa Rica provides nesting grounds for several kinds of turtle including **leatherback**, **green**, **loggerhead**, **hawksbill**, **ridley**, and **Pacific green**.

The Tortuguero area on the Caribbean coast and Ostional National Wildlife Refuge on the Pacific coast are the most famous turtle areas. Leatherbacks nest in the Caribbean in April and May; green turtles come in vast numbers from July through mid-October. The beaches can be absolutely thick with turtles at times, but don't expect to be able to frolic among them like in a dolphin-petting water park.

Turtles can lay eggs up to three times per season.

It's forbidden to be on many of the beach areas at night, but small, guided tours to view turtles nesting are conducted by National Parks Service trained guides. Bright lights, motors and movement disturb turtles at a critical time. Turtles don't seem to like to be peered at with flashlights while they are laying eggs.

Turtle Terms

- ◎ ***Barricadas:*** groups of egg-laying turtles
- ◎ ***Tortuga baula:*** leatherback
- ◎ ***Tortuga blanca, tortuga verde:*** green turtle
- ◎ ***Tortuga bocado:*** snapping turtle
- ◎ ***Tortuga carey:*** hawksbill turtle
- ◎ ***Tortuga jicóte:*** mud turtle
- ◎ ***Tortuga negra:*** Pacific green turtle
- ◎ ***Tortuga cabezona:*** loggerhead turtle
- ◎ ***Tortuga lora, tortuga carpintera:*** Pacific ridley

Many turtles build nests outside the borders of any national park or sanctuary and, in some areas, eggs can be legally collected and sold. Although almost any Tico you meet in the area makes their living either directly or indirectly from eco-minded visitors wanting to see turtles, they still occasionally profit from legally and illegally collected turtle eggs bought by middle men for sale in bars as snacks with beer.

In the Caribbean, there is a small private sanctuary near Barra de Matina where leatherback, green and hawksbills nest. Another sanctuary, the **Gandoca-Manzanillo Wildlife Refuge**, is south of Puerto Limón past Punta Uva. ☎ 506-754-2133.

Turtle eggs are occasionally served with beer as appetizers in bars.

Helping the Turtles

Several conservation efforts are underway in Costa Rica to help boost turtle reproduction success. Volunteers spend week- or month-long visits helping to patrol beaches, tag turtles and monitor nests. Volunteers usually pay for their own transportation and modest amounts for lodging and food. Some conservation groups involved with turtles and accepting paying volunteers include: **Caribbean Conservation**, ☎ 800-678-7853 or 352-373-6441, www.cccturtle.org/; **Caribbean Organization for Tropical Education and Rainforest Conservation**, ☎ 905-831-8809; and **Earth Island Institute**, ☎ 415-788-3666. **Foundation for Field Research**, ☎ 619-445-9264, has five- and 15-day programs.

Whales

Few of nature's creatures are more awe-inspiring than whales, and Costa Rica is one of the best places in the world to see them up close. In my travels I have had numerous encounters with whales. The most memorable one was when I was walking along Playa Hermosa near Jacó watching the surfers. As I watched their seal-like antics, I noticed a spout of water jetting up in a perfectly symmetrical plume just like a whale spout you see in the cartoons. It was only a few hundred feet out past the crowd of surfers and, even though the beach was crowded with people watching the surfers, no one else seemed to see the spout. I continued watching and soon saw more spouts and caught glimpses of shiny black whale backs as they swam in an arc to surface briefly for a blow. It seemed a small pod of whales was moving south just off the beach. I followed along for a mile or so watching them spout and blow before they disappeared.

August through December is the prime whale-watching season, but they can be seen year-round.

I've gotten much closer to whales in boats, but seeing them so close to shore and so close to the surfers moved me more than other encounters. Since then I've been informed that such perfect spouts are typical of sperm whales, common along the southern Pacific coast.

Humpback whales are probably the most common whale species encountered in Costa Rica with **sperm**, **pilot** and **orcas** (killer whales) also seen frequently. **Blue** whales are less common. Top whale-watching spots include the Ballena Marine National Park near Uvita and Drake Bay at the base of the Osa Peninsula.

Climate

Two Seasons

Costa Rica really has only two seasons: the **dry**, or high season, and the **rainy**, or "green" season, as the local travel industry likes to call it. Dry season runs from December through April, although the Northern Caribbean coast is pretty rainy almost all year. There are scattered dry periods during the so-called green season and there are definitely wet periods in the dry season. Some areas are so densely forested that even during the dry season it rains inside the forest continually as the humid air condenses on the leaves and the moisture drops off as "rain." The temperature doesn't change much between the seasons. It is hotter and more humid from May through September, but trade winds cool things down in some areas.

What Europeans and North Americans call winter is summer in Costa Rica.

Altitude affects the temperature more than anything else. The central highlands around San José enjoy a delightful climate, with temperatures rarely dipping below 65° F or above 85° F. Because of its altitude and tropical location, San José has one of the most comfortable climates in the world with an average temperature of 72° F. The Caribbean and Pacific coasts can be very hot and humid. Temperatures in the 90s are not unusual. The Osa Peninsula receives around 25 feet of rain per year. That works out to an average of almost one inch of rain per day. The northern Caribbean coast can get more than that. Some mountain areas actually get snow and ice, but that is extremely rare and something few visitors to Costa Rica will see.

A light jacket may be needed in Monteverde in the evenings & occasionally in San José.

Top 10 Attractions

- ☀ Arenal Volcano
- ☀ Beaches & surfing
- ☀ Birding
- ☀ Cocos Island
- ☀ Fishing for billfish on the Pacific Coast
- ☀ National parks & wildlife refuges
- ☀ Scuba diving
- ☀ Tarpon & snook fishing in the Tortuguero area
- ☀ Turtle watching
- ☀ Whitewater rafting

Planning Your Trip

Getting Ready

The high, or "dry" season runs from the end of November to April. The rainy season, more commercially referred to as the "green" season, runs from May through November. Of course, there is some overlap and, in some parts of the country, the dry season is quite wet by most people's standards.

When to Visit/What to Wear

Start packing with a high-quality **raincoat** and **umbrella**. I find poncho-style raincoats not very effective. If you're planning on fishing or being outside a lot, I suggest a full rain suit with pants and top. Humidity and heat are big issues, so buy the lightest weight, vented rain gear you can find.

Sunscreen and mosquito repellent are less pricey and easier to find in the US.

Casual attire is the norm, but don't get too casual outside your hotel or lodge. Shorts are okay for the beach and resort areas but are not appropriate in San José. Leave the ties and shiny shoes at home. You might want to pack some trendy glad rags if you plan on visiting some of the more upscale discos and nightspots in San José.

Topless bathing by women is rare and is frowned upon by locals.

Ticos are very friendly and tolerant people but are more conservative in dress than North Americans or Europeans. Ticos almost always dress neatly and are usually better dressed than tourists. Tourists are on holiday and tend to dress comfortably in shorts and a favorite T-shirt. If you see a man wearing a shabby bathing suit and dirty T-shirt or shirtless and needing a shave, it is almost certainly a North American tourist.

Stuff that is easy to dry is good to have in the tropics. **Cotton-polyester** shirts with high polyester content dry quickly and don't show wrinkles too much. Hawaiian shirts look great (some think), are cool and dry easily. A **hat** is essential. Hats that cover the ears are good if you're going to be on the water fishing or playing golf.

Short rubber boots can be bought in local hardware stores (*ferretería* or *abastecedor*) for about $10 and will keep your feet dry on all but the wettest forest walks and hikes. This is what the local farmers wear. I prefer them.

Hiking boots or **rubber boots** are absolute essentials unless you are only going to be engaging in the most delicate urban pursuits. If you insist on bringing only sneakers, bring two pairs and be prepared for one or even both pairs to be wet almost all the time. The country is wet and muddy and you won't have as much fun if your feet are constantly wet. Bring extra socks and underwear because you'll find yourself wanting to change them frequently. **Flip-flops** for the beach and pool are a good idea.

Bring zip-lock bags in several sizes for storing wet and smelly things.

Seasonal Prices

Rates are higher during high season, which theoretically corresponds to the dry season, or Costa Rican "summer," and runs from December to April. You can count on everything being booked in the last two weeks of December. You should make an early reservation if you intend to be in the area during that time. The rest of the year is the so-called "green season," when the rain can be rather intense. You should plan for some rainy days and occasional thunderstorms even during the dry season.

Telephones

The country code is 506. There are no area codes in Costa Rica. From the US, dial 011, then 506, then the local number.

Holidays & Festivals

The Costa Rican Tourist Board (☎ 223-1733; 800-343-6332 in the US; fax 223-5452; www.tourism-costarica.com), can provide more details.

Official Holidays

☀ January

January 1: **New Year's Day**. Generally, New Year's Eve and the following day are considered quiet days of reflection, not occasions for parties and drinking.

☀ March

March Festival is an arts festival in Puntarenas.

March 19: **Saint Joseph Day**

☀ April

April: **Easter** week (*semana santa*)

April 11: **Battle of Rivas anniversary**

☀ May

May 1: **Labor Day**

☀ June

June 29: **Day of Saint Peter & Paul**

☀ July

July 25: **Annexation of Guanacaste Province Anniversary**

☀ August

August 2: **Virgin of Los Angeles**

August 15: **Mothers' Day**

☀ September

September 15: **Independence Day**

☀ October

October 12: **Día de las Culturas**

☀ December

December 8: **Conception of the Virgin**

December 25: **Christmas Day**

Passports, Visas & Customs

Americans, Canadians and most Europeans automatically obtain 90-day visas at the airport on arrival. The visa is just a stamp in your passport and is not something you even need to think about in advance. Most visitors don't even realize they received a visa. Passports are required for most nationalities but, officially, US citizens can enter with a driver's license or birth certificate. I've never tried coming in without a passport and I'm not sure how easy it would be in reality. Extending your stay past 90 days involves navigating stupefying layers of bureaucracy and many find it much easier and quicker to simply leave the country for a day or two and re-enter.

Customs for tourists is usually pretty straightforward. Import taxes for consumer goods are high, and if you're obviously carrying a bunch of new stereos, small kitchen appliances and other consumer goodies you may be searched and asked to explain your intentions. Surfboards, diving gear, cameras, expensive binoculars and fishing equipment are perfectly normal items for tourists to be dragging along with them and should not cause any problems. US residents may return home with US $400 worth of goods per person, duty free. Canadians can bring home CAN $500. No fruit or uncanned foodstuff allowed, but you can bring back coffee. US residents are not allowed to bring back Cuban cigars.

Time Zone

The time zone for Costa Rica is the same as Central time in the US. Costa Rica does not do Daylight Saving Time, so Central time in the US does not coordinate with Costa Rica in the summer – add yet another hour.

Sunset is between 5:15 and 5:45. It's usually pitch-black by 6.

Learning Spanish

Even though Ticos are famous for their creative use of the Spanish language, Costa Rica is a great place to learn Spanish since the people are so outgoing and willing to listen as you stumble through verb conjugations. Schools and professional tutors teach not only localisms but also proper Castilian. Prices vary considerably but rarely get over $7 per hour for individual, one-on-one instruction and are much less for small classes.

Some schools offer home stays with local families and intensive "deep immersion" programs. Although any amount of language study is beneficial, it takes a few months of intensive study and daily use to become reasonably fluent.

Ticos have an amusing habit of "pointing" with their lips – try doing it yourself.

Even if you can take only a half-day of instruction, you will benefit from what you learn. Ticos respond with enthusiasm to anyone who tries, even on the most basic level. Basic courtesies and numbers can be learned in an hour or so and will add tremendously to your experience. A small Spanish-English dictionary is a great way to figure out what some of the strange signs you see mean. If you decide to spend a few days in taking formal Spanish lessons, I suggest getting out of San José for your studies and spending time in one of the many more salubrious locations as you expand your language power.

Using a few Spanish expressions such as Mucho gusto *(when being introduced), or* pura vida *(okay) will bring a smile.*

Costa Rica Nature Escape (☎ 506-257-8064, see page 56) is the most active agency arranging educational activities. A small but very high-quality local tour operator, they specialize in educational tours, including Spanish language study with lodgings arranged with local families or in the very best lodges. They can arrange all your travel, including air and hotels from the time you leave home, all through the country and back home again, or just single-day private lessons.

Other well-known schools include **Escuela del Mundo** (☎ 506-257-8064, www.speakcostarica.com) in Jacó and **Centro Panamericano de Idiomas** (☎ 506-265-6866, www.cpi-edu.com) in Monteverde, Heredia and Playa Flamingo.

Getting Here

Getting to Costa Rica is relatively painless. Several major airlines have scheduled flights, some cruise lines feature Costa Rica as a stopover, and it is even possible for the intrepid to drive there on the Interamerican Highway.

By Air

Due to recent security concerns and the subsequent drop in the number of travelers, flights to Costa Rica have been scaled back by some airlines. Most US flights come through Houston, Miami or Los Angeles (usually connecting through Mexico City). American, Continental, Delta, LACSA, Mexicana, TACA and United are the usual carriers. From Europe, there are flights from Madrid on Iberia. Havana is a popular hub for flights from Europe and South and Central America.

By Car

It is possible to drive from the US to Costa Rica along the Interamerican Highway, but such a drive is an adventure itself. If you hurry, you can get from Texas to Costa Rica in a bit under two weeks. A fairly new, stout vehicle is a must. The best route is to travel along the Gulf of Mexico to Guatemala and avoid the highlands and El Salvador. Of course, use extreme caution when driving through Guatemala and Nicaragua. Do not drive at night. If you like the idea of this driving adventure, you should read ***Driving the Interamerican Highway to Mexico and Central America***, by Audrey Pritchard, to get the lowdown.

Planning Your Trip

Local airlines flying within Costa Rica have a 25-lb. weight limit on luggage.

By Ship

Several cruise lines stop in the Caribbean port of Limón or the Pacific port of Puntarenas. Limón has been undergoing a serious renovation to accommodate the cruise ship passengers, but is still a bit on the seedy side, as is Puntarenas.

Most passengers are whisked away on one-day tours to nearby sights such as Tortuguero National Park, rafting on the Pacuare or Rentevazón, Arenal Volcano, and the Monteverde Cloud Forest Preserve. Trips are arranged on board or through local tour operators, such as **Costa Rica Expeditions** (☎ 506-257-0766) and **Costa Rica Nature Escape** (☎ 506-257-8064). Some lines make multiple stops along the Pacific coast, or include a trip through the Panama canal, visiting both sides of Costa Rica. Cruise lines stopping in Costa Rica include the following.

CLIPPER
11969 Westline Industrial Ave.
St. Louis, MO 63146
☎ 800-325-0010
www.clippercruise.com

Clipper offers a trip beginning in San José going to Pavas, Puntarenas and down the Pacific coast to Manuel Antonio, Drake Bay, Darien and back through Panama. They emphasize eco-tourism and provide experts on board, such as biology professors from Harvard and bird experts.

CUNARD LINES
6100 Blue Lagoon Drive, #400
Miami, FL 33126
☎ 305-465-3000; 800-7-CUNARD in US
www.cunard.com

HOLLAND AMERICA
300 Elliot Avenue W.
Seattle, WA 98119
In the US, ☎ 800-426-0327
www.hollandamerica.com

NORWEGIAN CRUISE LINE
95 Merrick Way
Coral Gables, FL 33134
In the US, ☎ 800-327-7030
www.norwegiancruiseline.com

PRINCESS CRUISES
10100 Santa Monica Blvd.
Los Angeles, CA 90067
In the US, ☎ 800-421-0522
www.princesscruises.com

RADISSON SEVEN SEAS CRUISES
600 Corporate Drive #410
Ft. Lauderdale, FL 33334
In the US, ☎ 800-333-3333
www.rssc.com

REGAL CRUISE LINES
4199 34th St., Suite B
St. Petersburg, FL 33711
In the US, ☎ 800-270-SAIL
www.regalcruises.com

ROYAL CARIBBEAN CRUISE LINE
1050 Caribbean Way
Miami, FL 33132
In the US, ☎ 305-539-6000
www.royalcaribbean.com

SILVERSEA
110 E. Broward Blvd.
Ft. Lauderdale, FL 33301
In the US, ☎ 800-722-9955, www.silversea.com

Planning Your Trip

Where to Stay

Hotels, Lodges & B&Bs

Five-star hotels in the grand European sense do not exist in Costa Rica. Star systems you might observe there should be used as no more than a very rough guide to quality. What you do find are dozens of imaginatively designed luxury lodges and boutique hotels, with very high levels of service and facilities. It is difficult at times to figure out why some places call themselves "lodge," "inn" or "hotel." The terms are used quite loosely.

Many hotels & lodges think having "eco" in the name will attract nature-oriented tourists, so you will see the word "eco" on everything from luxury beach resorts to laundromats & coffee bars.

The term "B&B" in Costa Rica is used much the same as elsewhere and can cover everything from a room or two in someone's small house to luxury suites with champagne breakfasts in "eco" lodges. The best approach is to read the descriptions provided here and visit the listed websites to get a better feel for what accommodations are like. Costa Rica offers everything from small bungalows with ceiling fans on the beach to enormous, all-inclusive family resorts with golf, casinos, swim-up bars, multiple restaurants, beauty salons and activities managers for the kids. All have their charms and detractions.

Howler monkeys make a huge racket early in the morning and will often be your only wake-up call.

The accommodations listed in this guide have been selected as the best in the country and the best in each area. The "best" does not necessarily mean the most expensive or most luxurious. Many hotels in Costa Rica do not have air conditioning; some don't have electricity, except for a few hours every day. Some of these bare-bones places are wonderful to stay in and make up for lack of modern conveniences with spectacular views or by being located by a deserted beach or in the middle of a rainforest. Expect a few rooster crows in the morning and a few barking dogs.

In some hotels the noise from the disco can be unsettling, so ask for a room away from it.

Many guidebook authors visit as many as five or six hotels in one day in an attempt to be "complete" or "comprehensive." I have personally stayed in almost all of the hotels listed, most of them for at least two nights and any that I have not stayed in have been highly recommended by trustworthy friends or family. I have slept in the beds. The few mentioned here that I do not have close personal knowledge of are indicated as not having been visited. In most of the areas covered, there are many more hotels I do not cover than hotels that I do cover. I try to determine the best ones in each area.

All the prices in the book are based on double occupancy during high season. Taxes and meals are not included in the prices, unless so mentioned. Hotels and lodges marked with a ☆ are my personal favorites. "The Best of the Best" choices earn their title by offering top-quality lodging and services. Look for the special icon (on the right) indicating these.

Planning Your Trip

BEST OF THE BEST

Spas

Costa Rica has a variety of hotels offering everything from volcanic mud baths to world-renowned cosmetic surgery. Few hotels can be categorized as being a just a "spa." Although many hotels have the word "spa" in their promotional material, only a few hotels in Costa Rica offer more than a few exercise machines and massages arranged if you make a special request.

Hotel Martino Spa & Resort, ☎ 506-433-8382, in Alajuela just outside San José offers full spa services and is the only spa in the country that truly deserves the name. (See page 139.) **Hotel Si Como No** in Manuel Antonio, ☎ 506-777-0777, has extensive spa facilities offered as part of its honeymoon packages (see page 294). **La Mansion**, ☎ 506-777-3489, also in Manuel Antonio, offers a sophisticated range of health and beauty treatments (see page 298).

Extended Vacations

Apartment & Vacation Rentals

Look in the classified section of the Tico Times *for vacation rentals.*

If you are going to stay in one area for an extended period, renting a house or bungalow can be economical and more comfortable than staying in a hotel. **Aparthotels** have rooms with kitchen facilities and can be suitable for extended stays. Many of them are little more than block buildings with gas hobs and laundry sinks, but some are quite elegant affairs with maid and concierge service. Some of the top hotels have larger suites with kitchens and offer better rates for extended stays. I have had wonderful times in the Osa Peninsula near Matapalo staying in a vacation rental near the beach. You can see my favorite vacation rental, **Casa Miramar**, at www.bosquedelcabo.com.

⚡ WARNING

Be sure you know what a vacation rental house offers in the way of electricity and hot water before you pay a deposit; many of the locals renting vacation homes consider such things to be frills and don't mention their lack on their websites or advertisements.

Here are a few places to try: **Costa Rica Rentals International**, Apdo. 1136-1250, Escazú, ☎ 506-228-6863; **Tropical Waters**, Dominical, ☎ 506-787-0031, www.aspensites.com/tropical-waters; and **Pacific Coast Realty Suites Presidenciales**, Playa Flamingo, Guanacaste, ☎ 506-654-4068, www.acquirecostarica.com. Prices range from $50 to over $500, depending on size, location and comfort level.

Where & What to Eat

There are many restaurants in Costa Rica which would be well received by sophisticated diners in any large, international city, but don't expect five-star restaurants in the European sense. You can certainly find restaurants that serve nouvelle cuisine, with small mounds of fussy food served on large plates, drizzled with colorful sauce. In hotels and lodges you'll find great seafood, including fish, lobster and shrimp, as well as steaks, pork chops, pasta and lots of fresh vegetables.

Frozen food is almost unknown. If you favor bacon and eggs for breakfast, cheeseburgers for lunch, and familiar North American meals at dinner you should have no problem. If you want to experiment with local specialties, your palate will be delighted with seafood, pasta, meals based around rice and beans and tropical tubers such as yucca. Sweet bananas and cooking bananas (similar to plantains) are prepared in a wide variety of tasty ways.

Typical Costa Rican food is interesting and wholesome. It is almost always made with the freshest ingredients.

Italian, Chinese and Mexican restaurants can be found in even the smallest towns. McDonald's, Pizza Hut and a host of the usual fast food emporiums are found in the larger cities. A trip to Costa Rica is a good chance to try new and interesting foods and

Seafood is almost always excellent.

gorge yourself on seafood – McDonald's tastes exactly the same everywhere in the world.

Dorado (mahi-mahi), **snapper** and **tuna** are almost always very fresh and excellent. **Shrimp, lobster** and *langostinos* (small, lobster-like crustaceans similar to crawdads) are wonderful, but usually expensive. Beef is not normally grain-fed, aged or loaded with hormones in Costa Rica, and usually only the tenderloin is served in tourist-oriented hotels. Even the tenderloins are a bit tougher than most US steaks, but I find them tastier and feel better eating beef knowing the local cattle is free range. It hasn't spent time in feed lots being fattened with additives and dubious feed, as it can be in North America. Much of the chicken seems to be battery raised, but sometimes you do get a nice tasty, although a bit chewy, free range chicken. Some of the upscale eateries serve export-quality, tender steaks.

No matter what you like to eat, you'll eat very well and will find plenty of familiar favorites.

Desserts tend to be oriented around fruit, with the ubiquitous Latin **flan** appearing on many menus. *Queque* (cake) is a fairly dry, sweet cake similar to North American pound cake. **Ice cream** is everywhere and good.

It's a rare restaurant that has windows with glass in them, and many don't even have doors (it rarely gets cold enough to need them).

Dining in Costa Rica at restaurants aimed at tourists is not cheap. Prices are similar to what you would find in North America. If you feel comfortable enough to try local eateries, you can have wonderful, safe and healthy meals at bargain prices. Don't be alarmed to see a hefty 25% added to your restaurant bill. A 15% tax is charged on all meals and 10% charge for service is added automatically to all restaurant tabs. Resist the impulse to tip in addition, unless you have been particularly pleased with the service. It may seem odd to walk away without leaving a tip, but remember – you already have paid 10%

when you pay the bill. Few restaurants outside San José take credit cards, so have some cash ready.

Prices listed in the *Best Places to Eat* sections are the average price for an entrée or main course before the taxes and service have been added. Although the law says restaurants must show prices on the menu with taxes included, many do not. Menus that include taxes almost always say so.

Organized Excursions

Planning Your Trip

Costa Rica is probably best known to tourists for nature and adventure tours. Birds, turtles, whales, cloud and rainforests provide an immense variety for nature lovers. Whitewater rafting, sea kayaking, mountain trekking, scuba diving and surfing keep the adventurous excited. A wide variety of tour companies make it all seem easy.

Tours & Tour Operators

Although independent travel has definite charms and advantages, the particular advantages of organized tours include not only safety and predictability, but also simplicity and guides with local knowledge. A local guide can show you things you never would have suspected existed. They can provide insight and information almost impossible for the independent traveler to obtain. Tour companies vary widely and are difficult to evaluate in advance. Although recommendations from friends are extremely valuable, one person's great tour could be a restrictive bore for someone else.

Two companies in Costa Rica stand out for organizing a broad range of quality tours. **Costa Rica Ex-**

peditions is by far the largest. **Costa Rica Nature Escape** is a smaller tour operator that offers personal guides, educational tours and all the usual nature expeditions. The **Costa Rican Tourist Board** is also a source of information and basic maps (see page 155).

⊘ TIP

If you want the personal services of a highly trained guide dedicated just to you, **Marcel Lichtenstein**, forestbp@hotmail.com, is an expert in birds, plants, trees and medicinal uses of tropical plants.

COSTA RICA EXPEDITIONS

Calle Central & Avenida 3, San José
Apdo. 6941-1000, San José
☎ 506-257-0766 or 506-222-0333; fax 506-257-1665
www.costaricaexpeditions.com

Costa Rica Expeditions (CRE) started out organizing rafting tours on the world-famous Pacuare River and has expanded into the largest tour operator in the country, offering every conceivable type of tour. They own and operate the Monteverde, Tortuga and the Corcovado Lodges. I have found their certified guides to be exceptionally knowledgeable, informative and helpful. The quality of their food and accommodations is of the highest standard. If you are looking for a one-day trip around San José and the surrounding area or a three-week multi-sport tour of the best Costa Rica has to offer, they can arrange it all. Details of their services are listed in each appropriate section.

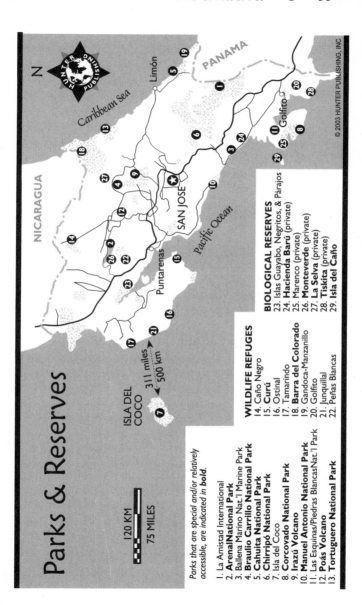

Parks & Reserves

Planning Your Trip

120 KM
75 MILES

*Parks that are special and/or relatively accessible, are indicated in **bold**.*

1. La Amistad International
2. **Arenal National Park**
3. Ballena Marino Nat.'l Marine Park
4. **Braulio Carrillo National Park**
5. Cahuita National Park
6. **Chirripó National Park**
7. Isla del Coco
8. **Corcovado National Park**
9. Irazú Volcano
10. **Manuel Antonio National Park**
11. Las Esquinas/Piedras Blancas Nat.'l Park
12. **Poás Volcano**
13. **Tortuguero National Park**

WILDLIFE REFUGES
14. Caño Negro
15. **Curú**
16. Ostinal
17. Tamarindo
18. **Barra del Colorado**
19. Gandoca-Manzanillo
20. Golfito
21. Junquillal
22. Peñas Blancas

BIOLOGICAL RESERVES
23. Islas Guayabo, Negritos, & Pàrajos
24. **Hacienda Barú** (private)
25. Marenco (private)
26. **Monteverde** (private)
27. **La Selva** (private)
28. **Tiskita** (private)
29. Isla del Caño

© 2003 HUNTER PUBLISHING, INC

COSTA RICA NATURE ESCAPE
Apdo. 11997-1000, San José
☎ 506-257-8064; fax 506-257-8065
www.crnature.com

This is a small but high-quality local tour operator. Costa Rica Nature Escape can arrange all your travel, including air and hotels from the time you leave home, all through the country, and then back home again. They specialize in educational tours that include Spanish language study with accommodations arranged with local families or in the very best lodges. They have a wide variety of programs for teenagers, children and families, so if you want to drop the kids off in surfing school or send them on their own horseback riding or rafting trips, you can go off on a second honeymoon. You'll know the kids are having more fun than if you had dragged them along with you. Guides are available who speak fluent English, Spanish, German, French and Japanese. Particular guides are trained in history, biology, entomology and zoology.

Costa Rican Adventure Tour Companies

CULTOURICA
El Marañon
☎ 506-249-1761, 506-249-1271
www.cultourica.com

Specializing in nature tours involving community and local people interactions.

HORIZONTES
Calle 28, Avenidas 1 & 3
☎ 506-222-2022; fax 506-255-4513
www.horizontes.com

One of the original nature tour companies in Costa Rica and covers all types of tours and areas.

SERENDIPITY ADVENTURES
Apdo. 90-7150, Turrialbo
☎ 506-556-2592; fax 506-556-2593;
In US, toll-free 877-507-1358
www.serendipityadventures.com

All types of tours to all Costa Rican locations.

US Adventure Tour Companies

COSTA RICA CONNECTION
1124 Nipomo Street, Suite C
San Luis Obispo, CA 93401
☎ 800-345-7422, 805-543-8823
www.crconnect.com

PREFERRED ADVENTURES
One West Water St, Suite 300
St. Paul, MN 55107
☎ 800-840-8687, 651-222-8131; fax 651-222-4221
www.preferredadventures.com

RICO TOURS
9901 Capital Of Texas Hwy, Suite 220
Austin, Texas 78759
☎ 800-955-8064; fax 512-418-0237
www.ricotours.com

"Soft" eco-tourism with some slightly different itin-eraries, including Selva Bananito Lodge, pre-retirement tours and treks to off-the-beaten-path Chirripó.

VOYAGERS INTERNATIONAL
PO Box 915
Ithaca, NY 14851
☎ 800-633-0299, 607-273-4321; fax 607-273-3873
www.voyagers.com

Planning Your Trip

Scuba Diving Trips

Even though there are few living coral reefs here, diving in Costa Rica is world-class; however, snorkeling is not the best due to turbulence in easily accessible areas. Even though it is a two-day boat ride to get there, **Cocos Island** attracts hard-core, world-roaming divers to see enormous schools of scalloped hammerhead sharks and other pelagics.

The northern Pacific region around the **Nicoya Peninsula** has numerous dive sites and sophisticated dive operators. The visibility can be poor, but huge swarms of fish, rays, turtles and sharks make up for it. In the south Pacific area, **Drake Bay** and **Caño Island** offer excellent diving with good visibility and the possibility of being in the water with manta rays and whale sharks.

On the Caribbean side, in the south, **Puerto Viejo de Limón** has coral reefs and quite good diving.

Some lodges are dedicated to diving, and have their own dive boats, on-site dive shops and a trained staff.

Many lodges send diving guests to local operators who offer their services directly to the public and to multiple area lodges as well. Most travel agencies will organize diving trips all over the country. The biggest dive operator is **Bill Beard** (☎ 506-877-853-0538). He operates in the Papagyo area and, although he arranges complete dive tours throughout Costa Rica, he subcontracts to independent operators for areas outside his base in Nicoya. If you are planning a dive trip covering the best spots in Costa Rica, I would suggest working with Bill Beard, **Costa Rica Expeditions** (☎ 506-257-0766), or **Costa Rica Nature Escape** (☎ 506-257-8064), all of whom can arrange everything from flights from the US, internal flights, hotels and lodges and arrange for all the diving.

In 2002, there were only two companies operating trips to Cocos Island: the **Aggressor Fleet Ltd.** (☎ 800-348-2628, in the US) and the **Undersea Hunter** (☎ 506-228-6613, 800-203-2120 in the US). These are typically one-week to 10-day trips on liveaboards with food, cabins and all diving included in the price. Prices run from $2,500. You can book with them directly or let agencies like Costa Rica Expeditions or Costa Rica Nature Escape set up the whole thing for you.

AGRESSOR FLEET LIMITED
PO Box 1470
Morgan City, Louisiana 70381
In US, ☎ 800-348-2628; 506-385-2628
www.aggressor.com

They specialize in seven- and 10-day liveaboard trips to Cocos Island aboard the *Okeanos Aggressor*.

DIVING SAFARIS DE COSTA RICA
Apdo. 121-5019, Playa del Coco
☎ 506-672-0012, 800-779-0055 US; fax 506-672-0231
www.costaricadiving.net

Based in the Sol Playa Hermosa Hotel, this is a well-established operator.

MUNDO AQUATICO
Apdo. 7875-1000, San José
☎ 506-224-9729; fax 506-234-2982
mundoac@racsa.co.cr

Certification, trips to Bat Islands, Catalina, Isla del Caño.

UNDERSEA HUNTER
Apdo. 310-1260, Plaza Colonial, Escazú
☎ 506-228-6613; in the US, 800-203-2120
www.underseahunter.com

Two liveaboards run to Cocos Island.

Planning Your Trip

BILL BEARD ADVENTURE TRAVEL
☎ 877-853-0538
www.billbeardcostarica.com

Runs liveaboards to Cocos Island and arranges dive
packages all over Costa Rica. One of the oldest and
best established dive operators in the country.

What to Expect
Getting Around

In general, Costa Rica is an easy place to find your way around in. In San José, taxis are rarely far away, are reasonably priced and are much less hassle than driving your own car and finding a place to park. Many people complain about the poor condition of the roads in the country but, compared to other Central and South American countries, they are pretty good. Enormous potholes big enough to hide a cow in dot even the best roads. Rutted and bridgeless dirt roads are the only means of access to some of the most interesting parts of the country. Don't let this bother you. Rent a four-wheel-drive and drive the whole country as you please.

Road signs (or the lack thereof) can be confusing and asking for directions can lead you astray as Ticos will always give you a positive answer even if they have no idea of what they are talking about.

> ### ⊚ TIP
>
> Be sure you know exactly where you are going before you set out; there are at least three towns called Puerto Viejo, several places called Flamingo, a couple of Matapalo, and several named San Pablo and San Pedro.

Schedules for ferries, buses and air transport often run on *hora Tica* (Tico time) rather than on *hora Americana*. Relax and enjoy your stay. You're on holiday and probably don't really need to be in a hurry.

Internal flights can get you close to most places and rural taxis are almost always available to get you to your final destination.

From the Airport

Taxis into San José cost approximately US $15 and about $5 to Alajuela. Some hotels will provide pickup service if you request it in advance. There are no regular hotel limo services like in a large US city.

Taxis

Taxis are common and efficient. They are a bit hard to hail in San José at times, especially when it's raining, but hotels and restaurants will call them for you. Be sure to agree on a price before setting off and don't be afraid to bargain. Taxis are one of the few things people bargain for in Costa Rica. Taxis drivers are required to use their meter (***maría***), but sometimes don't have one. Around US $20 should get you from the airport to almost any hotel in the San José area. About US $15 should get you to most of them. You can bargain if the driver doesn't have a meter (or claims it's broken), but you need to have an idea of what the metered price would be. An extra 20% is often added at night.

Tipping taxi drivers is rarely done and not expected.

Taxis in San José are so cheap and parking so hard to find that it does not make sense to rent a car for the time you are in the city.

Car Rentals

As in most countries, you'll need a valid driver's license, passport and credit card to rent a car. Rental companies have different minimum age restrictions – be sure to check before you go, since some of them are as high as 25 years. For insurance reasons, cars rented in Costa Rica cannot be taken over the border into Panama or Nicaragua.

Because of the numerous pot-holes, a car driving straight may be a sign the driver is drunk!

Road conditions may seem bad to people used to driving only on paved roads in North America or Europe. Potholes and lack of guardrails are only part of the problem. Although this may sound discouraging, there are few better ways to see the country than with the freedom of your own vehicle. Just make sure you get the right vehicle for where you plan on traveling.

Most car rental agencies are located in San José only. Major tourist centers do not necessarily have car rental offices but many of the San José-based agencies will deliver and pick up in other parts of Costa Rica for a fee ranging from $40 to $100. Do your research beforehand so you won't be surprised when you are there.

Europcar's customer service can be lacking when you most need it. I've spent hours on the phone with them trying to resolve some customer service issues, sometimes serious ones. I avoid them.

See each section's *Getting Around* for more agencies.

Gasoline runs about US $1.75 per gallon.

What to Expect

> ## ⚡ WARNING
>
> Be sure you make rental agents inspect the car carefully for dents, scratches, missing spare tires or jacks before you set off. Get any issues you find in writing on the contract. Some companies' cars are a bit run down, to say the least, and they may not remember the problems the car had when you return it. Be sure the tank is really full of gas before you set off or make sure the correct level is noted on the contract.

Car Insurance

The Costa Rican government has a monopoly on the car insurance business and requires rental cars to carry a minimum of collision and liability no matter what. Many rental companies will quote you very good rates, but when you actually get ready to sign the rental agreement you find you must pay an additional $10 to $20 per day for insurance, even if you are covered by insurance through your credit card. There is no way around this, so be sure you are comparing apples to apples when you select your rental agency. The minimum government required insurance has only a $1,500 deductible, but your insurance company or credit card company may cover you additionally at home. You cannot avoid the government insurance, no matter what sort of deal you have through your homeowner's insurance or credit card.

Gasoline, Petrol, Diesel

Fuel is relatively inexpensive in Costa Rica. Although sold by the liter it runs about $1.75 per gallon. It's a good idea to fill up before leaving San José (or other towns), since gas stations in the hinterlands can be hard to find. All fuel stations in Costa Rica are owned and operated by the government, so prices are pretty much the same everywhere. Gasoline stations are called **bombas** or **gasolineras**. If you find yourself in remote parts and really hard up for gas you can sometimes find locals who keep a supply on hand to sell to people just like yourself – for a small premium. Look for hand-lettered signs that say **gasolina**.

Driving Tips

In all of Costa Rica the act of driving is an opportunity for the usually reserved and careful Ticos to throw restraint to the wind and let their inner madness and aggression emerge unchained. Perhaps it's just the coffee. Since the roads are peppered with huge potholes, it is sometimes impossible to drive on the proper side of the road for more than a few feet, so the concept of driving only on the left or right side of the road sometimes seems to have been abandoned.

Turn signals, brake lights, headlights, seat belts and even windshields are considered optional items for rural Tico vehicles, and are not necessarily used even if a vehicle has them. Brakes and tread on tires are comparative luxuries – not necessities. Trucks passing two abreast on blind mountain curves is perfectly normal and should be expected. Driving at night is not a good idea. Ticos often turn their lights off to pass on blind curves at night – that way they

Gas stations can be scarce in remote areas, so fill up when your tank is half-full.

can more easily see the headlights of someone coming around the curve from the other direction.

Buses

 An extensive and complicated system of buses and *colectivos* operate all over the country, extending to the remotest areas. The main bus station in San José is called **"Coca Cola."** ***Colectivos*** cost a bit more and usually consist of pickup trucks with a canvas cover and wooden benches. Some run regular routes but usually leave only when full. *Colectivos* can be more comfortable than buses but you often see extra passengers hanging outside the back in the breeze. *Colectivos* usually are found near the central plaza of most towns. Ask at your hotel.

Luxury coaches do exist and are usually operated by tour agencies. Local "chicken buses" can be an interesting way to get to know the country. If you are adventurous, head for Coca Cola in San José for this one-of-a-kind experience.

★ DID YOU KNOW?

Unfortunately, trains are almost nonexistent in Costa Rica. The famous banana train line from San José to Limón was almost completely destroyed by earthquake and has been only partly restored.

Ferries

There are ferries operating from Puntarenas to Naranjo and Paquera on the Nicoya Peninsula.

The waits can be very long since the boats are small and can be easily filled by a couple of trucks or large tourist buses. When that happens everyone just continues to wait in line for three or four hours until the next ferry comes. A few river crossings are served by ferry. Most leave only when a customer arrives at the riverbank. These can be primitive-looking craft attached to a cable running across the river. Be sure to take a picture of your crossing to show to friends back home.

The Tempisque ferry was replaced by a bridge, shortening the drive time from San José to the resort area.

Internal Flights

SANSA (☎ 506-233-2714, www.flysansa.com) and **Travelair**, (☎ 506-232-7883, www.travelair-costarica.com) are the two main airlines offering flights within Costa Rica. Both fly to the main cities and a surprising number of small towns and villages. SANSA has flights from the main Juan Santamaría international airport and Travelair from Tobías Bolaños Airport. Tobías Bolaños is a half-hour cab ride ($10) from Juan Santamaría international airport.

What to Expect

Charter Airlines

AEROBELL
Tobías Bolaños Airport
☎ 506-290-0000; fax 506-296-0460
aerobell@racsa.co.cr

Internal air charters and sightseeing excursions.

Weight limits for baggage on flights to some remote places may be as low as 25 lbs.

SKY TOURS
☎ 506-296-3600; fax 506-228-9912

Sky Tours offers charters to all parts of the country. Based in San José, they offer tours in small planes of all the major sights in Costa Rica, including both coasts. The best excursion is "Dance on the Volcanoes," a tour by air of Arenal, Poás, Barva, Irazú and Turrialba. This may be the only way to see the top of almost perpetually clouded-over Arenal belching smoke and ash and tossing boulders into the air.

AVIONES TAXI AEREO
Juan Santamaría Airport
☎ 506-441-1626; fax 506-441-2713

Aviones has scheduled and charter flights to all airports within the country.

The Basics

Communications

Telephones

There are no area codes in Costa Rica. The international country code is 506. To call Costa Rica from the US, dial 011, then 506, then the local number.

Within the country, calls are cheap, but realize many hotels will add a hefty markup to calls made from your room.

To call other countries from Costa Rica, dial 00, then the country code of the country you are calling, followed by the number. For the US, you would dial 001, then the area code and number.

Phone Cards

Most US phone credit cards can be used, although buying local cards is always vastly cheaper. Access numbers are:

AT&T . . . . ☎ 0800-011-4114
MCI. . . . . ☎ 0800-012-2222
Sprint . . . . ☎ 0800-013-0123

Dial **113** for local information and **124** for long distance information (Spanish only).

Bilingual information for international calls **116**.

To make an international call, including collect calls, dial **175** to be connected with an operator (usually bilingual).

Faxes

Due to the unreliability of local mail service, faxes are a popular way to send documents. Many hotels will ask you to fax your details to them and will send a fax in reply for confirmation.

Internet Access

There are a couple dozen Internet cafés in San José; some of the smaller towns will have one. Only the fanciest hotels have phones in their rooms and few hotels offer modem jacks. Phone jacks are US-style. Dial-up services can be had on a short-term basis from several local suppliers. A good idea is to use one of the free e-mail services from Yahoo or Hotmail. The website **www.web2mail.com** allows you to check almost any e-mail account. That way you can check your e-mail from any browser, without needing a local dial-up service. **AOL** has local access numbers. Remember that hotels often charge hefty

What to Expect

fees for using phones in your room. A spell in an Internet café may end up being cheaper if you need more than just a few minutes online. See the *Appendix* for Internet dialup services.

Money Matters

Costa Rica is more expensive than most other Central American destinations but generally the value for money is higher; food and accommodations are better. While budget travelers may be able to scrape by on $20 a day or less, that kind of budget would mean not being able to take advantage of many of the most interesting experiences Costa Rica has to offer.

Currency

Bargaining is rare in Costa Rica except for unmetered cab rides.

Currency in Costa Rica is the **colon**. In late 2002, the exchange rate was 350 colones to US $1, but the rate fluctuates due to local inflation. US dollars are widely accepted throughout the country. Conceivably you could get away with using nothing but dollars but you may lose a bit as transactions are calculated in colones, translated to dollars and change recalculated back to colones. Change is rarely given in dollars. The colon is usually represented by a ¢ sign.

Where & When to Change

There is no set rate that all money-changing places must use, but there is very little difference. Banks, hotels and money-changing booths all set their own rates. You may want to check around but I find there is not much variation. Since dollars are widely accepted (especially in San José), it is a good idea to either change a small amount at the airport on arrival

or simply check the rates there. Get a general idea of
what to expect and wait until you have a feel for the
rates before changing a large amount. In San José,
next to Banco Lyon on the 2nd floor of the Schyfter
Building, **Villalobos Brothers Money Traders**
often has good rates. US dollars are much easier to
change than other currencies. You may have to hunt
around a bit to change your pounds, marks or Canadian dollars.

⚡ WARNING

People who approach you on the
street to change money usually offer only slightly better rates than
other places and often are more
interested in ripping you off in
some clever way than actually doing a straightforward transaction
– beware.

Although **ATMs** (money machines, cash points) are
common in San José and some of the larger towns,
they are scarce in small towns and nonexistent off
the beaten path. In spite of this, I believe they are
the best way to handle your cash requirements. The
rates are usually a bit better than changing cash
and you don't have to bring too much money with
you. The credit card companies handle huge
amounts of foreign exchange and are able to negoti-
ate good bulk rates. Unbelievably, some of that benefit may flow down to the individual. **Bank of Costa
Rica** (BCN) has ATMs all over the country, but they
work only if you have an account with the BCN to
draw from.

What to Expect

Colones devalue against the US dollar by as much as 15% in a year so. If you are staying a while, exchange money a little at a time.

Cash is king in Costa Rica, and many establishments do not take credit cards or will charge extra if you insist on using them. Outside San José, you may find yourself in a pickle if you don't have cash.

Traveler's Checks

Traveler's checks in small denominations are best. Small or isolated hotels may have trouble with large bills or large amounts. You will usually need your passport and sometimes a receipt from the place you bought the checks to change them. The rate for traveler's checks is usually less than for cash. American Express, Thomas Cook, Barclays and Citibank are about the only brands easily changed. Most stores do not accept traveler's checks. Only banks will take them.

AMERICAN EXPRESS
TAM Travel Agency
Calle Central, Avenida Central 1, San José
☎ 506-256-0203; fax 506-222-8092

To report lost or stolen American Express traveler's checks, call (US) ☎ 800-011-0080.

THOMAS COOK

To report lost or stolen Thomas Cook traveler's checks, call (US) ☎ 800-223-7373.

Credit Cards

Relying on plastic for your whole trip may work in the US or Europe, but in Costa Rica it is important to have cash – especially outside San José. Using bank cards to obtain money from ATMs is a good source for cash. Visa seems to be the most widely accepted card, although American Express is also common.

AMERICAN EXPRESS
☎ 506-233-0044

To report lost or stolen American Express credit cards, call (US) ☎ 800-528-2121.

MASTERCARD
☎ 506-253-2155

To report lost or stolen MasterCard credit cards, call (US) 800-011-0184.

VISA INTERNATIONAL
☎ 506-223-2211

To report lost or stolen Visa credit cards, call (US) ☎ 800-011-0030.

Tipping

Tipping is not generally done in Costa Rica. Most Americans find this hard to handle, feeling guilty if they don't tip as they do at home. However, a 10% service charge is built into almost all restaurant prices and it is just not necessary to add more. If you feel the service has been exceptional, an extra tip is always appreciated, but try to get over the idea that 15% to 20% is mandatory. Taxi drivers do not expect a tip but, if they have been nice and you feel like it, why not round up what's on the meter to the next even hundred colones? Porters and hotel staff should be tipped a dollar per bag if they do more than hold the door for you.

Keeping Your Money Safe

Don't flash your money. If you need to take out some cash to pay for something, make sure a big wad of bills is not revealed for all to see as you do it. It is a good idea to put a few small denomination bills in a front pocket for quick use so you don't have to pull out your whole roll just to buy something minor. Use the hotel safe if they have one.

Media

Newspapers

The *Tico Times* is a great English-language weekly with local news and things of interest to visitors. Even if your Spanish is good enough to read the Spanish-language papers, the *Tico Times* is worth a read because the news and articles are specifically aimed at English-speaking residents and visitors. They have perhaps the best fishing reports available for Costa Rica and have a good website that is updated weekly: **www.ticotimes.net**.

La Nación is a quite conservative daily. *La Prensa Libre* and *La República* are the other dailies – also on the conservative side. *Costa Rica Today* is an English-language weekly that is usually worth a read.

Magazines

Spanish-language weeklies *Esta Semana* and *Universidad* offer more balanced news reporting than do the dailies. Many US magazines can be found in the larger towns. The gift shop in the Hotel Camino Real in San José usually has a good selection.

Radio

Salsa and US pop rock are the normal radio fare. If you like this sort of thing, you're all set. I can handle these stations for only a few minutes at a time. Try **Radio Viva 850 AM**, **Radio Fabulosa 95.1 FM** or

Radio Azul 99 FM (plays some jazz). Station **95.5** plays smooth jazz with few commercial breaks. Their play list seems a bit limited and I find it's repititive after a couple of days.

Postal Service

Internal postal service is abysmal but mail generally gets there eventually. Locals rely on faxes, phone calls or express services. It can take quite some time to wait in line for stamps, as there is a puzzling amount of bureaucracy involved in even the simplest transaction.

Express Shipping Services

Both **FedEx** (☎ 506-293-6431) and **UPS** (☎ 506-290-2828) offer services in Costa Rica. Rates are somewhat higher than you would expect for shipping within North America. Both ship worldwide and have offices in most of the major cities. Call their main numbers for information about local offices.

Electricity

The current in Costa Rica is 110 volts/AC and plugs are the same as you'll find in the US. However, some of them are two-prong only, with no ground, so you may need an adapter to make a three-prong plug fit the two-prong outlet. There's no need for other adapters if you have US electrical devices, but you'll need a transformer and plug converter if you have European devices (hotels rarely have them).

What to Expect

Laundry

Most Ticos do their laundry at home so laundromats are a relatively foreign concept and are rare. As in most countries, having your laundry done at a hotel is often almost as expensive as buying new clothes. Lodges in remote areas are sometimes reached only by air and, since there are usually weight restrictions on baggage on internal flights, they may do laundry for guests economically and quickly, but don't count on it. Fortunately, you can get by without a bunch of fancy outfits. The seasoned travelers' trick of taking a shower with your clothes on and hanging them up to dry overnight is a problem in the humid tropics. It's a good way to end up with a bag full of sour and rotting garments if practiced in most parts of Costa Rica. You can sometimes find a local person who will do your laundry economically but, since drying the clothes is the hard part here, it can take a couple of days to get them back.

Bring about a dozen clothespins with you for hanging up shirts & bathing suits.

You can also try holding wet items of clothing over the air vent in your car while driving along with the heat on and the windows wide open.

The Metric System

The metric system is used in Costa Rica. You learned it in school; now it's just a matter of dragging the details out of your memory and putting them to everyday use. Some shortcuts: a **liter** is a bit more than a quart; a **meter** is a bit more than a yard; a kilometer is .6 mile. Therefore, 100 kilometers is 60 miles and 50 kilometers would be 30 miles. Here's a chart to help you out.

Going Metric?

To make your travels a little easier, we have provided the following charts that show metric equivalents for the measurements you are familiar with.

GENERAL MEASUREMENTS

1 kilometer	=	.6124 miles
1 mile	=	1.6093 kilometers
1 foot	=	.304 meters
1 inch	=	2.54 centimeters
1 square mile	=	2.59 square kilometers
1 pound	=	.4536 kilograms
1 ounce	=	28.35 grams
1 imperial gallon	=	4.5459 liters
1 US gallon	=	3.7854 liters
1 quart	=	.94635 liters

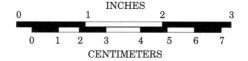

INCHES / CENTIMETERS ruler

TEMPERATURES

For Fahrenheit: Multiply Centigrade figure by 1.8 and add 32.

For Centigrade: Subtract 32 from Fahrenheit figure and divide by 1.8.

CENTIGRADE		FAHRENHEIT
40°	=	104°
35°	=	95°
30°	=	86°
25°	=	77°
20°	=	64°
15°	=	59°
10°	=	50°

Heath & Safety

The emergency number is **911** all over Costa Rica. Police are **127** and the fire brigade (*bomberos*) is **118**. Each regional chapter in this guide has local emergency numbers. Costa Rica is a healthy country and it is probably not necessary to avoid uncooked food and drink only bottled water. The Centers for Disease Control recommend travelers use Chloroquine as a malaria preventative and take precautions to avoid insect bites. Consult the **CDC Travel Health Hotline** at ☎ 888-232-3228, or www.cdc.gov/travel for more information.

Where to Get Medical Attention

In San José, the new **Cima hospital** is quite modern and up-to-date. In other areas, a **pharmacy** (*farmacia*) can direct you to a doctor (*médico*), or give general medical advice.

AIDS & Other STDs

Some locals believe lime juice applied to their private parts after intercourse eliminates the risk of AIDS and other sexually transmitted diseases. Besides probably being painful, it doesn't work.

Although prostitution is legal here and prostitutes are required to be examined regularly, sexually transmitted diseases are regrettably common – and not just among professionals. Just as in any other country you should always use a condom.

Street Crime

Costa Rica is probably safer than most Western countries, but you must take care as you would anywhere. Big cities are where the desperate and dishonest often congregate and San José is no exception. ***Chapulines***, street gangs, prey on tourists in San José. Groups of small children surround the unwary and snatch purses and cameras in the confusion they cause. Occasionally, there are reports of drugs slipped to the unwary in drinks or food. Thefts from parked cars are common. A few rapes and deaths of tourists are reported every year.

Of course you must be careful as you would in any city, but I have encountered more street crime in Paris than I have in San José or Limón.

Outside the big cities things are more casual. In some remote areas hotel lodge rooms do not even have keys. There is often no glass in the windows, only screens, so what would keys do for you? It is always a good idea to keep a substantial portion of your cash in the hotel safe. I try to carry only a bit more than what I think I will need for the day in my wallet along with one credit card. I also keep some cash and a credit card someplace other than in my wallet so that if the unthinkable happens, and I lose my wallet or am mugged, I will have other resources to fall back on. It is also wise to make photocopies of not only your passport details page but your credit cards, too. Keep a copy in your luggage and leave one at home or with a relative you can call if you ever need the information in an emergency. Visible fanny packs are a terrible idea since tricky fingers in a crowd easily rifle them without your even being aware someone has targeted you as an easy mark. Clever thieves can slice open fanny packs and purses with a razor blade and catch whatever falls out. I have friends who keep purses with razor slices in them as souvenirs of holidays gone wrong.

What to Expect

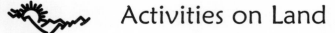

Activities on Land

One of the main reasons Costa Rica is such a popular tourist destination is the vast array of sports, nature and outdoor activities available. Extreme sports enthusiasts, bird-watchers and everyone in between can find the very best of their obsessive interest satisfied here.

Bird-Watching

As one of the premier birding destinations in the world, the wide variety of climates and ecosystems in Costa Rica provides habitats for a very broad range of bird types.

The low-lying, mangrove-thick costal regions are year-round and winter home to sea birds. Costa Rica's northern Caribbean coastal region is directly in the flyover path of the North-South America migratory route. You may see some of the same birds you are used to feeding in your garden alongside brilliant green parrots and toucans in Costa Rica.

Costa Rica is one of the very top birding destinations in the world, with over 400 species reported.

There are some 400 species of birds in the northern Caribbean area, including kingfishers, three species of toucan and eight parrot species. You can routinely expect to see hawks, herons, egrets, anhingas, cormorants, aricaris, jacanas, oropendolas, and frigate birds. The very lucky sharp-eyed visitor may see agami herons, hummingbirds or a great green macaw. Mountain and volcanic regions are home to unusual species such as the resplendent quetzal and ferruginous pygmy owl. Trogons and numerous varieties of parrots are found almost anywhere in the country.

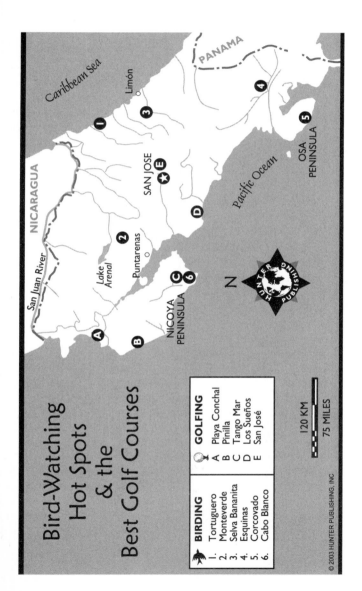

Bird-Watching
Hot Spots
& the
Best Golf Courses

BIRDING
1. Tortuguero
2. Monteverde
3. Selva Bananita
4. Esquinas
5. Corcovado
6. Cabo Blanco

GOLFING
A. Playa Conchal
B. Pinilla
C. Tango Mar
D. Los Sueños
E. San José

120 KM

75 MILES

© 2003 HUNTER PUBLISHING, INC

What to Expect

If you want good-quality pictures of birds or animals and not just the usual "find the animal" pictures, you'll need to bring the biggest telephoto lens you can afford (at least 300mm), fast film and a small, solid tripod. Birds and animals are small and almost always far away. The forests are dark places and are challenging for photographers.

Golf

Although not usually thought of as a golfing destination, Costa Rica has three world-class courses and several other excellent courses. The tropical weather means you can play comfortably year-round, although you may want to bring a good rain suit. Monkeys sometimes run out onto the course to grab golf balls and run off with them, which adds a little local spice to the game.

The best courses are generally considered to be (in order of greatness): **Playa Conchal** near Flamingo, designed by Robert Trent Jones II (☎ 506-654-4123. www.playaconchalresort.com); **Hacienda Pinilla**, south of Tamarindo, designed by Mike Young (☎ 506-680-7000, www.haciendapinilla.com); **Los Sueños**, close to Jacó, designed by Ted Robinson, Jr. (☎ 506-630-9000, www.marriott.com); and the **Melia Cariari** outside San José near the airport; designed by George Fazio (☎ 506-293-3211).

Tennis

Tennis opportunities abound with many hotels and lodges having adequate courts and a few having competition-quality courts. The *Copa del Café* (Coffee Cup) is an international-level competition held annually in San José during the first part of

January. It is hosted by the Costa Rica Country Club (☎ 506-228-9333, www.costaricacountryclub. com) in San José and attracts world-class players and sell-out crowds. The tournament is covered live on local television.

Activities on Water

Fishing

Costa Rica is one of the premier fishing destinations on the planet. Tarpon and snook on the Caribbean side and sailfish, marlin, dorado and rooster fish on the Pacific side come in giant sizes, and fishermen can expect lively action. Fishing charters and lodges are discussed in the regional chapters. Anglers like to state that a day spent fishing, even if you don't catch anything, is better than a day in the office. This seems pretty obvious and not worth stating but some fishermen seem to feel they need an excuse for indulging in their habit.

It is a rare day fishing in Costa Rica when nothing is caught and, during peak season, catching and releasing 15 or even 20 sailfish in the same day is not unusual. I've been on trips where clients asked the captain to head back to the dock since their arms were too tired to tangle with any more sailfish. I've come close to that point myself fighting tarpon out of Silver King Lodge. On one trip my brother and I were simultaneously battling enormous tarpon only to land them and discover that the other two rods we had out both had tarpon on them that we had to deal with. We spent almost two hours fighting tarpon non-stop. The best one was well over 100 lbs.

What to Expect

We groaned at the thought of fighting yet another giant tarpon. Of course, we released them all.

Almost any hotel or lodge can set you up with a guide for a day or half-day trolling or casting for the game fish.

Most visiting fishermen head for **Quepos**, **Flamingo** or **Golfito** on the Pacific coast, and **Barra del Colorado** and **Parismina** on the Caribbean. Some freshwater fishing is done on **Lake Arenal**.

> ★ DID YOU KNOW?
>
> In Costa Rica, all billfish, including sailfish and marlin must be released live. To establish an International Game Fish Association world record, a fish must be weighed on a certified scale. This means no new billfish records will be set in Costa Rica.

It is quite easy to line up a day's fishing. Snapper, dorado, kingfish and grouper are usually brought back to the dock for an evening meal, but billfish, rooster fish and other game fish are released. Costa Rican guides are fastidious about handling fish carefully so they can be released in a healthy condition.

Windsurfing

Arenal volcano is located at one end of the Lake Arenal and, on clear days, you can watch smoke, ash and lava flying through the air with a roar.

As in other areas of the world, windsurfing (although still extremely popular) seems to be fading rapidly in Costa Rica as the more dramatic kite surfing replaces it. Windsurfing is done in many areas of Costa Rica, but **Lake Arenal** is on the list of the best windsurfing destinations in the world. The lake is high, narrow and long, and the 55- to 70-knot winds simply blasts along it all year long.

Several lodges in the area rent equipment and offer lessons. The area around the lake is extremely humid and rainy. Dense tropical rainforest cascades down to the very edges of the lake. Heavy rain sometimes washes out the paved road around the lake requiring long detours on muddy cowboy trails passable only by four-wheel-drive (or horse). **Costa Rica Expeditions** (☎ 506-257-0766, www.costaricaexpeditions.com) and **Costa Rica Nature Escape** (☎ 506-257-8064, www.crnature.com), can arrange windsurfing expeditions to Arenal including transportation, lodging and equipment rental.

Surfing

Costa Rica is one of the hottest places for surfing in the world. The movie *Endless Summer* brought the amazing breaks to the attention of surfers who have made it one of their dream destinations. Surfers young and old flock to the beaches and it's a rare flight that comes into San José without a couple of surfboards in the hold. Long-boarders have to rent Jeeps or vans, or arrange for tour buses to get them to their beach destinations, since internal flights can't handle the big boards. Almost all the beach lodges and resorts, as well as the cheapest of budget hotels cater to surfers, and funky surfer towns with reggae-throbbing surfer bars are part of the Costa Rica beach flavor.

If you're not into the scene, most surfers are friendly and harmless and are to be admired from afar as they frolic like seals in the waves. Many surf shops also arrange kayaking, fishing and diving trips, so be sure to check them out. If you like loud shirts and flowery beachwear, head to the closest surf shop. Hawaiian-style shirts are a great choice for the tropics since they offer a loose, cool fit and dry out

What to Expect

Most local airlines won't accommodate long boards; you'll have to rent a van or Jeep to get around.

quickly. "Walk softly and wear a loud shirt" is the motto of someone famous, and, as an aging Bohemian, I've adopted the saying as my own and have worn out many treasured loud shirts.

Good surfing hot spots are found almost anywhere on either coast.

Many of the best spots are well-kept secrets accessible only by four-wheel-drive or by hiking for many miles along deserted beaches, fording raging tropical rivers and battling mosquitoes swollen to the size of grapefruits. The most popular spots on the Pacific coast include **Potrero**, **Playa Coco**, **Playa Naranjo** and **Playa Langosta** near Tamarindo in the Nicoya region, **Jacó** and **Manuel Antonio** in the mid-Pacific, and **Pavones** in the Osa Peninsula. The main Caribbean spots are **Puerto Viejo de Limón**, **Playa Bonita** and **Portete**. Ask the local crowd where the best places are.

In the Northern Pacific areas, there is good surf pretty much all year long; the Caribbean surf seasons run from January to March and from July to October. The Central Pacific area is fairly dependable year-round, and the Southern Pacific areas, Matapalo, Pavones and Zancudo, are considered best from July through November. Almost any time of the year in almost any season you may find the biggest and best waves you've ever surfed, so don't worry too much about timing.

Whitewater Rafting

Costa Rica offers some of the finest whitewater rafting found anywhere ranging from class I to class V+ in difficulty. Most of the rafting is done on the **Pacuare** and **Reventazón rivers**, but other rivers, including the **Savegre**, **Corobici**, **Sarapiquí**, **Naranjo** and **El General** are also open to rafters. Tours run from one to five days. The Pacuare and

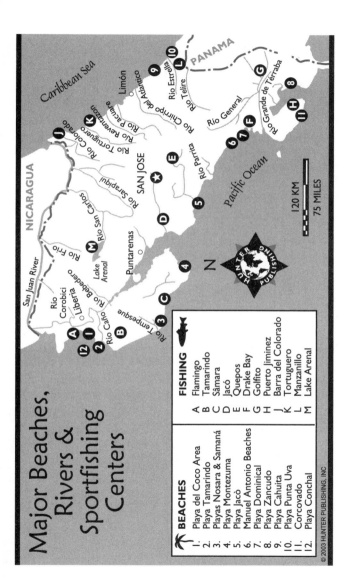

Major Beaches, Rivers & Sportfishing Centers

BEACHES
1. Playa del Coco Area
2. Playa Tamarindo
3. Playas Nosara & Samaná
4. Playa Montezuma
5. Playa Jacó
6. Manuel Antonio Beaches
7. Playa Dominical
8. Playa Zancudo
9. Playa Cahuita
10. Playa Punta Uva
11. Corcovado
12. Playa Conchal

FISHING
A Flamingo
B Tamarindo
C Sámara
D Jacó
E Quepos
F Drake Bay
G Golfito
H Puerto Jiminez
J Barra del Colorado
K Tortuguero
L Manzanillo
M Lake Arenal

© 2003 HUNTER PUBLISHING, INC

Reventazón are both within an easy drive of San José and, although several companies offer two- and three-day trips on these rivers, there is little reason to spend more than one day. The overnight trips usually cover the same amount of river – they just involve hikes into the jungle and walks to an assortment of waterfalls and jungle pools.

Ríos Tropicales (☎ 506-233-6455, www.riostropicales.com), offers the most comfortable and complete tours, especially on the Pacuare. Their riverside lodge is a good place to rest up halfway down and explore the surrounding almost-untouched forest.

Class Conscious

- ◎ **Pacuare** is an 18-mile run with class I-IV rapids and class V on the upper end.

- ◎ **Reventazón** is a 12-mile run with mostly class III and some class V at the upper end.

- ◎ The **Sarapiquí** in the Northeast is about 15 km (nine miles) long with class II and some class IV rapids.

- ◎ **El General** in the Southwest near San Isidro de El General is not visited as often as the others and has class IV and V rapids.

None of the rafting outfitters offer anything approaching luxury accommodations, although **Costa Rica Expeditions** (☎ 506-257-0766), offers private gourmet raft trips, but they have no lodge – camping or one-day trips only. Most of the outfitters take clients through class I-IV rapids only, although they can arrange more extreme trips for qualified rafters to class V+ rapids. Most of the rivers have some sections of class V on the upper ends. The scenery on these trips is spectacular. You don't really see much wildlife as you move down the river since you are kept busy most of the time but the tropical forest along the riverbanks is stunning.

All levels of experience can be accommodated. Most operators pick you up at your hotel early in the morning around 6 am or 7 am, provide breakfast and lunch, and drop you off back at your hotel in the evening around 6 pm.

These wonderful trips should not be missed. If you are fearful of white water rafting, just book a gentler trip.

Costa Rica-based whitewater rafting tour operators include **Aventuras Naturales** (☎ 506-225-3939; 800-514-0411, in the US; www.toenjoynature.com), **Costa Rica Expeditions** (☎ 506-257-0766, 506-222-0333, www.costaricaexpeditions.com), and **Ríos Tropicales** (☎ 506-233-6455, www.riostropicales. com). US-based whitewater rafting tour operators include **California Native** (☎ 800-926-1140), **Mariah Wilderness Expeditions** (☎ 800-462-7424), **Mountain Travel** (☎ 800-227-2384), **Pioneer Raft** (☎ 800-288-2107), and **Wildland Adventures** (☎ 800-345-4453). Costa Rica Expeditions is the oldest and probably the most respected rafting outfitter in the country. See the *San José Tours* section (page 108), for more details on these tour operators and their offerings. Most agencies and hotels can book whitewater rafting trips through these same outfitters.

Shopping

Costa Rica is not usually thought of as a destination for shopping. Some **crafts** are worth buying

What to Expect

and the world-class **coffee** is spectacular and something almost every visitor takes home.

Where to Go & What to Buy

Business Hours

Changing cash in banks can take hours and the rates aren't much better than what you can get in your hotel.

Most businesses are open at times similar to what you would expect in North America. Store hours from 8 am to 6 pm is common, except for banks, which are open from 9 am to 3 pm. Some private banks are open until 5 pm. Government offices close at 4 pm. Most restaurants close before midnight and will serve meals all day.

Antiques

Few true antiques are to be found in Costa Rico, but it is possible to find colonial or old world furniture. Expect to pay a premium price. The San José *Shop Till You Drop* section (page 118) lists a few places where hard-core antique hunters might look.

Carts (Carretas)

The genuine antique carts from the town of Sarchí are treasured and can be quite expensive.

The town of **Sarchí** in the central plateau is known for its highly decorated bullock carts (*carretas*), examples of which you will see in hotel lobbies all over the country. A visit to the workshops that produce these beautiful constructions creates a desire in some people to buy one to put in their lawn back home. Shipping can be arranged. These carts are uniquely Costa Rican handicrafts and can be exquisitely detailed and brightly colored.

Believe it or not, in the old days, such fancy carts were actually used by everyday farmers, who still take pride in their beautiful carts. An annual cart parade and competition is held in Sarchí every year in February. Half-day tours to Sarchí are commonly coupled with trips to Poás Volcano or to one of the coffee plantations. Many other handicrafts are available in the town. Even though it is a pretty touristy scene, the town is beautiful and worth a visit.

Ceramics

Most of the interesting ceramic bowls, plates and figures sold in Costa Rica come from **Guatíl**, a small town in the Nicoya Peninsula with a thriving ceramics industry. Individual craftsmen are organized mostly by women who operate small shops and cooperatives. The prices are quite a bit lower if you actually go to Guatíl, but don't expect to bargain much. The quality is excellent; designs tend to earth tones and traditional geometric. Many shops around the country can arrange shipping, but many of the pieces are large and heavy. See page 170 for more details.

Coffee

Justifiably famous for delicious coffee, Costa Rica exports most of the best they produce, so sometimes you'll get a lame cup in the country. But you can still buy great coffee locally. Ticos like their coffee extremely sweet and, if you buy it ground, it sometimes comes with sugar already in the bag. Whole beans are your best bet unless you are sure the ground coffee you are buying is *sin azúcar* (without sugar) or *puro* (pure). Grocery stores sell good coffee in bags at probably the best prices you'll find. I like

What to Expect

Store your coffee beans in the freezer as soon as you get home. Beans can develop a slight rancid flavor if left at room temperature.

Tres Generaciones (from Doka Estates) and **Café Britt**. **Volio**, **Américo** and **Montaña** are also acceptable. Hotel gift shops sell cute little bags at very high prices but, unless you want to give cute little gifts to someone, you can buy a half-pound bag of better coffee for half the price in the grocery store.

★ DID YOU KNOW?

Ticos traditionally make their coffee in an interesting sock-in-a-stand arrangement. It's basically a little iron tripod with a thin sock dangling in the middle. Coffee is put in the sock, a cup or pot underneath and boiling water is poured on top of the coffee. These stands, called **chorreadotes**, make great gifts and conversation pieces for impressing your friends when you get back home. Buy several of the socks so you can continue enjoying coffee à la *Tico*. The contraptions make excellent coffee.

Duty-Free Information

Tourists are rarely bothered about bringing things into the country but there are limits on the amount of film and consumer goods that can be imported. Many Costa Ricans returning from trips abroad are loaded down with highly taxed electronics and consumer goods. Customs inspectors seem to have their eyes peeled for these travelers and let tourists get through with no hassle even though they may be carrying similar items.

Photography

Tips for Shutterbugs

Only places like Kenya and the Galapagos rival Costa Rica for wildlife and nature photography opportunities. Bring plenty of film! Realize that wildlife is one of the most difficult (but rewarding) photography subjects. Powerful telephoto lenses and extreme patience are needed to get high-quality close-ups of monkeys, other mammals and birds. Frogs, flowers and tropical forest scenes are usually easier subjects and can provide spectacular shots. Light levels are usually quite low in the forest so bring low light film (ISO 400 or higher) and use an integrated flash if possible.

Butterflies are hard to photograph as they flit about randomly just before you press the shutter release.

As soon as you step out into the humidity after riding around in your air-conditioned car your camera and eyeglass lenses fog up instantly. It can take up to 20 minutes for temperatures to equalize and the condensation to go away. If I'm riding in the car and think I may encounter sudden photo opportunities, I keep the air-conditioning set to include outside air and keep the driver's side window wide open to minimize condensation on my lenses. I like to carry my cameras inside plastic, zip-lock bags when trekking through the rainforest and bring several soft cloths to help keep my lenses free from moisture. Be careful when changing film in the forest that you don't drip sweat off your face into the inside of your camera. This may seem to be strange advice but a couple of drops of salty sweat falling on to your shutter can ruin your photo session.

What to Expect

Bring plenty of low-light film, ISO 400 or higher, for use in the rainforest.

Film and developing are more expensive in Costa Rica than in the US, Canada or Europe. The best plan is to buy your film before you leave home, wait until you return to develop it, and bring spare batteries, etc. with you. Life isn't always simple, so if you need film, photographic supplies or camera repairs, there are three reasonably competent shops in San José, **Equipos Fotogrficos Canon** (Avenida 3 between Calles 3 and 5, ☎ 506-233-0176); **Dima Color** (Pavas Avenida Central between Calles 3 and 5, near the US embassy, ☎ 506-222-3969, 506-231-4130); and **Rapi Foto** (Calle Central at Avenida 7, ☎ 506-223-7640).

Are your landscape shots pale and washed out? Use a polarizing filter to make colors brighter.

Some lodges and small local stores sell film, but experienced photographers prefer not to buy film in Central America. It can be poor quality after spending long periods of time in hot shipping containers on its way to Costa Rica by freighter.

Normally Costa Ricans don't mind having their picture taken but it is only polite to interact a bit before taking a shot. A couple of Spanish words and phrases can go a long way. I like to think about it this way: "If I were at home in my country, how would I feel if a tourist were taking this picture of me?" If the situation is appropriate, simply saying *¿Permiso?* (May I?) may be quite enough.

San José

– & The Central Valley –

Overview

San José sits in a lovely valley, overlooked by old and crumbling volcanoes: **Poás**, **Irazú** and **Barva**. The few interesting attractions in San José are in the **central** part of town. The city is a bit rundown and not particularly attractive, but the area around it, the *Meseta Central*, or Central Valley, is full of things to do and see. There are many possibilities for great day-trips from San José. The suburbs are more pleasant than the city and I advise staying outside of the central part of town where things are quieter, safer and generally nicer.

The most interesting sites are outside of town. The suburbs of **Escazú** and **Alajuela** (close to the airport) are more pleasant and less busy than central San José. Almost any hotel can arrange day-trips to coffee plantations, cloud forests, volcanoes, or whitewater rafting adventure. and even a day at the beach. There are numerous agencies anxious to help you. Some people take day-trips from San José to the Monteverde Cloud Forest Preserve, but it is a bit much to do in one day. Besides, there are more fun and less-crowded parks closer to town.

Climate

Due to altitude (1,400 meters/4,600 feet), the temperature in San José averages about 75°F (22°C)

Bring a good rain coat & an umbrella.

year-round and never gets much below 65°F (18°C) or above 80°F (28°C), in spite of being in the tropics. Rain is to be expected almost every day, even in the so-called dry season (December though April). Torrential downpours are common, and often last for several days.

Don't get the wrong impression; the climate is really lovely and is one of the best in the world. It's never too hot or too cold, and you don't have to worry about watering the grass.

Getting Here

Airlines serving San José usually come through Houston, Miami and Los Angeles (connecting through Mexico City). **American**, **Continental**, **Delta**, **LACSA**, **Mexicana**, **TACA** and **United** are among the carriers. From Europe, there are flights from Madrid on **Iberia**, and from Amsterdam on **Martin Air**. Havana is a popular hub for flights from Europe and South and Central America.

Getting Around

Central San José is fairly compact and you can walk to most places of interest. Crossing streets is very dangerous, even at marked crossings with traffic lights. Be sure to look both ways at least twice before crossing any street, and consider running across. Drivers seem to take great joy in aiming straight at you – if you're in the road, you're fair game. Taxis are relatively cheap and usually easy to flag down, except during a rainstorm.

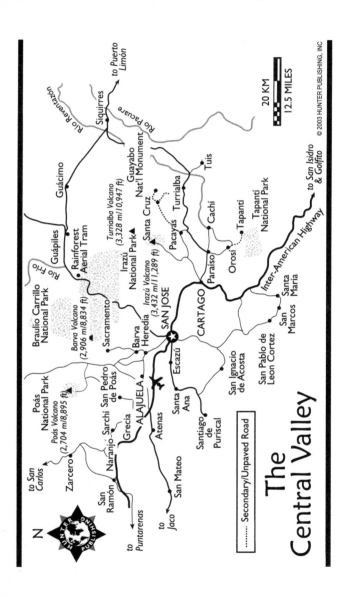

The
Central Valley

N

.... Secondary/Unpaved Road

20 KM
12.5 MILES

© 2003 HUNTER PUBLISHING, INC

San José

Driving a car in San José is not recommended for tourists.

If you are comfortable driving in cities like New York, Paris, Rome or Mexico City, you'll be okay here. But since parking (and theft from cars) is such a problem, it usually makes more sense to leave your car in the hotel parking lot and take taxis.

The bus system can seem incomprehensible, but is actually fairly well organized. Buses usually run on time and are often packed. The legendary Third World "chicken buses" are mostly found in the countryside. Of course, the more you're willing to use public transportation, the more likely you are to meet interesting locals, and experience the parts of Costa Rica that tourists never see. Special tourist buses hit the most popular attractions. Inquire at your hotel.

Getting Your Bearings

In spite of what you may think at first, there is some logic in San José's layout. The downtown area is a grid, with the pedestrian-only streets – **Calle Central** and **Avenida Central** – crossing more or less in the middle. *Avenidas* (avenues) run east and west. *Calles* (streets) run north and south. The avenidas north of Avenida Central are odd-numbered and the ones south of Avenida Central are even-numbered. The calles east of Calle Central are odd numbered and calles west of Calle Central are even.

*Downtown San José has numbered streets (*calles*) and avenues (*avenidas*).*

Paseo Colon leads west from downtown toward Parque La Sabana and is considered the main street in town. There are some hotels and tourist-oriented travel offices in that direction. To the east of downtown are **San Pedro** and the **university** area. **Escazú** is a pleasant suburb to the west of town, overlooking the city. The **airport** is northwest of

Central San José

1. Coca-Cola Bus Terminal
2. Bus for Alajuela & airport
3. Parque La Merced
4. Central Market
5. Children's Museum
6. Melico Salazar Theater
7. Parque Central
8. Metropolitan Cathedral
9. Aurola Holiday Inn
10. National Theater
11. Cultural Plaza
    (Gold Museum & Tourism Office)
12. Esmaralda
13. Hotel Don Carlos
14. Parque Morazán
15. Serpentario indoor zoo
16. Edificio Metálico (Metal Building)
17. Parque España
18. National Cultural Center
19. Casa Amarillo
20. INS Building (Jade Museum)
21. Parque Zoologico Simon Bolivar
22. El Pueblo shopping complex
23. Parque Nacional
24. National Library
25. Democracy Plaza
26. National Museum (Fort Bellavista)
27. Criminology Museum
28. National Train Museum

N

Paseo Colon

500 METERS
200 FEET

San José

town. Most streets downtown are one way. Simple, right?

The problem starts when you realize that locals use more than the street number alone to specify a location. Quite logically (to the Ticos), particular addresses are expressed as "between Calle 2 and 4, Avenida 4" or "Calle 3, 50 meters south of Banco Popular," for example. City blocks are considered to be 100 meters, whether they are or not, so 50 meters means in the middle of the block.

You may have to walk a few blocks, or ask someone, before you know what street you are on. Addresses expressed as distances from major landmarks are common. The problem for visitors is when the landmarks are no longer there, but everyone (except you) knows where they used to be, like the old Coca-Cola bottling plant. This actually works if you make sure to use the local system and don't try to refer to places using street numbers, even if you somehow find them out. If you tell your taxi driver you are going to the Jazz Café in San Pedro, *frente de Farmacia Fischel*, you'll get there.

Rental Cars

Street signs are often nonexistent, obscured or even painted over.

It is not necessary to rent four-wheel-drive vehicles, unless you are going to be off the main roads or well out of the Central Highlands area. Monteverde, Arenal or some of the more remote areas in Osa and Nicoya can be challenging, or impassable, in regular vehicles. If you are going out of the San José area, a four-wheel-drive will be a comfort. The following are the biggest operators.

Rental Agencies

ADOBE RENT A CAR
Store no. 20, Plaza Ventura Shopping Center
Apdo. 325-1000, San José
☎ 506-221-5425; fax 506-221-9286
www.adobecar.com

AVIS
Apdo. 508 Centro Colón
Behind the Lizano factory in La Asunción de
Belén
Calle 36, Avenida 7
☎ 506-239-2806; fax 506-293-1111
www.avis.co.cr

BUDGET
Paseo Colón, 30th Street
Apdo. 255-1007 Centro Colón
☎ 506-232-3284; fax 506-255-4966
www.budget.co.cr

DOLLAR
Paseo Colón, between 30th and 32nd Street
Apdo. 184-1005 San José
☎ 506-257-1585; fax 506-222-1765
www.dollarcostarica.com

THRIFTY
One kilometer (half-mile) east of San José
Airport
Apdo. 750-1007 Centro Colón
☎ 506-394-3257
thrifty@racsa.co.cr

San José

ECONOMY LIMO SERVICE
☎ 506-231-5410
They offer chauffeured airport pickups and hourly service to take you on tours of the city and surrounding areas. Their drivers are uniformed and bilingual.

Some of the more interesting restaurants are found outside town and are expensive to reach by taxi.

Outside San José, driving yourself begins to make more sense, but most day-trips organized through hotels or agencies will include pickup at your hotel. Lunches, snacks, etc., are usually part of the deal, so a car is really not needed unless you want the freedom provided by having your own transportation.

Traffic in and out of San José can be a nightmare and road signs are not dependable. It's easy to get turned around, and find yourself heading in the wrong direction but, if you have a map and a sense of adventure, exploring the Central Valley by car can be a joy. If you are staying in one of the suburban hotels (recommended), a rental car is worthwhile.

 # Sunup to Sundown

Seven-Day Itinerary

Day 1

If you're coming from North America, you probably won't experience jet lag, so you can jump right into exploring the city and your surroundings. If your hotel is in town, take an afternoon walk around town and visit the **Central Market** (page 118) and stop for lunch or dinner at one of the centrally located restaurants, such as **Machu Pichu** (page 147).

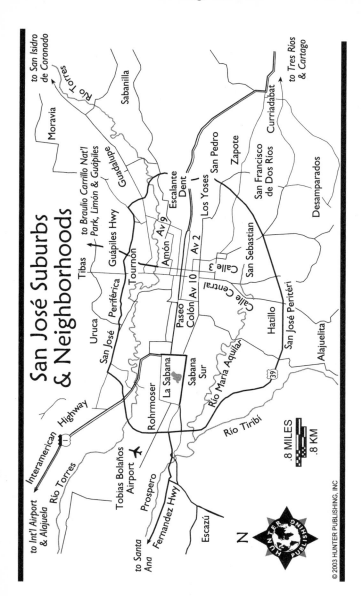

San José Suburbs & Neighborhoods

to San Isidro de Coronado

Río Torres

Moravia

Sabanilla

to Tres Ríos & Cartago

Curriadabat

to Braulio Carrillo Nat'l Park, Limón & Guápiles

Guadalupe

San Pedro

Zapote

San Francisco de Dos Ríos

Desamparados

Escalante

Dent

Los Yoses

Tibas

Guápiles Hwy

Tournón

Amón

Av 9

Av 2

Calle 3

San Sebastian

Uruca

Periférica

San José

Paseo Colón

Av 10

Calle Central

Hatillo

San José Peritéri

Alajuelita

Interamerican Highway

Río Torres

Rohrmoser

La Sabana

Sabana Sur

Río María Aguilar

Río Tiribi

39

.8 MILES

.8 KM

Tobias Bolaños Airport

Prospero

Fernandez Hwy

Escazú

to Int'l Airport & Alajuela

to Santa Ana

N

© 2003 HUNTER PUBLISHING, INC

HUNTER PUBLISHING

San José

An **organized tour** is also a good idea, especially if your hotel is located in the suburbs. Central San José is difficult to navigate and the traffic can be daunting. Spend the afternoon exploring more of San José, or indulging in your favorite sport (golf, tennis), or leisure activity (pool, tropical cocktails). On arrival, I always buy a copy of the English-language *Tico Times* to check out the nightlife and live music options for the evening.

Day 2

A variety of **combination tours** (usually with lunch) covers attractions in the Meseta Central surrounding San José (page 108). I suggest taking at least two of these while in the area. Start off with a trip to **Poás volcano** (page 114), in the morning, followed by a visit to **Doka Estates** or **Café Britt** coffee plantation (page 111).

An evening visit to the **Jazz Café** (page 124) is best scheduled for a light sightseeing day, as the music usually doesn't start until after 10 pm, and often goes on until well after midnight. Take a late nap and then go. They serve excellent food, so you can make a whole night of it.

Day 3

A day-long visit to the **Caribbean lowlands** (page 108) is a must. Wildlife is easy to see on guided boat trips through the canals. Tour agencies can handle all the details and arrange to pick you up at your hotel in the morning, and zip you down by air or bus to Tortuguero for bird-watching and eco-tours. You'll be well fed and back in your hotel for another evening on the town.

The new casino at **Hotel Martino Spa & Resort** (page 127), near Alajuela, is a good choice for an excellent Italian meal and an evening at the tables.

Day 4

If you had an easy night the night before, schedule a **whitewater rafting trip** (see page 116) on one of the Class IV or IV rivers outside San José. Rafting trips cater to all levels of expertise, from complete newbie to rafting expert. Costa Rica is a world-class rafting destination, and several excellent rivers are an easy day-trip from San José. Rafting tour operators arrange for early morning hotel pickup, breakfast, bus, all equipment, guides, lunch, and get you back to your San José hotel before dinner. Be sure to bring a change of clothes, since you are guaranteed to get soaked from head to toe. The water is refreshing and spending a few hours soaking wet is actually quite pleasant in the warm tropics. Have dinner close to your hotel and sleep late in the morning.

Day 5

By now, you probably have a good feel for the things you want to take home for mementos or gifts. Spend the day shopping. A trip to **Sarchí** (page 113) or the **Central Market** (page 118) for handicrafts, clothes and specialty items will take up a morning or afternoon. If you haven't loaded up on coffee from a tour of a coffee plantation, stop by a local supermarket for top-quality coffee at bargain prices. Both **Doka Estates** and **Café Britt** have very good buys on coffee and will ship it back home for you for a small fee.

San José

Day 6

Big-time **sportfishing** (page 83) or a trip to the **Monteverde Cloud Forest** (page 166) are both popular trips, but can be a bit much to get accomplished in one day. Tour operators can pick you up at your hotel, and zip you down to the coast for sailfish, or over the notorious (but now improved) mountain roads, to the cloud forest, and get you back around dinnertime, but it is a long day. An alternative is to choose another combination tour and visit **Zoo Ave** (page 118), near Alajuela, for wildlife photo opportunities, **Irazú volcano** (page 22), **Sarchí** (page 113) or, if you still haven't done it, visit one of the coffee plantations (page 111).

Day 7

Buy any last-minute souvenirs still on your list, eat a seafood lunch at **El Banco de Los Mariscos** (page 153), and head to the airport.

Bullfights

The object of fights seems to be to smack the bulls on the butt without being butted in return.

Costa Rican bullfights are completely unlike those in Spain or Mexico, or anywhere else in the world, but still are probably not for sensitive souls. In the Costa Rican version, the bulls frequently get the best of the bullfighters. It's actually quite an entertaining event – not nearly as cruel as you might expect. The ring is crowded with young bullfighters that seem to delight in causing their fellow bullfighters to get into often amusing difficulties with the bulls.

The bullfighters spend most of their time running away. Most bullfights are held during the Christmas holiday season in a ring just outside San José. Local television stations carry the "fights" during this time. Don't miss it – it's a hoot.

Fútbol (soccer)

Costa Rica has probably the best Central American team, although it has never made it to the World Cup. **Estadio Ricardo Saprissa stadium** (in Tibás) holds the matches on Sundays during the season (September to June), and **Estadio Nacional** (near La Sabana Park) holds games on Wednesdays. Most Ticos are enthusiasts, supporting either *El Monstro* (San José) or one of the regional teams. The games can get rowdy and only the true *fútbol* fanatics should go.

Golf

There are limited golfing opportunities in San José, although both the **Hotel Meliá Cariari** and **Hotel Herradura** have golf courses, but are not really open to non-guests. Sometimes your hotel can make arrangements to get you a tee time. Ask your concierge. In Santa Ana, just outside town, there is an 18-hole course at **Parque Valle del Sol**, ☎ 506-282-9222, www.vallesol.com. The **Costa Rica Country Club** (☎ 506-228-9333, www.costaricacountryclub.com) has a fair course.

San José

Museums

People used to visiting world-famous museums in other countries may be disappointed in San José's more modest offerings.

Tennis

Parque La Sabana is a large public park at the end of Paseo Colón. It has courts and hosts the ***Copa de Café*** (Coffee Cup), an international-level competition held annually in San José during the first part of January.

Day-Trips & Tours

*S*an José is a great place to base yourself to explore the surrounding **Meseta Central**. Although a fascinating and bustling city, San José is not a developed tourist destination and the few sights worth seeing can be explored mostly by walking around on your own.

You can reach almost any place in the country on a half-hour flight from San José.

There are dozens of full-day and half-day tours you can take. **Costa Rica Expeditions**, **Costa Rica Nature Escape** and **Grayline Tours Costa Rica**, all offer a variety tours. You can combine two half-day tours into an entire day's expedition, including lunch. The most popular tours are to **coffee plantations and factories** (not to be missed), **volcano tours** to Poás and Irazú, the **rainforest aerial tram** and the **butterfly farms**. A day-trip to **Monteverde** is perhaps a bit much to do, considering the four-hour horrendous ride to get there. **Sarchí** is a short trip if you're in the market for some attractive yard art.

Escazú

to San José
via Highway

27

Ferretería
Bello Horizonte

to
Hotel Alta

traffic light

Back road
to San José

Car Wash

El Cruce
Shopping Ctr

Periféricos
Supermarket

Soccer Field

Quiub Q'tal

SAN RAFAEL
DE ESCAZU

traffic light

Mas y Menos
Supermarket

to Costa
Verde

SAN ANTONIO
DE ESCAZU

Bello Horizonte

to
Tiquicia

N

Biesanz
Wood Showroom

to
Tara Resort Hotel

HUNTER PUBLISHING

NOT TO SCALE

© 2003 HUNTER PUBLISHING, INC

San José

Some tour operators can arrange trips to areas a bit farther from San José for fishing, diving, birding, etc., and get you back in time for dinner. If you have a small group and want to arrange a charter flight (see *Getting Around*, page 67 for charter airlines), you can comfortably do almost anything the country has to offer from a San José base.

Most hotels and lodges can arrange for any tours offered in the area. Both **Costa Rica Expeditions** (☎ 506-257-0766, www.costaricaexpeditions.com) and **Costa Rica Nature Escape** (☎ 506-257-8064, www.crnature.com), can make all arrangements for tours in advance.

Butterfly Farms

Covered by light netting, butterfly farms range from a few square feet to several acres in size and consist of gardens planted with the tropical plants each type of butterfly needs to eat and reproduce. Some include displays of the reproductive process. An excellent one is the **Costa Rica Entomological Supply**, better known simply as the Butterfly Farm. Tours run continuously from 9 am-5 pm. The cost is $15 per adult. ☎ 506-438-0400, www.central-america.com/cr/butterfly/bflybus.htm.

Canopy Tours

Canopy tours (around US $55), usually involve either elevated walkways through the forest or zip-line rides whizzing through the trees. They are quite popular and fun, but don't expect to see much in the way of wildlife – they are more about an exhilarating ride than ecology. The screams of punters often drown out any songs from birds and scare off all but the most jaded jungle inhabitants. **Sky Trek** in Monteverde (see page 169) has slides and walkways in a fantastic cloud forest setting.

City Tour

Grayline Tours Costa Rica, ☎ 506-220-2126, offers a "Discover the Capital City" tour. You'll visit the National Theatre, National Museum, downtown and residential neighborhoods. Hotel pickups are included in the $25 fee. Most hotels and lodges can arrange for any tours offered in the area.

Coffee Tours

The **Café Britt** tour is on almost every visitor's itinerary. It's a wonderful tour, but consider visiting the prize-winning **Doka Estate** (see below), if you want to know how the very best coffee is grown and prepared. You may have to call Doka directly to arrange a tour, as almost all the hotels and agencies in town steer tourists to the Britt tour.

CAFÉ BRITT
Just outside Heredia
☎ 506-260-2748
www.cafebritt.com
$20 for tour only, $15 for transportation from most San José hotels

Café Britt presents a very slick, fun tour of a coffee farm, and a look at their roasting operation, along with hijinks by professional actors. Part of the tour takes the form of a play, which happens to be the longest-running play in Costa Rican history. This is an entertaining tour with an opportunity to buy coffee and gifts at great prices.

San José

You'll get to taste a wide variety of fresh roasted coffee. The tour is given at the Britt roasting operations just outside Heredia. This is in a rundown area and is very hard to find. I suggest you pay for the transportation from your hotel. If you drive, ask them to fax you directions, but beware: there are gross inaccuracies in the map. There are hundreds of signs in the area pointing to the tour, but signs are missing at some key intersections. Although $20 is a bit much for the two-hour tour, it is fun. Tours are at 9 am, 11 am, and at 3 pm. The 11 am tour includes lunch and lots of coffee. They do have decaf. You can easily combine this tour with a trip to Poás volcano.

Café Britt will ship coffee home for you, or will provide carry-on containers for your purchases.

DOKA ESTATE
Alajuela
☎ 506-449-5152
www.dokaestate.com
Tours: Monday-Friday, 9:30 am & 1:30 pm; Sat., 9:30 am; Sun. with reservations. Coffee shop is open Mon.-Fri., 9 am-5 pm; Sat., 8 am-1 pm
$15

To learn about how coffee is grown and prepared and have a chance to taste and buy the very best coffee in Costa Rica (and perhaps in the world), visit Costa Rican-owned Doka Estate. It's just outside Alajuela near Sabanilla.

For two years running, Doka has won both first and second prize in the annual national competition for the best Costa Rican coffee. This is a prize not lightly given. It is interesting to note that although Doka's premier *Tres Generaciones* brand won first place both years, their second-quality *Medio Luna* brand won second place. This means that the best of Café Britt, Volio and all the other Costa Rican coffees could not match the second-best from Doka. About

Doka Estate has been producing coffee on their 450-acre plantation for 80 years and still uses the same, water-driven mill and traditional methods they started out with. Only coffee beans grown on their own land is used for their *Tres Generaciones* brand. The excellent quality is said to be due to their use of only the *arabica* species *caturra*, *catuai* and *Costa Rica 95* plants, the high altitude and volcanic soil the beans are grown in, and the company's insistence on sun-drying them. The *Tres Generaciones* brand is sun-dried for five days, while their *Medio Luna* brand is partially dried in wood-fired dryers.

About 90% of Doka's output is exported prior to being roasted, with about 65% going to Starbucks.

Tours are given at 9:30 am and 1:30 pm, and include visits to the old water-driven processing facility, drying pans, fields, packaging facility and gift shop. Of course, you can buy some their very best coffees, and either ship it home or take it with you. You can also order coffee on their website. The tour is educational – there is no dog-and-pony show. Tour guide Julia Bravo starts off by, surprise, surprise, offering visitors a cup of coffee. At the end of the tour, visitors are again given a chance to taste the best coffee in Costa Rica. This tour should not be missed.

Sarchí

Sarchí's claim to fame is the highly decorated, typically Costa Rican (at least they were typical 50 years ago) **ox cart**. The **Chevarri Oxcart Factory** is a common destination for tourists wishing to see or buy these interestingly decorated carts. You are sure to see some of the better examples in hotel lobbies in San José and other places. Many North Americans like to buy them and display them in their yards at home filled with flowers. Sarchí is about 16 km (10 miles) past the airport and is a nice

way to spend a morning or afternoon on your own or
with a group.

Tortuguero National Park

*The forest in
the Tortuguero
area is truly
tropical and it
is very likely to
rain, but the
boats are cov-
ered.*

Day-trips through the canals by boat start at US
$75, including breakfast and lunch. The park is one
of the best places in Costa Rica to see wildlife. You
can expect to be amazed by the birds, monkeys,
sloths, caimans, crocodiles and other wildlife. The
bus ride each way is about three hours and the hotel
pickups in San José are usually at 6:30 am.

Volcanoes

There are four massive volcanoes within a short
drive of San José. They are not usually active, but do
blast off a bit from time to time in a minor way. See
the *Volcanos* section (page 22) for detailed descriptions. **Poás** and **Irazú** are two of the few volcanoes
in the world where you can drive right up to the
crater and peer inside.

Grayline Tours Costa Rica, ☎ 506-220-2126,
Costa Rica Expeditions, ☎ 506-257-0766, and
Costa Rica Nature Escape, ☎ 506-257-8064, offer
day-trips from San José to Arenal, Irazú, and Poás,
with hotel pickups. Arenal is a bit of a long haul to do
in one day and the cone is often obscured by clouds.
Tours from San José run from $45 and up and usu-
ally include pickup from your hotel.

Volcán Poás National Park

Volcán Poás National Park is the most visited park
in Costa Rica, which is not surprising, given its location close to San José, and the ability to get up close

to a steaming volcanic crater. The park is well developed and the facilities are similar to US national parks, with a visitors' center, interactive displays and video room. The gift shop is loaded with the typical carvings of toucans and coffee-related items you will see all over the country. The café offers fantastic coffee, served in all the ways popular with North Americans: latte, cappuccino, espresso, American-style coffee, and, all the usual flavoring syrups if you must have them. The food is best skipped, although the tamales wrapped in banana leaves are nice.

The walkways and trails are short, easy and well maintained. You can go only to an overlook of the crater, and on a short walk to the Green Lagoon, a small crater with a sort of green lake. The lagoon is hardly worth the effort, being a small lake with a slight green tint. The overlook of the crater is a good photo opportunity. There is a viewing platform perched on the crater rim, but it can be rather crowded with families with young children at times. You can comfortably observe *fumaroles* spouting sulphurous smoke, and there are signs explaining what the different craters are all about.

The crater is often clouded in, meaning all you get to see is the inside of a cloud – a bunch of fog, in other words. Many tours to Poás leave San José very early in order to get to the crater by eight or nine in the morning. The park closes at 3:30 pm. On the way up, be sure to stop at the small roadside **Casa de Café**, which sells absolutely wonderful coffee and a few coffee-oriented souvenirs. The drive takes you through some of the finest coffee-growing regions in Costa Rica and you can see hundreds of acres of screen-covered fields of coffee plants. The area is also famous for growing strawberries and you can buy them at roadside stands.

San José

Although the park is mostly about the volcano and the crater, there are many associated acres of cloud forest preserve that are not accessible to the public. Some wildlife can be seen from the walks, but the times I've been there I was lucky if I saw squirrels.

There are few volcanoes in the world where you can actually peer down into the crater without a lot of hiking and danger involved. While Mona Loa Volcano in Hawaii is bigger and more spectacular all the way around, Poás is worth a trip. You can easily combine an early visit to Poás with a tour of the nearby Doka or Café Britt coffee plantation and get back to San José in time to freshen up for a night out.

Whitewater Rafting

Several outfitters offer one- to three-day rafting trips (see *What to Expect*, page 86), to the **Pacuare** and **Reventazón rivers**. Levels range from class I-IV, although class V trips can be arranged for experienced rafters. Scenery on these trips is spectacular. You don't see much wildlife since you are kept busy most of the time, but the tropical forest along the riverbanks is stunning. These are wonderful trips and you shouldn't miss them, even if you're afraid of the idea of whitewater rafting – just book a gentler trip.

All levels of experience can be accommodated.

Most operators pick you up at your hotel early in the morning around 6 am or 7 am, provide breakfast and lunch, and drop you back at your hotel around 6 pm.

AVENTURAS NATURALES
Apdo. 10736-1000, San José
☎ 506-225-3939, fax 506-253-6934;
In US, 800-514-0411
www.toenjoynature.com
$95, one-day Pacuare trip

Aventuras Naturales offers one and multi-day trips. The multi-day trips are on the Pacuare and stops at the company's Pacuare Lodge, which offers basic accommodations in the rainforest at the river's edge. The website gives a good explanation of the packages and trip levels.

COSTA RICA EXPEDITIONS
Calle Central & Avenida 3, San José
Apdo. 6941-1000, San José
☎ 506-257-0766, 506-222-0333; fax 506-257-1665
www.costaricaexpeditions.com

CRE started out organizing rafting tours on the world-famous Pacuare River and has expanded into the largest tour operator in the country, offering every conceivable type of tour. They offer rafting trips to all the main rivers in Costa Rica, with camping and even special gourmet rafting trips.

RIOS TROPICALES
☎ 506-233-6455; fax 506-255-4354
www.riostropicales.com
$95, one-day Pacuare trip

One- , two- and three-day trips down the Pacuare and Reventazón with stops at their riverside lodge on the Pacuare if you feel like lingering. The lodge is quite basic. The overnight trips include side trips through the rainforest and visits to tropical waterfalls and jungle pools – you don't cover any more river if you go for more than one day. Once you get past the annoying river sounds and pop-ups, their website gives a good explanation of the packages and trip levels, but you have to dig around a bit to get the full picture. Turn your speakers down before you go to the website.

San José

Zoo Ave

The monkeys at Zoo Ave offer a good photo op, but don't stand directly under a tree branch full of them!

Zoo Ave Wildlife Conservation Park (☎ 506-433-8989, www.zooave.org) is a small, non-profit bird and wildlife sanctuary just out side Alajuela near the airport. The park is open from 9 am-5 pm and charges a modest $10. They specialize in rescuing birds and animals that have been injured, or abandoned as pets, and reintroduce them to the wild after rehabilitation. A walk down their concrete paths through the forest is a comfortable way to get an up-close look at animals and birds you'd be lucky to get a brief, remote glimpse of in the wild. If you have an extra couple of hours between planes, you can catch a taxi and be here in just a few minutes. Where else are you going to see a ferruginous pygmy owl? Zoo Ave is a good place to get easy pictures of toucans and parrots without getting your feet muddy.

Shop Till You Drop

Costa Rica is not usually considered to be a shopper's paradise, but there are some interesting things to buy. A few local artists' work are worth a look and possible purchase. Most handicrafts you see for sale in San José are imported from Guatemala or Peru. Some items of interest can be found downtown in the **Central Market**, but keep a close hold of your purse.

The **Multi Plaza mall** in Escazú is a modern and American-style mall with all the stores you would expect back in the US. Liz Claiborne, Tommy Hilfiger, TCBY – they're all here. If you forgot hiking boots, sun screen, holiday reading material, or if you want to buy an elegant ball gown (why, in Costa Rica?), Multi Plaza is a comfortable, comprehensive place to shop.

Antiques

Although not usually considered as a place for antique shopping, there are a few shops in San José that may have special treasures.

ANTIGUEDADES GOBELINO
Avenida 9 between Calles 3 & 5
☎ 506-223-9552

They have large furniture, jewelry and glass.

ANTIGUEDADES CHAVO
Calle Central between Avenidas Central & 1
☎ 506-258-3966

Look for chests and colonial furniture, some real and some almost real.

Art

If you are a collector, there area couple of galleries worth looking at.

ARTE LATINO
Calle 5 and Avenida 1
☎ 506-258-3306

Original Central American art featuring a variety of primitive artists.

GALERIA 11-12
Avenida 15 and Calle 35, Escalante
☎ 506-280-8441
www.galeria11-12.com

San José

Costa Rican masters and trendy contemporary artists including Ricardo Morales, Rolando Garita and Guillermo Porras.

Prominent Tico Artists

Traditional and contemporary artists are creating beautiful works. Taking advantage of tropical hardwoods that have fallen or otherwise been harvested inan ecological way, **Barry Biesanz** (☎ 506-289-4337, www.biesanz.com) creates amazing wood sculptures, bowls and intricate freeform boxes. His showroom is in Escazú and is a bit hard to find. His website has a good map or ask for directions at your hotel.

Rolando Garita, **Ricardo Morales** and **Guillermo Porras** are also noted Costa Rican artists. **Sara Morales**, represented by Sharon Hernández (☎ 566-383-7479), is known for huge and striking oils of stylized horses. **Gerardo Valerio Trigueros** (☎ 506-240-8315, 506-297-1970) creates detailed, almost iridescent ecological art, wildlife, dolphins and still lifes, oils and acrylics. **Luis Chacón**'s work can be seen in the lobby of the Real Intercontinental Hotel in San José. **Maria Fonseca** has her studio in Naranjo with woodcarvings in exotic tropical woods. You can see her work at the Hotel Martino in Alajuela. The lobby and hotel public areas are graced with dozens of her carvings and she carved every door in the hotel individually. **Lil Mena**, who creates handmade paper products, and some of the artists listed above, have their work displayed in some of the galleries below.

Handicrafts

ATMOSFERA
Calle 5 between Avenidas 1 and 3
☎ 506-222-4322

The shop is a maze of high-quality Costa Rican masks, bowls, bird-embroidered clothing, gold and pre-Columbian jewelry, priced from $25 to $1,000.

BOUTIQUE ANNEMARIE
Calle, 9 between Avenidas 7 and 9 in the Hotel Don Carlos
☎ 506-221-6063

Collection of leather, jewelry and paintings.

GALERIA NAMU
Avenida 8 between Calles 5 and 7
☎ 506-256-3412
www.gallerianamu.com

Pefi Figueres and local women artists are features.

MERCADO NACIONAL DE ARTESANIA
Behind the Soledad Church, Calle 11, Avenida 4
☎ 506-221-5012

Manager Guillermo Guido has collected a variety of wooden candelabra painted by local artists.

Books

If you have a heavy reading habit and the *Tico Times* isn't enough, bring your reading fix with you. There are a couple of places you can by English-language books. US magazines are plentiful.

7TH STREET BOOKS
Calle 7 between Avenidas Central and 1
☎ 506-256-8251

LEHMANN
Avenida Central between Calles 1 and 3
☎ 506-223-2122

Has a good selection of maps and a few books in English.

San José

Coffee

There are a couple of specialty shops in San José that coffee addicts should check out. The tours at **Café Britt** and **Doka** both offer opportunities for buying lots and lots of coffee at good prices. Both can ship it back home for you. See pages 111-112 for more details.

LA ESQUINA DEL CAFE
Avenida 9 at Calle 3
☎ 506-257-9868

Good selection of fresh-roasted beans, also serves meals. They offer coffee from six different regions of Costa Rica, all fresh roasted. Try a few to see what you like and then stock up before you fly home.

Handmade Guitars

Near **Iglesia La Dolorosa**, mostly on Calle 2, there about 10 guitar shops specializing in handmade acoustic, classical, and flamenco instruments. The quality can be quite high and, as you must expect, high-quality means correspondingly high prices. There are some budget guitars sold. The most prestigious of these luthiers are **Emmanuel Mora Torres**, **Aristides Guzmán**, **Edgar and Rodrigo Garro**, **Olman Arguedas**, **Martin Prada** and **Omar Corrales Guzmán**.

Markets

Look for **Mercado Central** between Avenida Central and Avenida 1, and between Calles 6 and 8. This is a huge food and crafts market with all the Costa Rican and imported goodies sold in a confusing maze of small stalls. This is a great place to get a feel for what can be bought in small shops around the country. The usual smelly fish and slimy tripe are part of the experience. There are more interesting and complex markets in Central America and this one is a bit claustrophobic. Watch your purse.

After Dark

San José has a lively nightlife. The Latin sound predominates in the discos, bars, casinos, and live music and dance venues. There are quiet spots for serious music fans, such as the Jazz Café, and rowdy strip bars, such as Key Largo. Most of the larger hotels offer nighttime entertainment, but some of the best hotel bars can be the habitat of rather seedy lounge lizards and their ilk.

At night, stay away the bars downtown unless you are exceptionally adventurous.

Prostitution is legal in Costa Rica but not noticeably regulated and strip clubs and bars catering to them and their clients are justifiably famous. AIDs and other STDs are on the increase and hustles, scams, drugging and robberies occur. Be careful.

Live Music

There is an active live music scene in San José specializing, as you might guess, in salsa and merengue. Jazz, rock and what passes for blues can also be found. Most of the nighttime action is in the area between **Calle 4, Avenida 9** and **Calle 23**, **Avenida 2**. There is the usual-to-any-big-city sleazy area more or less around downtown late at night. Here are some places to try.

San José

INTERCONTINENTAL HOTEL

In front of Multiplaza shopping center, Escazú
☎ 506-273-4783

Primarily Latin music from 9 pm.

JAZZ CAFE

In San Pedro opposite Farmacia Fischel
☎ 506-253-8933
jazz.cafe@terra.com

Occasional appearances by jazz greats like Chucho
Valdez spice up the mix of local artists and visiting
mid-level jazz dignitaries. The Jazz Café is one of
the real hot spots in San José for the "young professional" crowd, although you'll see plenty of aging
hipsters adding to the atmosphere as well. It is the
stereotypical dark, low, smoky room, with tiny tables and traditional jazz club ambiance. Stylized
busts of the jazz greats like Duke Ellington and Ella
Fitzgerald add to the atmosphere. The full dinner
and bar snack menus are great – you'll need to ask
the waiter to light another candle to read them. I
make a point of ending up here on evenings when I
stay out past my usual "milk and cookies" time of
10 pm.

If disco is not your thing, stop at the Jazz Café.

Opening hours are 6 pm-2 am, but the music generally doesn't start before 10 pm. It would be wise to
make a reservation on Friday or Saturday nights.

EL TOBOGAN

Just off the Guápiles Highway near the
República office
☎ 506-257-3396

Huge dance floor with live bands, aimed at the local
couples scene. Open from 8 pm-2 am.

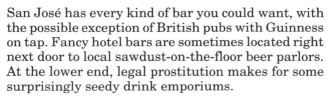

Bars, Discos & Nightclubs

San José has every kind of bar you could want, with the possible exception of British pubs with Guinness on tap. Fancy hotel bars are sometimes located right next door to local sawdust-on-the-floor beer parlors. At the lower end, legal prostitution makes for some surprisingly seedy drink emporiums.

Beers usually sell for between US $1 and $2.50. Mixed drinks run from US $2 to $5, depending on the ambiance and assumed sophistication of the establishment. The younder the crowd, the later the action starts. Some clubs may open as early as 6 pm. Call before you go and ask when the crowds arrive.

ALL STAR BAR AND GRILL
Centro Commercial Cocón, San Pedro
☎ 506-225-0838

Regular old sports bar, like you find in any North American town, featuring reasonably good hamburgers and occasionally live music.

BLUE MOON
Los Yoses

Gay and lesbian bar.

BUENAS VIBRACIONES
Paseo de los Estudiantes

Gay and lesbian crowd.

EL CUARTEL DE LA BOCA DEL MONTE
Avenida 1 between Calles 21 and 23
☎ 506-221-0327

Yuppie meat market makes for a lively after-work scene. Live music on the weekends packs them in. Open 6 pm-1 am.

San José

LA ESMERALDA
Avenida 2 between Calles 5 and 7
☎ 506-221-0530

Mariachi-flavored bar and restaurant. Open 11 am-5 am. Closed Sunday.

LA VILLA
Near the church in San Pedro
☎ 506-225-9612

Left-wing revolutionaries hang out with an artsy crowd.

COCLOCO
☎ 506-222-8782
In the Centro Commercial El Pueblo

Latin sound, dancing on two floors. Closed Sunday and Monday.

COYOTE
In the San Pedro Mall (downstairs)

Dancing.

DEJA VU
Calle 2 between Avenidas 14 and 16A
☎ 506-223-3758

The crowd is well dressed, young, gay techno and primarily male. This is a very hot, happening spot, high on the list of Latin "in" spots.

INFINITO
In the Centro Commercial El Pueblo
☎ 506-221-9134

Techno, funk and a young crowd.

PLANET MALL
In the San Pedro Mall (upstairs)

Expensive, but oh, so trendy, with varied music depending on the night.

LA PLAZA
Near El Pueblo shopping center
☎ 506-222-5143

Caters to a younger disco crowd, with a $5 cover. Open 7 pm to 4 am.

SALSA 54
Calle 3 between Avenidas 1 and 3
☎ 506-233-3814

High-end salsa dancing for the real aficionados, or those who just want to watch how the experts do it. Classes are offered early in the evening. Open from 7 pm-4 am.

Casinos

Most of the major hotels have casinos. Gambling is legal in Costa Rica, but the games can be quite a bit different from what you may have experienced in Las Vegas or in European casinos. Be sure you understand the rules before jumping in. The atmosphere in most casinos is fairly casual. Few people come to Costa Rica specifically for the gambling and most casinos seem to be filled mostly with Ticos.

CASINO COLONIAL
Avenida 1, between Calles 9 and 11
☎ 506-258-2827

One of the few casinos with a US sports book.

HOTEL MARTINO SPA & RESORT CASINO
La Garita Road, Alajuela near the airport
☎ 506-433-8382; fax 506-433-9052

This place opened in early 2002. Alfonso Martino has created a casino with a European feel, including late night live music and excellent food and wine selections. The casino overlooks the elegant hotel pool.

San José

TARA CASINO & POKER CAFE

Escazú in the Tara Resort Hotel, Spa & Casino, 10-minute cab ride from downtown San José
☎ 506-228-6992; fax 506-228-9651
www.tararesort.com

Tara Casino and Poker Café, which opened in 2001, is one of the few true, dedicated casinos in San José. While most of the casinos in Costa Rica are little more than a few slots in a hotel lobby, Tara has built a large, elegant, stand-alone casino with a poker room, roulette, rummy, tute (similar to black jack), pai-gow and slot machines.

The casino attracts an international crowd, unlike most of the other casinos. The adjacent Poker Café is a late-night spot (closes at 4 am, or whenever) for a quiet drink, gourmet sandwiches, soups and snacks.

Shows

The **Pueblo Antiguo Dinner Show** in Lurica (☎ 506-231-2001) includes an unremarkable dinner with Costa Rican folkloric dancing and enactments of local history. The show is $6 or $20 for dinner and show. A bit sappy, but this is a regular stop on the package tour group itinerary. My suggestion is skipping this twee evening and catching up on sleep or writing postcards.

Lowlife

*The best and most famous lowlife bar is at **Hotel Del Rey**, Calle 9, Avenida 1.*

San José is famous for its lowlife and rightly so. Easily avoided if you are not so inclined, the doubtful delights of dubious ladies of the night and low bars are easily found.

Best Places to Stay

San José has a plethora of hotels, ranging from el cheapo to very expensive. Even the very cheapest accommodations are usually quite clean and neat. The high-end does not offer any true "five star" establishments, but quiet luxury is definitely available.

Alive Prices

Prices are based on double occupancy during high season, and given in US $. Taxes and meals are not included, unless so noted. Hotels and lodges marked with a ☆ are my personal favorites. "The Best of the Best" choices earn their title by offering top-quality lodging and services.

Central San José

AUROLA HOLIDAY INN
5th Avenue & 5th Street
☎ 506-222-2424, 506-233-7233; fax 506-233-0603, 506-222-2621
www.aurola-holidayinn.com
$150

With 188 rooms and 12 suites, this is just like a Holiday Inn anywhere: dependable and unexceptional. The rooms are slightly shabby, but clean. Buffet meals are overpriced, but palatable. It is practically downtown, so it's convenient.

San José

BARCELO SAN JOSE PALACIO SPA & CASINO

500 meters southeast of Juan Pablo II Bridge along General Cañas highway
☎ 506-220-2034; fax 506-220-2211
www.barcelo.com
$130

Barceló operates a chain of upscale business/vacation hotels in San José, and in some of the better resort towns. It is located on the road into town from the airport and offers all the usual business hotel amenities, including meeting rooms and concierge service. It seems a bit rundown in comparison to some of the newer business-oriented hotels, such as the Camino Real, but is clean and comfortable.

LE BERGERAC

Calle 5 in Los Yoses
☎ 506-234-7850; fax 506-225-9103
www.bergerac.co.cr
$95

The mostly small, but comfortable, rooms overlook gardens, or have balconies with a view of the city. The suites are larger and decorated with period furniture. There is a good restaurant, Isle de France, known for their French menu and ambiance.

BRITANNIA HOTEL

Calle 3 & Avenida 11, Barrio Amón
☎ 506-223-6667, 506-290-2878; fax 506-223-6411, 506-290-2853
www.centralamerica.com/cr/hotel/britania.htm
$120

The Britannia, located partly in an old coffee baron's house, combines a British feel with tropical gardens. The new wing is basically a four-story motel of modest pretension. Try for a room in the older section.

DON CARLOS
Calle 9 and Avenida 9
☎ 506-221-6707; fax 506-255-0828
www.doncarlos.co.cr
$70

The Don Carlos, one of the first guesthouses in San José, is located in a nice residential area, but still close to downtown. Their style is an attempt at colonial tropical elegance but, although clean and neat, the hotel is in need of renovation.

☆ GRANO DE ORO
Calle 30, Avenida 2/4, No. 251, near Paseo Colón
☎ 506-255-3322; fax 506-221-2782
www.hotelgranodeoro.com
$85

The Grano de Oro, a few blocks from the center of San José on a quiet street, offers elegance and luxury in an old renovated tropical Victorian mansion. The hotel is a member of the Small Distinctive Hotels of Costa Rica, and has 32 unique and tastefully decorated rooms and three suites. All the rooms are elegantly decorated with wrought iron beds, dark hardwood paneling, handpainted Italian tile and damask fabrics. The warmth of a private home is maintained throughout the hotel. There is a sundeck with Jacuzzis and several courtyards with fountains. Public areas and rooms are loaded with a jungle of potted tropical plants, including orchids, bromeliads and heliconias. The indoor plantings are so extensive the hotel requires one full-time employee just to keep up with them.

Before becoming an elegant hotel, the house was home to a prominent San José family that owned the country's largest cookie factory. Canadian owners Eldon and Lori Cooke renovated the old home in appropriate style and maintain that way.

San José

Standard rooms are a bargain at $85, and the three suites have vastly more charm than equally priced "standard" rooms at other San José hotels. The **Vista de Oro suite** is a large, hardwood-paneled room on the top floor, with an marvelous, full-wall view of the city skyline and surrounding volcanoes, private Jacuzzi overlooking the sundeck and city, and elegant antique furnishings. Other hotels in town offer mere standard rooms at prices similar to the $240 for the top-quality suite at the Grano de Oro.

Many people use San José hotels as resting places after flights from Europe and North America before heading on to other areas of Costa Rica. The Grano de Oro is well suited to such a role as it is within easy reach of the airport and the staff is accustomed to helping visitors plan tours and make travel arrangements. The restaurant (same name as hotel) is well known as being one of the very best in Costa Rica (see *Best Places to Eat*, page 145).

This is one of the nicest hotels in Costa Rica and, if you consider the standard rooms are the same price as the very ordinary rooms at the Hampton Inn near the airport, it is a stone bargain as well.

HOTEL SANTO TOMAS
Avenida 7 between Calles 3 & 5
☎ 506-255-0448
www.hotelsantotomas.com
$ 80

This wonderful B&B is located conveniently close to downtown. The renovated home was originally built in 1910 by a former coffee baron. Its current North American owner Thomas Douglas saved it from demolition 12 years ago and restored it. Amenities include a solar-heated pool, 30 minutes of free Internet access, and a restaurant in the garden courtyard patio. The staff is very helpful.

RADISSON EUROPA HOTEL
& CONFERENCE CENTER

Central Street & 3rd-15th Av, Edificio Central
☎ 506-257-3257; fax 506-257-8221
www.radisson.com
$200

The Radisson has 107 rooms aimed at business travelers, with junior and presidential suites. There's a restaurant and coffee shop, bar and casino, spa and Jacuzzi, pool, basketball and soccer, jogging track, and putting green. Centrally located.

Suburbs of San José

☆ **THE ALTA HOTEL**

Two km (1.2 miles) west of Escazú,
on old road to Santa Ana
☎ 506-282-4160; fax 506-282-4162
www.thealtahotel.com
$110

The contemporary Mediterranean-style Hotel Alta is in a quiet, upscale suburb of San José on a mountainside overlooking the Valley of the Sun. On a clear day you can see all the way to the Pacific. The maize-toned, stucco building was handcrafted (literally) in 1998, to the design of architect Rolph Ruge. With the accompanying **La Luz** restaurant, this is a hotel for people who enjoy the very best of accommodations, service, and food. The restaurant would be a standout in any major international city. The breakfasts go far beyond the regular continental (available at an $8 supplement), and are the best I've had outside of England (see *Best Places to Eat,* page 150).

There are 23 rooms, including four suites, and the penthouse, all with central air conditioning. The penthouse, or a combination of suites, can be iso-

San José

lated to create private, multi-bedroom apartments with kitchens for honeymooners, families or corporate events. All the suites have working desks with Internet connections.

It is difficult to describe the attention to detail New York designer Keler Henderson and the architect have lavished on the rooms and public areas. The hotel has been featured in *Estilos & Casas Costa Rica* (Costa Rica's *Architectural Digest*) and is a combination of contemporary mixed with traditional Mediterranean design. During construction, what is now the restaurant was a woodworking shop, where each detail of tropical hardwood molding, flooring, doors and windows were built one by one to fit each room. Being a bit of a handyman, I spent some time marveling over the craftsmanship and beautiful woodwork. The tiled public areas and rooms have elaborate wrought iron light fixtures made by the same craftsmen. Exhibitions of local artists are held in the lobby and hall with wine and cheese during "Meet-the-Artists" evenings (hotel guests are invited).

All of the rooms are large with private balconies or terraces. Huge doors open up to the valley view. I didn't even have to raise my head off my pillow to gaze out over the hopefully named Valley of the Sun. Big, monogrammed fluffy towels and, in keeping with the climate, lightweight bathrobes are supplied in all the bathrooms.

Corporate events and weddings are held in the banquet room, or outside overlooking the valley and lush hotel grounds. Intimate dinners are arranged on the Moroccan Terrace, where more than one successful proposal of marriage has been made. Up to 50 people can be seated in the banquet room.

Facilities include a business center with Internet access, fax, copy machines and printers, gift shop, dry sauna, exercise room, weight room, on site (and fast) laundry service, and in-room massages. Flamenco dancing and yoga classes are also held.

Airport pickup service is offered with advance notice. The pool is beside an enormous Guanacaste tree in lush grounds with ginger, bromeliads and small palm trees in large, terra cotta pots. Butterflies flit about while fully laden orange and papaya trees seem ready to drop fruit at any moment. The most popular TV aerobics show in Costa Rica (*Aerobics with Ale*) frequently shoots from the pool area.

Though I tried hard, I found nothing to complain about. The concierge expertly handles tour and travel arrangements.

☆ CAMINO REAL INTERCONTINENTAL

In front of Multiplaza shopping center, Escazú
☎ 506-208-2202; fax 506-289-8980
www.interconti.com
$245

The Intercontinental is a world-class luxury hotel oriented towards the business traveler. It has 261 rooms and suites, pool, tennis, business and conference center, live music, bars, and two restaurants. It is very comfortable and very luxurious. The modern **Multi Plaza shopping mall** is conveniently located across the street, and is a great place to buy things you forgot.

Used by major banks and multinationals, the extensive meeting and conference facilities are complete, first-class and the best in Costa Rica, by far. The large meeting areas in the pool cabana are used for weddings and elegant corporate dining. The hotel organizes special themed events such as a "Coffee

San José

and Orchid Encounter" and "Sounds of the Forest" evenings. Kosher food is available upon request.

The health club features personal trainers, a variety of exercise machines and weights, dry saunas, full beauty salon and massage room. For only $20 more, you can snag a room on the primo **Club International** where the suites are located. It takes up the entire fifth floor, with concierge service, breakfast buffet, bar, library, coffee in the afternoon and happy hour in the evenings.

With several bars and three excellent restaurants (see *Best Places to Eat*, page 144), you can enjoy fine dining or have a hamburger by the pool. Daily evening specials in the **Azulejos** restaurant include lobster (my favorite), family and Italian Nights. The formal **Mirage** restaurant offers Mediterranean cuisine and is one of San José's premier dining experiences.

Airport pickup and drop-off service is complimentary. Non-smoking rooms area available. The extensive breakfast buffet is an additional $15. While the Intercontinental does not offer the quirky charm of some of the area boutique hotels, it is unmatched in luxury features and business facilities. Check their website for specials.

FINCA ROSA BLANCA

BEST OF THE BEST

One kilometer (about a half-mile) northeast of Santa Barbara de Heredia

☎ 506-269-9392; fax 506-269-9555; In US, 800-327-9854

www.finca-rblanca.co.cr

$155

Don't try to locate Finca Rosa Blanca at the end of a long day or at night. Even though they have signs along the way, it is very hard to find. Be sure to get them to fax you a map or, better yet, take a taxi.

Don't let this bother you, though – it is definitely worth the effort.

When I went, after a long drive from the coast, it took me two hours to find the hotel. I eventually enticed a Costa Rican gentleman to show me where it was. I finally arrived a few minutes after the time I was told dinner was supposed to start. I was tired, cross, hungry and not in the mood to like the place. I was already thinking up horrible things to say. As soon as I stepped through the front door, though, and smelled the smoke from the fireplace, saw the artwork everywhere, sensed the peaceful nature of the room, and saw the owner chatting quietly with a couple of guests, my tension dropped away. My mood changed and I was ready to enjoy my stay.

The hotel is unique, quirky, artfully planned, and the service is designed to make guests feel at home and pampered. Americans Glenn and Teri Jampol, both creative and fascinating people, opened it. The architectural style brings to mind Gaudi with a Mediterranean influence. Everywhere you look, each nook and cranny is decorated with works of art and objects collected from around the world. Local artists have painted the walls with tropical scenes. The stucco walls are sculpted into bizarre yet pleasing shapes. There seem to be no square windows, or anything else square. It doesn't look like anything came from Home Depot!

Each of the nine rooms is completely different. King-size beds, interesting tile showers, Jacuzzis, unusual balconies and artwork make the rooms special. This is not the Hilton. This is a hotel for people who appreciate the quirky nature of artists. Finca Rosa Blanca is luxurious and caters to people who appreciate luxurious accommodations and enjoy fine dining. It brings out the bohemian in you.

San José

The food is served at a large dining table and is exquisite, thoughtfully prepared and elegantly presented. Soups, salads, breads, meats, fish and unusual desserts, mango crumble for example, are all prepared from scratch with organic ingredients. Many of the vegetables are raised in the hotel's own greenhouse. Soon, they should start serving organic coffee grown right outside the dining room window. Expect the unusual. Expect absolutely delicious meals.

Opened to the public in 1989, Finca Rosa Blanca is probably the oldest boutique hotel in Costa Rica. Due to the huge effort by the owners, it's earned the highest possible Certification for Sustainability in Tourism rating for the hotel's recycling programs, community involvement and environmental awareness.

Many people fly in late in the day at the beginning of their trip to Costa Rica and need a place to stay overnight before flying or driving on to more remote areas of the country. Convenient to the airport and away from the bustle of San José, Finca Rosa Blanca is a fantastic place to start your trip. It is also a great place to base yourself for several days while you explore the Central Valley around San José on daytrips. Many people who use it for their overnight stopover regret not being able to stay longer and enjoy the beauty and hospitality of this unique hotel – perhaps the nicest in Costa Rica.

HAMPTON AIRPORT INN
Autopista General Cañas, near the airport
☎ 506-443-0043; fax 506-442-9532
www.hamptonhotel.co.cr
$100

The Hampton is only two minutes away from the airport, and is a good spot for a quick sleep in familiar surroundings between flights. It's just like any

Hampton in the States, but is getting perhaps a bit long in the tooth. The 56 rooms are well insulated for sound, so getting a good night's sleep is not a problem. A basic breakfast buffet is included in the price. The hotel has a free shuttle to and from the airport, but be sure you call in advance so they will expect you. You're really paying for the convenience of being right next to the airport since, even though the service is good, there is nothing of particular charm or note here. It seems a bit overpriced compared to some of the farther away, but more interesting competition. There is a basic, lozenge-shaped pool surrounded by rose bushes – a good place to listen to the jets blasting off nearby. There is a small bar, but no restaurant. American fast-food restaurants are a short cab ride away. Pizza delivery is available. A coffeemaker, iron and hairdryer are in each room. The new Hampton Inn Suites opened next door in early 2002 and has standard rooms and suites at $140. It is new, big, and again, just like a Hampton Inn back home, faceless and bland, but no surprises.

☆ HOTEL MARTINO SPA & RESORT
La Garita Road, Alajuela near the airport
☎ 506-433-8382; fax 506-433-9052
www.hotelmartino.com
$145

The Martino, built in a period of four years and completed in 1999, is a boutique resort, featuring 34 junior suites in Alajuela. It's only a short ride from the airport, but in a world full of the sounds of tropical birds and running water. This is a relaxing place to stay if you are just changing planes before going on to other areas of the country, or if you want to be in the San José area for some time. It is a good base for exploring the Central Valley in day-trips. The lodge is across the street from **Zoo Ave** reserve.

San José

The Martino has a classic Italian-style, with a mix of Italian and Costa Rican character thrown in. Loving attention to detail is evident in the construction, with superb woodwork. Local woods, such as *cedar amargo*, *caoba,* and other exotics, were used for paneling, trim and furniture, with flooring made from the wood of almond trees. The door to each suite is a unique carving by Costa Rican artist **Maria Fonseca** (see page 120). All the rooms are beautiful, down to the tiniest detail, with handmade trim to porcelain bathroom fittings.

The 20-acre grounds have tropical plantings selected for their beauty and aroma, including ylang-ylang, orchids, bromeliads, bamboo and hibiscus. As you arrive, a towering breadfruit tree in front of the lobby greets you, and gives you a hint of what you will find inside. Care was taken during construction to preserve local specimens of Guanacaste and Benjamin trees. Hummingbirds and parrots dart around as you enjoy morning coffee on the veranda, or a tropical drink by the pool in the evening. The neo-classical Italian pool, built with statues and hand-painted tile, is overlooked by **Le Gourmet** restaurant and lounge. It seems to have been carefully dropped into the middle of an exotic forest.

After building and running four hotels in Italy, amiable and philosophic owner Alfonso Martino retired here to enjoy the perfect climate and create his vision of the perfect resort. "Spending the money to build this was a pleasure. It is a gift I gave to myself that I share with my guests." The beauty of the wood itself, and love of the surroundings, influenced the design and execution of this remarkable structure. Staying here is sharing Mr. Martino's vision of paradise – ask him to explain. A chat with him should be part of every visit.

Facilities of the lodge include one of the largest casinos in Costa Rica with seven tables offering all the usual games. A large indoor and outdoor covered lounge is available for weddings, receptions and corporate events. Continental breakfast, included in the room price, features bread and preserves made in Mr. Martino's own kitchen. The coffee (Volio) and fresh fruit juices are superb.

Le Gourmet restaurant serves true Italian-style cuisine (see *Best Places to Eat*, page 151), and has the best cappuccino I found anywhere in Costa Rica. Much of the produce for the hotel restaurant is grown in the hotel garden (you can pick the vegetables you want to eat that night).

While most hotels offer an exercise room and sauna and declare themselves a "spa," the associated health club and spa is certainly the most luxurious and complete in the country. In addition to tennis courts and a wide variety of weights and exercise equipment, the spa here offers a long list of beauty and health treatments, including volcanic mud masks, aromatherapy, massage services, Roman steam bath (an exact replica of an archeologically unearthed steam bath in Italy), wet and dry saunas, reflexology, chiropractic, rehabilitation gym, cellulite treatment, anti-stress clinic, bio-thermic showers, acne treatment, negative ionized oxygen treatment, and full beauty parlor services.

TARA RESORT HOTEL, SPA & CASINO
Above Guardia rural de San Antonio de Escazú
☎ 506-228-6992; fax 506-228-9651
www.tararesort.com
$140

Tara, high in the clouds in the Pico Blanco mountains above San José, is as reminiscent of an Old English country hotel as it is of the antebellum

San José

southern mansion namesake Tara from *Gone with the Wind*. Rhett and Scarlett would be comfortable gliding around the halls. The owner, Rhett Butler look-alike Richard Shambley, is from North Carolina, and has brought old-style Southern charm with him to Costa Rica. If you like a hotel with character, and rooms furnished with period furniture, potpourri and oriental carpets, this is your spot. This was one of the most elegant homes in Costa Rica. It has been converted into a luxury spa, casino and hotel. Well-known as one of the most elegant of the luxury hotels in San José, Tara is located in the quiet suburb of Escazú.

Tara was built in 1978 for the Shah of Iran. Each of the 14 rooms and suites are unique and fully equipped with full baths, color TV and all of the other amenities you expect from a fine hotel. This is not a cookie-cutter, chain hotel. The **Scarlett suite** or **Miss Pittipat's** room are the most desirable rooms. The three-story mansion with huge white columns has been lovingly maintained and embellished with exotic tropical hardwoods such as *Coco bolo*. The large staff is attentive without being overbearing – again in the old Southern or British style. It is set high in the clouds, but on clear days the views of volcanoes Poás and Barva are stunning.

The immaculately maintained grounds contain luxuriant tropical plantings, including lilies, bromeliads, royal palms. White-railed terraces overlook the valley. The swimming pool is surrounded by tropical greenery with waterfalls, a Jacuzzi and a bar.

My only disappointment during my stay was that clouds often obscured the views – nothing really to grouse about considering everything else. The continental breakfast is tropical fruit with toast and *excellent* coffee. Internet access is available, and so is laundry and dry cleaning service. An elaborate,

Southern-style wedding was being conducted while I was there, and was truly a sight to see. Tara is one of the preferred venues for society weddings in San José, and complete wedding and reception-planning services are offered. The father of the bride, not to mention the bride herself, would not be disappointed at Tara.

The **Spa** offers a gym, aerobics classes, saunas, steam rooms, therapeutic massage, exfoliation therapy, body cocoons with volcanic mud, facials, aromatherapy, hand and foot treatments, and a wide variety of other ways to pamper yourself and improve your health and appearance. Professional trainers customize fitness, and health programs individually. Well-heeled visitors from South America and Europe fly in especially for the world-famous body restoration treatments. Cosmetic surgery and other beauty improvement services can be arranged after personal consultations.

The **Atlanta Restaurant** (see *Best Places to Eat*, page 148), a gleaming crystal, silver and lace table-cloth vision, offers continental cuisine equally as elegant and satisfying as the hotel itself.

The **Tara Casino and Poker Café** is one of the few true, dedicated casinos in San José (see *Nightlife*, page 128).

It's right on top of the continental divide next to a good alternative to Monteverde: **Los Angeles Cloud Forest Reserve**, that has all the same stuff, but no crowds.The hotel is owned by former Costa Rican president Rodrigo Carrazo.

San José

Best Places to Eat

If you must, you can find old favorites like Tony Roma's, Denny's and even TGI Friday's, but in a city full of interesting and innovative restaurants, why eat the same things you can eat any night back home? San José has some fantastic restaurants, but nothing you could call "gourmet." Still, the gustatory opportunities of San José are not to be scorned. There is some great food to be had. California/Asian fusion is about as wild as it gets but, if you stick to seafood and local specialties, even the most jaded foodie or diehard meat-and-potatoes person should be delighted with the dining opportunities.

Alive Prices

Prices are given in US $, and are the average price for an entrée or main course, per person, before taxes and service charges are added. Although Costa Rican law says restaurants must show prices on the menu with taxes included, many do not. Menus that include taxes almost always say so.

Central San José

AZULEJOS
In the Hotel Real Intercontinental, across from Multi Plaza shopping center in Escazú.
☎ 506-208-2202
$30
International

The Azulejos, open seven days a week for breakfast, lunch and dinner, is off the lobby in the Real Intercontinental hotel. The buffet breakfasts and lunch are complete, and nightly dinner buffet specials are legendary, ranging from Italian, family, to lobster nights. I was fortunate enough to experience lobster night, and what a feast it was. A full buffet with seafood salads and vegetables was only a warm-up to lobster served in seven different styles. Pig that I am, I tried all seven. Lobster was offered sautéed in garlic, "American" style, thermidor and "Azulejos," among others. The Azulejos sauce is made with pineapple, tomatoes, onion and peanuts. I found the steamed and broiled lobsters to be the best. Although delicious, the others seemed overcooked.

Five types of hot pepper sauce deserve respect. The chipotle is absolutely white-hot. Tenderloin, sea bass and tilapia are grilled to your specifications, and are included in the price of the buffet. The lobster night buffet checks in at a hefty $32, not including drinks, but hey, it's lobster, after all. The house wines are acceptable Chilean Concho y Toros.

☆ GRANO DE ORO

In the Grano de Oro hotel
Paseo de Colón, Calle 30, Avenida 2/4 No. 251
☎ 506-255-3322
$14
French

In keeping with the traditionally elegant style of the hotel, the restaurant of the Grano de Oro combines a French menu with fresh local ingredients, in a fusion of Old and New Worlds. Rated by the *Junta Gourmet Centroamérica* as one of the top restaurants in Costa Rica, the food and ambiance live up to the promise. The renovated 90-year-old Costa Rican family home that is the core of the hotel and restaurant provides a hushed elegance. The architecture of the old home has been preserved. A parlor with settees and damask-covered chairs is the lovely setting

San José

for before-dinner drinks and leads to the old home's traditional dining room. The inside dining room spills over to the sun porch and garden courtyard and is shaded by full-grown avocado and mango trees dripping with orchids and bromeliads.

Executive Chef Francis Canal Bardot puts his classical training to use preparing such fusions of traditional and local as *croquetas de camembert* (deep-fried camembert with blackberry sauce), *sorpresa de verano* (lettuce, oranges and local macadamia nuts) and *pollo al coco* (chicken breast in coconut sauce with pineapple). The *corvino con macadamia* is a sea bass filet crusted with ground macadamia nuts and served with an orange sauce. Fish of the day, shrimp, and salmon are presented *provenzal*, *en soufflé* and *meunière*, reflecting the chef's classical background. The *lomito piemontes* comes as two small filet mignons (quite tender, not the usual tough Costa Rican beef), stuffed lightly with Gorgonzola cheese and dressed with a sherry sauce. Delicious.

Desserts include the signature pie *Grano de Oro* (two layers of coffee cream on a chocolate cookie crust), and a variety of crêpes specially selected to include seasonal local fruits – the mango is quite special. Piña colada cheesecake covers the fusion side of things.

The wine list is a bit on the basic side, adequate with no real surprises. There are the usual Chilean wines seen all over Costa Rica (Chile has a trade agreement with Costa Rica that includes wine and apples), some Spanish, and a few French selections. Beaujolais is a shocking $30, but an excellent Penedés Reserva is only $27. I thought about not being so critical of the wine selection, since maintaining an attention-grabbing cellar is expensive. It is of interest to only a small percentage of customers but, considering the quality of the rest of the restaurant, the wine cellar should match it.

Fine dining can only be found in a few places in Costa Rica and the Grano de Oro deserves its reputation as just such an oasis.

MACHU PICHU
Calle 32, Avenida 1/3
☎ 506-222-7384
$8
Peruvian

Machu Pichu is the place for ceviche in San José. Ceviche is popular all over Costa Rica, but Machu Pichu prepares unique variations with a Peruvian theme. The décor is somewhat stark, but the interesting and well-prepared food makes up for it. The menu centers on pork, chicken, corn and seafood.

LA MESETA COFFEE SHOP
Calle Blancos across from Motorola
$1.50 per cup (worth it)

One of Costa Rica's largest coffee exporters, Tostadora La Meseta, runs this shop. It is not a fancy place, but they brew coffee individually to your taste and with your selection of local beans.

CAFE MUNDO
Calle 15 and Avenida 9
☎ 506-222-6190
$15
Closed Sunday
International

International flavors with good music. Californian Ray Johnson is the chef of this Costa Rican-style bistro. Even though it is on the expensive side, the sandwiches and full-course dinners are great.

San José

VISHNU
Avenida 1, near Calle 3
☎ 506-222-2549
$6
Vegetarian

Vishnu, an oasis of healthy eating in the land of food fried in lard, is a nice stop for lunch. You can see the food being prepared in the kitchen and, if you like things made out of soy, it would be hard to go wrong here. Soy burgers, soy pita sandwiches – you get the picture. The *refrescos*, fruit drinks made with a base of water, milk or yogurt, are tremendous. The prices are reasonable, and the place seems to attract healthy young Ticas, who are obviously trying to stay that way. You can buy packaged granola, breads and honey to take away.

Suburbs of San José

ATLANTA RESTAURANT
In the Tara Resort & Spa
☎ 506-228-9651
$18

The Atlanta overlooks San José with views of volcanoes Poás and Barva. The dining room is elaborately set with silver, crystal, lace tablecloths and understated, old-world elegance. The service, provided by immaculately tuxedoed waiters, is exceptionally attentive. For both lunch and dinner, Belgian chef Aurelio creates continental specialties based on regional ingredients.

Meals begin with starters such as lobster bisque, proper French onion soup, and proceed to beef filet with Gorgonzola cheese sauce (done in the Spanish style – not too strong), beef Wellington, duck (specialty of the chef), and a variety of local seafood entrees such as shrimp, *corvina* (sea bass) and *tilapia*.

Desserts range from the ubiquitous Tico dessert *Queque* (cake), to crêpes Suzette (how often do you see that on a menu?). I'm partial to a proper cheese plate, and the Atlanta somehow manages to come up with an interesting selection of local and imported cheeses. Hot rolls served with herbed butter accompany meals. The wine selection is adequate but, unless you're not fussy about your wines, I suggest you avoid the locally produced house red and spend a bit more for something nicer.

LA CASONA DE CERDO BBQ & CHICHARRONERA
Near Heredia on Rió Segundo Road
(close to the airport, on the road in front of the Hampton Inn)
$8
BBQ

A large stuffed pig greets worshipers as they enter this Western-style temple to pork and all the varieties thereof. It is a vast room with picnic-style tables and wooden benches. The waiters wear cowboy hats. The place is a hoot and resembles good ol' Texas-type BBQ places in the US (although not quite as good as my favorite BBQ joints back home in Tennessee). It is very popular with locals and gets crowded on weekend nights. Don't let that slow you down, since parking attendants wait by the main road to help you park and get you started in line. It's noisy, cheap and fun, with draft beer, shots of rum, and plenty of local color. Music tends toward Latino interpretations of Hank Williams favorites – strange but fun.

Meals come with corn on the cob, cole slaw and French fries. The ribs are short, wet and meaty. Specialties include pork chops, pork ribs, chopped pork, *chicharrones* (fried pork skin), and other pork standards. You can get a chicken if you must, but La Casona is for BBQ pork lovers.

☆ LA LUZ

In the Hotel Alta in Escazú
☎ 506-282-4160
$16
Continental, Costa Rican Fusion

Mâitre d' and chef Ronald Villalobos presents a combination of local ingredients with New World and continental traditions in new ways to produce some outstanding treats, while avoiding California trendiness – always a risk for innovative chefs. This is perhaps the best of the modern kitchens in San José. The menu leans heavily to seafood with shrimp done in a variety of interesting ways, including a spicy Tex-Mex preparation. Starters range from avocado crumble to the house specialty, a feta cheese tart made with dried tomatoes, sweet peppers, caramelized onions, and honey cilantro vinaigrette (US $5).

Moroccan chicken served over couscous with papaya chutney proves the sweet and sour idea behind most Moroccan dishes is sound and travels well. Tenderloins of both beef and pork are served in a variety of innovative sauces such as *fresa* (strawberry), balsamic vinegar and garnished with local vegetables. The dorado is served over champagne risotto with Portobello mushrooms, capers and a very light white wine sauce. When I tried it, the fish was fresh and flaky, with a delicate crust from pan-frying. I was impressed with the garlic prawns sautéed with sage, served with roast garlic potato cake, vegetables, tequila lime butter sauce and cilantro oil.

Desserts are special, with interesting tarts dominating. The *tartaleta* (short tart), stuffed with pineapple and macadamia nuts, is served with blackberry sauce. It's not at all what you would expect from Costa Rica and delicious.

I was particularly pleased to note they carry the wonderful Spanish Carlos I brandy, my favorite and rarely seen on North American menus. As expected, the coffee is great (Costa Rican, of course). The wine list includes the usual Californian labels with a few well-chosen Australian, Chilean and South African selections. Special wines not found on the wine list, such as a particularly fine Barbaresco and a Chateau Lafitte, can be had for a price for those special occasions. The cellar is without a doubt one of the best in Costa Rica.

A private room for eight diners is available for corporate or family meals. There's also a banquet room that can seat up to 50. Weddings and receptions are catered. Because of the intimacy of the hotel rooms and the fantastic views, on many evenings more than half the guests dine on their balconies rather than in the restaurant.

☆ LE GOURMET
In the Hotel Martino Spa & Resort
La Garita Road, Alajuela
☎ 506-433-8382; fax 506-433-9052; in US, 800-414-7004
$12
Italian

This is one of my favorite restaurants in Costa Rica. I've eaten here dozens of times and every single dish that has been put on the table in front of me has been fresh, delicious and perfectly prepared. I know I am going to have an excellent meal every time I visit.

Le Gourmet lives up to its name and is a truly classic Italian restaurant. Full-course meals consist of spectacular ciabatta, antipasto, pasta, a meat or

San José

seafood course, followed by delicate tarts filled with mysteriously delicious sweet cheese, all served on fine linen. Alfonso Martino grows much of the produce on the hotel's 20 acres (you can pick the vegetables for your meal if you like). He also bakes his own bread and makes all the pasta by hand. Frozen is not a word in his vocabulary. The glass-walled dining room is spacious and overlooks the hotel's Roman pool with neoclassical statues.

Mr. Martino is the former head of one of the most prestigious restaurant management and cooking schools in Italy. Alfonso believes only an incredibly skilled cook, after years of apprenticeship and experience, could possibly originate a new dish. You won't find cherry sauce on your steak. You won't find "interesting" Thai/Californian/Mexican concoctions. You'll find fettuccine alfredo prepared as it should be, fresh salads with greens from the hotel garden, mozzarella cheese, and palm hearts served with extra-virgin olive oil imported from Mr. Martino's family farms in Italy.

Desserts include the typical flan and the delightful tarts mentioned above. The coffee is Volio and is superb. You are unlikely to find a better cup of espresso anywhere in Costa Rica. Mr. Martino's attention to every detail in the dining room and kitchen is obvious. This is a restaurant run with care. Love of great, carefully prepared food is obviously an important menu item.

LE MONASTERE
Escazú, near the US ambassador's residence
☎ 506-289-4404
$25
Belgian and continental
Closed Sunday, dinner only.

Located in an old monastery (as the name implies), the restaurant is certainly not monastic, and neither are the prices. The view and surroundings are wonderful, but the food is not memorable. There is a tendency by the waitstaff to push expensive items like lobster, and overpour the wine so you'll buy another bottle. I don't recommend it.

☆ EL BANCO DE LOS MARISCOS

In Santa Barbara de Heredia
☎ 506-269-9090
$8
Seafood

If you're interested in eating huge amounts of delicious, fresh seafood at low prices, this is the place. Banco de los Mariscos has its own fishing fleet to supply the restaurant and they need it. The place is gigantic and feeds huge numbers of mostly Tico eaters for lunch and dinner. The acoustics of the barn-like structure are horrible, but don't let the hustle and bustle of seemingly hundreds of waiters running around shouting put you off your feed. This restaurant has probably the best seafood in Costa Rica.

Starters include eight different kinds of ceviche, along with a variety of shrimp and lobster cocktails. Shrimp is offered in a dozen different configurations, including in butter, in garlic (*ajillo*, my favorite), in tomato sauce, and in several sizes. There's *pequeño* (small), *mediana* (medium), *grande* (large), and *jumbo* (jumbo). The lobster selection is similar. Fish is served fried, sautéed, broiled, with mushrooms, with tomatoes, etc., etc. This is not what you would call fine dining, even though they do offer lobster thermidor. This is plain old good eating. The variety of lobster dishes run around $12, which is a bargain anywhere. If you have felt shortchanged on the lobster other places in Costa Rica, this is your

San José

chance to gorge yourself at a low price. They offer chicken, hamburgers and T-bones, in case someone in your party doesn't go for seafood (sad!).

El Banco de los Mariscos is a bit hard to find, but if you head straight into Santa Barbara de Heredía and turn left at the plaza, then go straight for a ways you should see their huge sign on the right. You may need to stop and ask. It's worth the effort to find it.

A to Z

Banks

There are numerous banks in town and in the suburbs.

> **◎ TIP**
>
> ATMs at the Bank of Costa Rica (BCN) work only if you have a local account with them; they do not accept international ATM cards.

Emergency Medical

Call 911 in all areas. The **Hospital CIMA**, located off the main road to Multiplaza Mall in Escazú, is the newest and most modern hospital in Costa Rica.

Police

Call 911 in all areas.

Post Office

The main post office is located at **Calle 2 Avenidas 1/3**. They have stamp machines in the main lobby, but you should be prepared for a long wait if you need any more complicated services.

> **◎ TIP**
>
> Many hotel gift shops sell stamps for postcards and letters.

Tourist Information

The Costa Rican Tourist Board (ICT) has an office at Avenida 4, Calles 5/7 in downtown San José and one at the airport. They offer some basic tourist maps and books. ☎ 506-223-1733, fax 506-223-5452; In the US, 800-343-6332; www.tourism-costarica.com.

San José

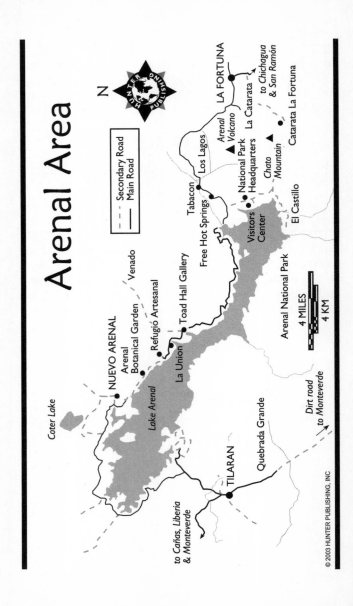

Arenal Area

© 2003 HUNTER PUBLISHING, INC

The Northwest

– Arenal & Monteverde –

Overview

Arenal

Arenal Volcano is one of the few active volcanoes in the world tourists can view and enjoy in comfort with little danger. At night, the sparks and tumbling hot lava makes for an unforgettable show. Numerous comfortable hotels are situated nearby, so you can see the cone doing its thing day or night from your room, the hotel pool, soothing hot springs, or even while dining in the hotel restaurant. Ominous rumblings sound like jets taking off, but there is no airport nearby.

The classic cone of Arenal spews smoke, ash & glowing lava every day.

Arenal is about a four-hour drive from San José, but there is one major problem with visiting it: the volcano is almost always clouded over. You can easily spend several days in the area and never see the cone at all. When the first eruption in modern times occurred in 1968, the locals were not even aware of it until it was too late for many to flee. This was due to the dense cloud cover. If you are really keen on seeing it, I suggest you plan on visiting the area more than once during your stay in Costa Rica. On three separate week-long trips, I never glimpsed the cone. But you never know.

A cinematographer I met had recently been on assignment to capture 30 seconds of spectacular Arenal volcanic activity for a TV commercial. He had planned on a week in the area to be sure of getting some footage. On day one, the film crew had just set up their equipment in view of the cone when the clouds parted, the volcano let out a neat puff of smoke, and a white horse trotted through a pond in the foreground. "That's a wrap!" he said, and the team loaded up for the trip back to San José.

The base of the volcano and the surrounding area are covered in dense rainforest and offer a number of hikes, birding trips and horseback rides.

Fortunately, there are many other things to do in the area. At the base of the volcano, **Lake Arenal** is a popular fishing spot, and the constant, almost overpowering winds make it one of the best **windsurfing** destinations in the world.

Monteverde

Monteverde is perhaps the most common tourist destination in Costa Rica, and although the main street is dirt and well-rutted, it shows. It's only a three- or four-hour drive from San José. Only Jacó and Manuel Antonio on the Pacific coast exceed it for tourist density. The area is quite oversold. **Monteverde Cloud Forest Preserve** is spoken of by local wags as the "crowd forest."

The area usually referred to by the tourist industry as Monteverde actually runs from the small town of **Santa Elena**, to the entrance to Monteverde Cloud Forest Preserve. I refer to this six-kilometer (four-mile) road as the "Monteverde strip." It is almost lined end to end with hotels, restaurants, gift shops, a few galleries, and dozens of places offering to arrange every sort of tour or activity known to man. There are plenty of gaps along the strip but, as soon as the road to the area is finished being paved, those gaps will inevitably close. It was originally settled by Quakers. Now an interesting community of re-

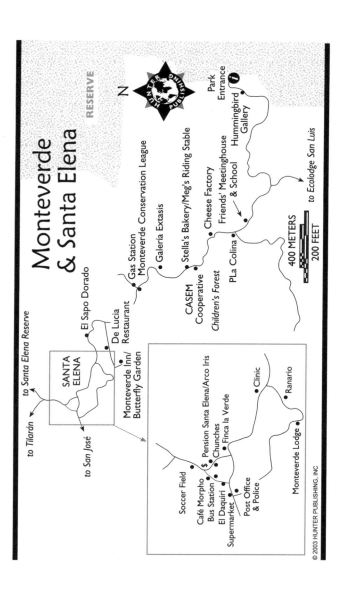

Monteverde
& Santa Elena

RESERVE

N

to Santa Elena Reserve

to Tilarán

to San José

SANTA
ELENA

El Sapo Dorado

De Lucia
Restaurant

Monteverde Inn/
Butterfly Garden

Gas Station
Monteverde Conservation League

Galería Extasis

Stella's Bakery/Meg's Riding Stable

CASEM
Cooperative

Children's Forest

Cheese Factory

Friends' Meetinghouse
& School

PLa Colina

Hummingbird
Gallery

Park
Entrance

to Ecolodge San Luis

400 METERS

200 FEET

Soccer Field

Café Morpho
Bus Station
El Daquirí
Supermarket

Post Office
& Police

Pensión Santa Elena/Arco Iris

Chunches

Finca la Verde

Clinic

Ranario

Monteverde Lodge

© 2003 HUNTER PUBLISHING, INC

tired, reasonably well-off North American arty types is flourishing among the tourist attractions.

The vastly overcrowded **Monteverde Cloud Forest Preserve** is certainly the main reason people come here. The park is so busy, at least in the areas open to the public, that you can feel like you're in Central Park in New York, instead of a nature preserve in Costa Rica. As you walk through the park, you are rarely out of sight of other groups. Sightings of the elusive **quetzal** quickly attract droves of jostling gawkers. The nearby **Santa Elena Cloud Forest Reserve** is much, much quieter and, although smaller, has all the same attractions. You can actually see Arenal Volcano on a clear day from Santa Elena. My recommendation is to skip Monteverde and its strip completely and view wildlife in Corcovado or one of the other, less-crowded parks. However, as much as I run the place down, there are plenty of interesting things to do in the area.

Many people come here to study Spanish either in classrooms or in deep-immersion home stays.

The community arts center has great, multilingual workshops.

An **international music festival** takes place in January or February in Monteverde and includes jazz, classical and Caribbean sounds. The festival is poorly promoted and, when I visited one February, I could find no signs, posters, nor anyone who could tell me much about the festival or its schedule. The hotels I visited in the area seemed unaware of the concert schedules.

Climate

The highland climate in the Arenal and Monteverde area can best be described as sodden. Even in the so-called dry season (December through April), it can rain every day. After a few days in the area, clothes start to smell of mildew and shoes refuse to dry out. Since this region straddles the continental divide, there is a constant parade of moisture-bearing clouds blowing heavily over. The clouds are low and dump copious amounts of rain. The wind is so heavy that a large number of electric generating windmills have been set up near Tilarán, and world-class **windsurfing** is done on Lake Arenal.

> ⊚ TIP
>
> Be sure to bring a good-quality **rain suit** – a poncho may not be good enough.

Getting Here

The main route from San José is the **Pan-American Highway** (head toward Puntarenas and Liberia on Route One). To go to **Arenal**, turn off at San Ramón toward La Fortuna.

To get to **Monteverde**, continue on past Punta-renas in the direction of Liberia. You don't actually go into the town of Puntarenas itself. There is a turn up into the mountains off the main road that was not marked the last time I was there, so ask directions at a *bomba* (gasoline station) about 15 minutes after you cross the Rió Barranca, just past Esparza. If you miss that turn, there is another a few miles farther along that goes along the Rió Lagarto, toward Pozo Azul. You need to look for signs to Santa Elena, as the actual town of Monteverde is tiny, and most lo-cals never refer to it – they talk about Santa Elena. The last time I traveled the road in mid-2002 it was paved for about a third of the way, and appeared that paving would be soon be done for the next third. The last third was being graded. This is one of the more notorious bumpy roads in Costa Rica (though it is not as bad as many roads I know in Tennessee).

Getting Around

Roads near Arenal are usually in good condition and are mostly paved. However, due to the huge amount of rain, ***derrumbes*** (mudslides) are common, and can block roads for days at a time. Sometimes the main road around the lake to Tilarán is closed, which means a torturous drive through cattle country on steep muddy roads, if you have a four-wheel-drive. If you have a regular car you might have to drive almost back to San José and come around from the other direction to get to the lodges near the volcano.

Roads in this area are poor, but are being paved one by one.

The main street from Santa Elena through Monteverde to the park is worse than any of the roads on the drive up. It is slippery, rocky and has enormous potholes most of the year. It is usually graded a bit in February, but quickly deteriorates back to its normal, deplorable condition.

You can drive in between Monteverde and Arenal through Tilarán on a rough, rocky, frequently muddy road, but you have to go all the way around Lake Arenal. This makes the trip about a three-to-four-hour drive. However, it is a fantastically beautiful drive through the rainforest, with views out over the lake. **Coatimundis** (a possum-like creature) lurk in the road hitting up passing tourists for handouts.

Sunup to Sundown

Seven-Day Itinerary

Day 1

After the long drive from San José to Arenal, explore some of the short **hiking trails**, near whichever hotel you have selected. If the sky is clear and you can see the **Arenal Volcano** (see page 20), take advantage of the opportunity to see it from several vantage points. The volcano is obscured most of the time by clouds, so grab any chance to drive through Fortuna, along the road toward the lake. Turn off the main road and head toward **Arenal Observatory Lodge**, if you have a four-wheel-drive, for views from the other side of the cone (see page 174).

Day 2

A variety of **hiking trails** around the base of the volcano are accessible from many of the area hotels (it is forbidden and extremely dangerous to hike near the crater). Many local guides have been trained to hold forth at length about the volcano's history and geology. The **rainforests** in the area are particularly lush and steaming. Morning or afternoon hikes are well worth the effort. The rest of the day can be spent enjoying the **hot springs** at Tabacón (see page 177), which is not as cheesy as it seems from the road. The springs are set in beautiful gardens and shouldn't be missed. The adjoining hotel is reportedly right in the path of future eruptions and pyroclastic flows so, unless you want a potential full volcanic experience, you may want to stay elsewhere.

Day 3

It's a good idea to plan on an extra day in the Arenal area in case the frequent clouds prevent viewing the cone. Be sure to schedule some time driving around beautiful **Lake Arenal** through the rainforest. The lake is at very high altitude, straddling the continental divide and is therefore extremely windy. **Windsurfing** (see page 84) is a definite option for those so inclined. The lake is also known for **fishing** (see page 83).

Day 4

Head to **Monteverde** and its famous **cloud forests** (see page 166). Even though it is a short distance, if measured by a crow, between Arenal and Monteverde, the twisting, rough roads mean it can be a four-hour drive. Some intrepid travelers make the journey more directly by **horse**, or even on foot. Tour operators can arrange this for you before you even get to the area, or ask at your hotel. Some of the horseback outfitters feature rough and hungry-looking animals, and have a bad reputation, so have a look at what you'll be riding before making a commitment, if possible. The afternoon can be spent checking out some of the interesting shops or the **cheese factory** (see page 166), in the Monteverde area.

Day 5

The **Monteverde Cloud Forest Preserve** (page 166) is the big deal in the area, but it can be crowded. Go in the early morning, retire to a local restaurant or your hotel for lunch, and return to the preserve in the late afternoon. With a bit of luck, you will find some relatively quiet time there. Be sure to visit the

Hummingbird Gallery (page 172) near the preserve entrance. There are literally clouds of hummingbirds flitting about. It's quite an amazing scene.

Day 6

If you can't arrange for a long stay at **Ecolodge San Luis** (see page 178), down the hill from Monteverde, you should at least visit overnight or arrange to go horseback riding. Or, try one of their excellent guided walks. Students and researchers staff the lodge and are involved in serious ecology research projects. They encourage visitors to participate in, or at least observe, what they are up to. It is hard to find more knowledgeable forest guides anywhere in Costa Rica. If you are serious about learning about the tropical environment, Ecolodge San Luis is not to be missed.

Day 7

Before heading back to San José, you should visit the **Santa Elena Cloud Forest Reserve** (page 169). It is much less crowded than the Monteverde Preserve, and is rich in quetzals and the other wildlife that makes Monteverde famous. The ride back to San José can take up to four or five hours and, although the roads have been vastly improved, some find it uncomfortable. You may want to get an early start and take it slow.

Attractions & Tours

Tourism is king in Arenal and Monteverde, and many types of tours and activities are available for visitors. Most hotels and lodges can arrange for any tours offered in the area. There are also a variety of tour offices in La Fortuna and on the Monteverde strip, which can arrange area activities and tours. Both **Costa Rica Expeditions** (☎ 506-257-0766, www.costaricaexpeditions.com) and **Costa Rica Nature Escape** (☎ 506-257-8064, www.crnature.com) can make all arrangements for tours in advance.

MONTEVERDE CHEESE FACTORY
On the strip between Santa Elena and Monteverde near the park.
☎ 506-645-5136

There is little to see, and no tour, but they do sell great cheese, yogurt and ice cream. The Cheese Factory was started by some of the Quakers who settled in the area some 50 years ago. Now it's run by their descendents.

MONTEVERDE CLOUD FOREST PRESERVE
☎ 506-645-5122
www.cct.or.cr
Open 7 am-4 pm
Cost: $8.50

In 1972, naturalist George Powell and area resident Wilford Guindon purchased 850 acres (328 hectares) of relatively untouched cloud forest land. They combined it a few years later with a 1,550-acre (554 hectares) watershed reserve, maintained by the local Quaker community, to form the Monteverde Cloud Forest Preserve. The preserve has since been significantly expanded. It is still privately owned and operated, by the non-profit Tropical Science Center, an educational and research association. The preserve has rapidly became one of the premiere tourist attractions in Costa Rica.

Straddling the continental divide, the park is only partly open to the public. A series of eight trails, a suspension bridge and three overnight shelters are maintained. Guided natural history tours, a night tour, special tours for birders, and an evening slide show about the rainforest are offered. There is a dormitory for researchers and student groups, a snack bar, restaurant, and a small gift shop.

The trails are wide, relatively free from mud, and can be classed mostly in the "easy" category for hiking. The forest is in turns sunny and gloomy. Ferns, bromeliads, orchids and huge numbers of hanging plants seem to encrust the trees and ferns. It's a wet and often windy place and, since the forest is at the very top of the Central American spine, clouds blow through dropping moisture picked up from the steamy Caribbean lowlands. Guides allowed in the preserve are licensed and well trained. I have found them to be some of the very best in the country.

There are six separate vegetation zones, over 100 mammal species, 400 species of birds, 20 types of amphibians and reptiles, over 2,500 species of plants, and perhaps as many as 60,000 insect species. In late February and early March, quetzals move to the Pacific side of the continental divide and are easy to see from the preserve's trails. This makes it a birder's paradise.

For all of these reasons, the preserve is overcrowded with visitors. It is relatively close to San José and the government and travel agencies have heavily promoted the preserve and surrounding area. A limited number of visitors are allowed into the park at any one time, but it is still rare to be out of sight of a guided tour group, or to be unable to hear the cackle of tourists as they excitedly point out the wonders to one another. When I visited with a guide, he located a couple of quetzals in some trees near the trail. Within five minutes a jostling crowd of over 75 people had gathered.

The preserve is a wonderful place to visit but, if viewing wildlife and tropical forest is your main interest, skip Monteverde and head to more remote parks like Corcovado (page 330), where you will see more wildlife and fewer fellow tourists.

☆ MONTEVERDE STUDIOS OF THE ARTS (COMMUNITY ARTS CENTER)

Just off the main road
☎ 800-370-3331; www.mvstudios.com

The arts center offers an interesting selection of workshops in basketry, ceramics, cooking, fibers, jewelry, painting, drawing, collage, photography, stained glass, writing, woodwork, yoga and music. There is an attached gift shop with items produced in the workshops and by workshop leaders.

Classes are offered on site and in artists' homes and studios. They're usually small and include field trips to the forest to study materials, and for photography sessions. If the locally produced furniture, bowls and sculptures charms you, you can participate in four-hour workshops for $50 that can put you on your way to producing masterpieces of your own. Longer, more intense courses can be negotiated with the artists. If you have an artistic inclination, call for a brochure before heading to Costa Rica.

RANARIO (THE FROG POND)

Just past Monteverde Lodge
☎ 506-645-6320
ranariomv@racsa.co.cr
$8
Open 9 am-6 pm

The best time to visit Ranario is in the evening, when the frogs are most active.

Poison dart frogs, with their iridescent blue, red and green colorings, may be the most colorful and photographed Costa Rican wildlife. The Ranario has over 20 species of Costa Rican frogs and toads, housed in large terrariums filled with tropical plants. Guided tours are delivered with an entertaining and educational dialogue that draws you in. You leave wondering why you haven't been completely fascinated by frogs and their froggy doings before your visit. Unfortunately, flash photography is not allowed, as it can blind the subjects.

SANTA ELENA CLOUD FOREST RESERVE
Open 7 am-4 pm
$7

The Santa Elena Cloud Forest Reserve, located next to Sky Trek (see below), is contiguous to the Monteverde Cloud Forest Preserve, and is run by a local high school. It is cheaper and vastly less crowded than the Monteverde Preserve, and has all the same wildlife and a couple of spectacular views of Arenal Volcano (on the rare clear days). It is also a little higher and a little wetter.

SKY TREK
In Monteverde, follow the signs past the Santa Elena High School
☎ 506-645-5238
www.skywalk.co.cr
Open 7:30 am-4 pm
$35

Sky Trek offers a zip-line and suspension-bridge trip through the cloud forest canopy, ostensibly in search of wildlife. There are 10 cables and two bridges. There is a bit of a walk through the forest to get to and from the main attraction – the zip-lines. Don't expect to see much wildlife, as lots of people traipse through the area, and many of them spend their time on the zip-lines screaming. The zip-lines are fun. They close at 3 pm. They also offer "Sky Walk Costa Rica" at the same location, which is a walk through the forest and over a series of seven suspension bridges.

Shop Till You Drop

There are few places to buy works of local artisans or souvenirs in Arenal, except for a skimpy selection in hotel gift shops. In La Fortuna, stores sell rubber boots, raincoats and the expected farming community supplies.

Monteverde offers a better selection, with several art galleries and a few souvenir venues.

CHEESE FACTORY
Monteverde on the strip
☎ 506-645-5136

Great cheese, mostly cheddar, as well as ice cream.

CHUNCHES
Santa Elena
☎ 506-645-5147

Chunches (Costa Rican slang for "things") has a very large selection of children's books in Spanish and English, as well as art supplies and coffee. Oddly, they also do laundry at reasonable prices.

COOPERATIVE DE ARTESANAS
SANTA ELENA Y MONTEVERDE (CASEM)
On the Monteverde strip, across from Stella's Bakery
☎ 506-645-5006

In 1982, several area women formed a cooperative to market the products of local artisans. There are now over 140 women and 10 men involved in the project. About 90% of the items in the gallery have been produced by Costa Ricans. Most of the work on display can also be found in other gift shops around the country. There is the usual selection of souvenirs, including beaded jewelry, T-shirts, postcards, mounted butterflies, wooden boxes and bowls. They have a good selection of ceramics from Guatíl on the Nicoya peninsula. In addition to the usual over-cute toucans carved out of a variety of materials, they have a unique selection of bird and animal mobiles made out of felt.

☆ GALERIA EXTASIS
Follow the signs on the Monteverde strip
☎ 506-645-5548
Call for hours.

Finally, a place to admire and buy wood sculptures and paintings by local artists, with no cheesy carvings of toucans! Galeria Extasis is probably the best place in the country to see high-quality work by some of the most talented sculptors in Costa Rica. The carvings are not cheap, and many of the designs can only be described as surreal. Wood from fallen trees and roots was used to create beautiful bowls, boxes and abstract sculptures of animals and people. If you have been admiring these in gift shops around the country, this is the place to buy the best. Almost every gift shop in Costa Rica has a selection of the boxes I am describing, but the ones on display at Galeria Extasis are many levels above what is normally seen. Most of the work is by Marco Tulio Brenes, who apprenticed with the famous Barry Biensanz. Several other, very talented artists also have work on display.

Warm up your credit cards before going inside. If you have a love for fine artwork and beautiful woods, and your taste runs a bit to the surreal and abstract, you will have a hard time leaving empty-handed.

HUMMINGBIRD GALLERY

By the entrance to Monteverde Cloud Forest Preserve

☎ 506-645-5030

wainmayn@racsa.co.cr

Call for hours.

The gift shop has souvenirs, film, coffee, textiles and books. They have a nice selection of framed wildlife photographs, and a room dedicated to watercolors of local interest. The best thing about the gallery is the numerous hummingbird feeders they have hanging from trees in front of the store. Dozens of humming-birds jostle for position around the feeders all day long. You can see literally hundreds of them up close. It is notoriously hard to photograph hum-mingbirds, but you can be sure to get some great shots here in just a few minutes, even with a simple camera. However, getting a nice clear shot of a hum-mingbird without the feeder in the frame is another matter. They land and leave in an amazing blur and sit relatively still only when perched on the feeders. Some never land at all, but stick their snouts into the feeders while hovering, with wings beating a million miles an hour.

MONTEVERDE STUDIOS OF THE ARTS (COMMUNITY ARTS CENTER)

☎ 800-370-3331; www.mvstudios.com

The giftshop, attached to the community arts center, has a selection of gifts and souvenirs made by artists that participate and lead in the workshops spon-sored by the center. On sale is a selection of jewelry, ceramics and funny little trucks made out of beer cans. It's a strange shop, decorated in quirky ways with scraps of iron and weird pieces of wood found in the forest. The arts center offers workshops in bas-ketry, ceramics, cooking, fibers, jewelry, painting, drawing, collage, photography, stained glass, writ-ing, woodwork, yoga and music.

After Dark

Live Music

Monteverde is home to the best music festival in the country from January until March. Heavy on jazz and Afro-Caribbean, there are also significant classical, folk and brass contingents. The Monteverde Music Festival (☎ 506-645-5053, www.mvinstitute. org/music) sponsors weekend evening concerts from January through April (check these dates as they may change).

Nightlife is very limited. I heard reports that the locals were trying to shut down the only "happening" type bar, La Cascada, which is only open on weekends.

Best Places to Stay

Hotels and lodges in Arenal are definitely not in the luxury category, but the better ones are comfortable and clean. Monteverde has a couple of nicer places, but nothing in a five-star category.

Alive Prices

Prices are based on double occupancy during high season, and given in US $. Taxes and meals are not included, unless so noted. Hotels and lodges marked with a ☆ are my personal favorites. "The Best of the Best" choices earn their title by offering top-quality lodging and services.

Arenal

ARENAL OBSERVATORY LODGE

From La Fortuna, look for a gravel road on the left four km (2.4 miles) past Tabacón.
☎ 506-290-7011, 506-695-5033, 506-290-8427
www.arenal-observatory.co.cr
$100

The Arenal Observatory Lodge was originally built for Smithsonian Institute and Earthwatch scientists and researchers as an observation post. It is perched on the edge of a small valley directly facing the enormous cone of Arenal. The volcano is right in the front yard. You just can't get any closer (1.8 km, about a mile, from the crater). The site was chosen as the best and safest place to view the volcano, and is still used to do just that by vulcan- ologists. There is a seismograph in an elevated observatory building (open to lodge guests) that records every rumble and belch of the volcano. Arenal is active – very active. It last blew in August of 2001 and is always putting out smoke and ash (read more about Arenal in the *Volcanoes* section, page 22). If you want to see red hot lava pouring down the volcano side, you don't even have to raise your head up off your pillow. Just glance out the window of your room (on a clear day). You can hear it rumbling and roiling and feel occasional tremors.

The views of fiery rocks flying out of the cone and lava pouring down the slopes at night are seen on postcards sold in tourist shops all over Costa Rica. There is one catch, though. Arenal and the lodge are located in the middle of a rainforest, which means it rains a lot (they don't call them rainforests for nothing). When it is raining, which is most of the time, clouds obscure the peak, and almost everything else.

The lodge is a basic, rustic mountain lodge (no phones in the rooms), but not all of the rooms have views of the volcano. Be sure to specify a room with a view of Arenal when you make reservations. It is comfortable, but by no stretch of the imagination could you call it luxurious. The sounds of howler monkeys echoing through the forest wake you up in the morning, if the volcano doesn't. The road into the lodge is long and rough. You don't have to have a four-wheel-drive to handle it, but it is be best.

The pool is the most imaginatively designed I have seen in Costa Rica, and the 870-acre grounds are surrounded by the Arenal Volcano National Park. The hotel is handicap-friendly, with specially designed bedrooms and bathrooms. You can take a wheelchair right into the pool, and the half-mile "Saino" (*peccary*) nature trail is completely accessible by wheelchair.

The forest itself is a wonderful reason to come here, and you can certainly enjoy exploring, even when it's raining.

There is one notable exception to what I just said about lack of luxury. In 1999, Apsinall Senior completed the spacious and creatively decorated **White Hawk Villa**. The secluded villa is over 4,000 square feet, with two large master suites upstairs, and two large bedrooms downstairs. It has its own well-appointed kitchen and bar and can sleep 10. The views of Arenal Volcano and Arenal Lake are breathtaking. There are two large sitting areas with comfortable couches and coffee tables made from local woods. They are arranged in front of picture windows overlooking the cone and lake. A helicopter pad is nearby; the trip from San José is done in about 20 minutes. The hotel restaurant will cater meals, provide a cook, or you can do your own cooking. At the time of my visit in 2001, White Hawk Villa was a bargain at $500 per night.

There is really no place nearby to eat, so all meals are taken in the lodge restaurant. The food is okay, but not memorable. The bartenders are friendly and will fix up all sorts of interesting drinks with volcanic themes, like Liquid Lava and Pyroclastic Shooters.

A variety of walks and horseback rides to nearby sites, such as the lake at Cerro Chato, La Fortuna Waterfall, and to view the volcano from spectacular vantage points, are organized through the lodge office. Guides are hotel employees trained in various specialties, which include volcanology, biology, entomology, and birds' tropical biology. Esteban is the manager; he speaks excellent English and will help you arrange everything with a smile on his face. This is a great base from which to explore the park and surrounding areas.

ARENAL PARAISO HOTEL
About eight km (five miles) west of Fortuna, just before Tabacón
☎ 506-460-5333; fax 506-460-5343
www.arenal-paraiso.com
$60

The volcano you may hear rumbling every now and then is just across the street.

The Arenal Paraíso a comfortable mountain lodge. The rooms are all in their own little bungalows scattered about the hummingbird-infested grounds. The 12 standard and 25 deluxe bungalows are beautifully crafted from tropical woods, but are lacking in some basic amenities, like lights over the mirrors in the bathrooms. It is extremely rainy and humid in this region; the hotel seems to be losing the battle against mold, and the smell of old, wet laundry permeates the rooms.

Deluxe bungalows are $87 and have a TV and phone. A few of the bungalows have private Jacuzzis. The hotel has three deluxe rooms suitable for handicapped access.

The **Rancho Paraíso Steak House** is on-site (see *Best Places to Eat*, page 183), and serves a decent breakfast (included with stay). The dinners are, of course, steak-oriented, but there's also pasta and a few fish items on the menu.

The hotel was a dairy farm until the volcano eruption made tourism a better bet. The local owner continues to add bungalows and amenities. The staff will organize area tours for you, and the hotel has the largest stables in the area. Guided or unguided nature walks begin at the hotel and meander through the nearby cow pastures and secondary forest. Since it is unwise to actually go near the top of the volcano, the trails don't get particularly high, and are not especially challenging. Nearby hot springs, emanating from deep underground, are tapped to heat the pool and spa and provide theoretically healthful baths. The spa and pool are not open to the public, as they are at the nearby Tabacon, so you don't get huge tour buses pulling up and the hoi polloi noisily piling in. The grounds are thick with orchids and hum with bird life.

TABACON LODGE
11 km (6.6 miles) west of La Fortuna de San Carlos
☎ 506-256-1500 (reservations), fax 506-221-3075;
506-460-2020 (hotel), fax 506-460-5724
www.tabacon.com
$140

The hot water for the lodge is piped in from the hot springs across the road. Vulcanologists told me the resort is built on top of the last recent lava flow, and is directly in the path of probable future pyroclastic flows. Vegetation grows so fast in the area you can't see much evidence the old lava flow – the place looks like it's in the middle of centuries-old jungle. In the case of a major eruption, if things go as some predict, guests could have as little as two minutes to get their act together and skedaddle, before being cooked or suffocated by hot gases. This is a risk you take if you decide to stay.

With almost 100 hardwood-finished units, the lodge seems a bit busy at times. It is well maintained and the rooms are air conditioned and modern with coffee makers. Some rooms have kitchenettes. There is a gym, lovely pool and of course, a view of the volcano from the restaurant and some of the rooms.

Monteverde

ECOLODGE SAN LUIS & BIOLOGICAL STATION
Turn right just before Monteverde, toward San Luis
☎ 506-380-3255; fax 506-645-5364
www.ecolodgesanluis.com
$162

Many visitors come to Costa Rica to view wildlife and enjoy pristine tropical forests. However, few manage to do more than take a couple half-day guided walks, tour the mangroves, or take a horseback ride. If you would like to get a bit deeper into things and spend quality time with tropical ecology experts, Ecolodge San Luis is the place. It offers one of the best opportunities for someone on a short trip to Costa Rica to do so.

The lodge is much more than a hotel where tourists can stay near a national park and go on tours. The main function of the lodge is research and education. Resident naturalists and researchers are involved in full-time tropical ecology research projects. Part of their mission is to interact with visitors, and to share their knowledge and love for the area. This means walks through the forest are guided by some of the most experienced experts in the fields of tropical botany, bird migration, reforestation, sustainable development and tropical agricultural. All the guides are active researchers.

Not only do guests have the opportunity to look over the shoulders of researchers, they are encouraged to help in the projects. They (and you) can be involved in reforestation projects, studies of tropical bird species and migration, population biology of bromeliads, seed dispersal by birds and mammals, collection and analysis of medicinal plants, and a wide variety of other research activities. Guests can join weeklong total immersion programs in tropical biology. You can enroll for credit, or as special students, in a variety of 10-day to three-week tropical study classes through North American and European colleges and universities. Guests are encouraged to sit in on lectures, classes and labs and can be part of any of the academic activities that catch their interest.

Activities available include guided or self-guided nature walks, horseback riding, world-class birdwatching with expert guides, observation of nocturnal creatures, hands-on farm activities, cultural and social events with the surrounding community, classroom lectures, volunteer research participation, day-trips to Monteverde, slide presentations, river walks and, of course, relaxation.

The lodge incorporates a working farm, and guests can participate in farm activities, such as coffee picking, tending the tropical organic garden, banana picking, cow milking – the list goes on and on.

Cabins are clean and comfortable, and have hot water. Delicious Costa Rican-style meals, cooked over a wood stove, are served in the dining room at large tables. Guests eat with the students and researchers, and the conversation runs from technical discussions of research projects, to who is going to the local dance that night. There are 12 cabins, four bungalows and a four-room bunkhouse that can sleep up to 30. Prices begin at $51 per person for the bunkhouse. All meals, naturalist guides and most activities are included in the room price.

Any birder can be confident of adding significantly to their bird life list.

A bird list presently includes more than 250 species, and the number continues to grow. While no promises are made, 50 species can easily be seen before breakfast by even casual birders.

The 162-acre (65 hectares) lodge is 15 minutes from Monteverde in the San Luis valley, away from the tourist bustle surrounding the park. It borders Monteverde Cloud Forest Preserve and the **Children's International Rainforest**, also known as the Children's Eternal Cloudforest (Bosque Nuboso de Los Niños). This was founded by Swedish schoolchildren. It is almost 75,000 acres (25,000 hectares) and is more of a preserve than a tourist attraction, although there are trails. It almost surrounds the preserve.

Founders Diana and Milton Lieberman are faculty members of the University of Georgia, and actively teach field courses in Costa Rica. They are both employees of the Costa Rica Park Service.

☆ MONTEVERDE LODGE
Main Monteverde road
☎ 506-257-0766, 506-222-0333, 506-645-5057; fax 506-257-1665, 645-5126
www.monteverdelodge.com
$116

Monteverde Lodge, run by Costa Rica Expeditions, is one of the very few, truly comfortable places to stay in the Monteverde area. It has the soft beds and hot showers you need at the end of a long day filled with adventure in the nearby cloud forest. The lodge is on 20 acres (eight hectares) of bromeliad-filled grounds. Local naturalist guide Arturo Jarquín and landscaper Sigifredo Altamirano designed the gardens to attract butterflies and hummingbirds, and include only plants native to the immediate area. A lover of bromeliads would be in paradise here – there are dozens of species about the grounds. Several trails wind through and around the lodge grounds, so guests can enjoy the tropical setting with little effort.

The rooms and main building overlook almost undisturbed forest. There are no distractions to the eye as you look down from the lodge toward the Gulf of Nicoya. As you enter the main building, you can't help but be drawn to the large glass enclosure beside the lobby that houses an enormous Jacuzzi. Guests can soak here after a wearying hike. Both the bar, with an open fireplace, and the restaurant, have good views out over the grounds.

Be sure to get a seat by the windows for breakfast, so you can watch the hummingbirds at the feeders.

There is a large room dedicated to computers for guests addicted to the Web and their e-mail. Rooms are large and all feature glassed-in sitting areas overlooking the gardens. They are cleverly placed, protected from the wind and mist that is so common in the cloud forest. My only complaint is the lack of TVs and telephones (which some consider distracting). The lack of air-conditioning is excused, since it is rarely needed in this mountain area.

All the lodges operated by Costa Rica Expeditions to do a top-quality job of providing expert guides and arranging activities for guests. The company is famous for having its own guide-training program, and employs only the best people, with advanced naturalist qualifications. The staff know which are the best places to go and don't steer guests to their favorites for the sake of a commission. For instance, for safety and liability reasons, the lodge does't recommend any of the nearby canopy tours. They inform guests of the features of each and give basic advice about how best to judge for yourself the suitability of each one. Slide show presentations covering tropical biology topics are offered to guests every night.

The menu in the restaurant is international and usually includes two or three starters, and two or three main courses. I found the food to be quite good and reasonably priced (see *Best Places to Eat*, page 185). The breakfast menu has basic continental, typical Costa Rican, or full American-style breakfasts. Coffee is quickly provided and quickly refilled – very important in the morning. The kitchen is flexible. I met a group from Israel who were served large salads at breakfast, which is a popular morning meal in their country.

Even the most pampered traveler should be pleased with the comfort level and good food. Most visitors to the area come to explore the Monteverde Cloud Forest Preserve, and Monteverde Lodge is a good base to do so. If you've hiked perhaps a bit too hard and return wet and cold, a soak in the Jacuzzi and a drink in the bar by the fireplace should warm you up nicely.

Best Places to Eat

Arenal

Tourist-oriented restaurants in the Arenal area go through the motions, but the food is just not up to the prices they like to charge. Big city prices are charged for tough steaks, bland fish and overcooked vegetables.

This is a good chance to try some of the smaller local restaurants. Fortuna has dozens of small sodas and tourist-oriented places to eat. Most of them are okay. La Vaca Muca, just outside Fortuna on the road to Arenal, is, for my money, by far the best eating in the area.

Alive Prices

Prices are given in US $, and are the average price for an entrée or main course, per person, before taxes and service charges are added. Although Costa Rican law says restaurants must show prices on the menu with taxes included, many do not. Menus that include taxes almost always say so.

There isn't any fine dining in the Arenal area, although hotel restaurants may argue.

RANCHO PARAISO STEAK HOUSE
At Hotel Arenal Paraiso, eight km (five miles) west of Fortuna
☎ 506-460-5333
$12
Steak

The Rancho Paraíso has one of the best selections of steaks in the area, including the *lomito* (tenderloin) filet mignon, T-bone, sirloin, and even an imported Argentinean sirloin. The usual boiled vegetables and baked potato round out the meal. The *palmito* salad is excellent. Service is brisk, and most of the waiters speak excellent English. An adequate wine list leans heavily toward Chilean reds; the house red is barely acceptable and comes in rather small glasses ($3). Desserts are no surprise and include flan, *tres leches* (a kind of bread pudding), and *queque* (cake). The view of the volcano (when not clouded over) is hard to beat.

☆ LA VACA MUCA

About one mile to the west of Fortuna
☎ 506-479-9186
$5
Local cuisine

La Vaca Muca, run by a local Tico family, serves up a better meal than any of the local hotel restaurants for about half the price, or less. You get a big platter of side dishes such as rice, beans, salad, fried plantains, fried potatoes, bread and cheese (this is called a *Casado*) with either chicken, beef or fish for about $6, with a beer, including tax and tip. The family is friendly, the service spot on, and the food fresh and hot. A large sign hangs in the place proclaiming "*escenas amorosas*" (love scenes) are not allowed. I didn't see any reason for that during my visits, but who knows what might go on late at night. La Vaca Muca is the best place to eat for miles around.

Monteverde

Monteverde is not really a place to look for fine dining either. Although there is a fair contingent of well-off gringos with homes in the area, and lots of tourists, there are few restaurants of real note.

DE LUCIA

On the Monteverde strip
$14
International
☎ 506-645-5976

The Chilean owner greets guests at the door and brings a selection of meats and fish to the table for diners to select from. Steaks, chicken, sea bass and vegetarian main courses are offered, along with wonderful, fresh tortillas with guacamole. The dining room overlooks a small garden and forest.

THE GARDEN
In Monteverde Lodge
$12
International

The Garden is in a large, high-ceilinged room with an open fireplace in the main building of the Monteverde Lodge. Hummingbird feeders have been placed strategically near the huge glass windows that encircle to room, so be sure you get a seat near the windows. The views are out over the forest valley toward Nicoya. The menu changes every day and usually includes two or three starters and two or three main courses. You should call to see what's on and make a reservation if you are not a guest of the lodge.

Service is good and the wine list is adequate. Desserts include such Costa Rican specialties as *tres leches*, a light cake with sweet milk poured over it, and coconut flan. Flan is a bit hard to describe but is basically an egg custard with a thin, sweet, brown sauce poured over it. The flan served at The Garden is not the flan your mother used to make – it has a crust like cheesecake and a coconut flavor. Menu prices include tax and service so you know exactly what you will spend – a big plus. Even though Costa Rican law says all restaurants must do this, few do.

PIZZERIA DE JOHNNY
Near the Sapo Dorado
☎ 506-645-5066
$8

Pasta and pizza made in a brick oven are the staples. The pizza is great, the salads large and fresh, and hot focaccia seems to come with everything. Skip the chocolate cake. The modern room has a fair view of the adjoining forest.

STELLA'S BAKERY
On the Monteverde strip across the street from the CASEM gift shop
☎ 506-645-5560
$8

Stella's has a wonderful selection of sticky things to eat that are made from scratch on the premises. Their pies, chocolate cake and sticky buns are a sinfully good way to ruin your diet. You can enjoy cinnamon rolls at breakfast, soups or sandwiches on fresh bread for lunch, and follow up later with an afternoon slice of blackberry pie. Lunchtime diners fill out a card with their selection of items to be made into a sandwich, and it's ready in a few minutes. There are four small tables inside and several out in the garden. The food is so good that I hate to complain about the smell of sewage as you step across a ditch to enter, or about the rude service. I rarely encounter surly service from Costa Ricans, but I did both times I visited Stella's. Perhaps their success has gone to their heads.

A to Z

Banks

Banco Nacional in Santa Elena, La Fortuna and Arenal.

Emergency Medical

Call 911 in all areas. There's a Monteverde doctor on call at ☎ 506-645-6264.

Police

Call 911 in all areas.

Post Office

In Santa Elena, Arenal and La Fortuna. Just ask and someone will point them out to you.

Tourist Information

Ask at **Chunches** in Santa Elena,☎ 506-645-5147, or go to the **Costa Rican Tourist Board** (ICT) in San José at Avenida 4, Calles 5/7, or the one at the airport. They offer some basic tourist maps and books. ☎ 506-223-1733, fax 506-223-5452; In the US, 800-343-6332; www.tourism-costarica.com.

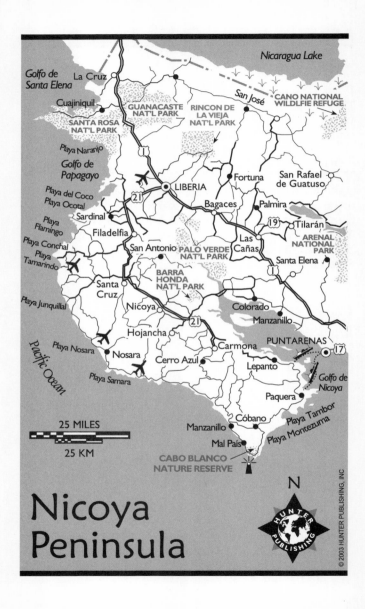

Nicoya
Peninsula

Nicoya Peninsula
Overview

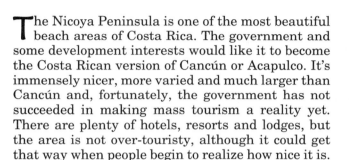

The Nicoya Peninsula is one of the most beautiful beach areas of Costa Rica. The government and some development interests would like it to become the Costa Rican version of Cancún or Acapulco. It's immensely nicer, more varied and much larger than Cancún and, fortunately, the government has not succeeded in making mass tourism a reality yet. There are plenty of hotels, resorts and lodges, but the area is not over-touristy, although it could get that way when people begin to realize how nice it is. At the moment it is a secret shared by fishermen, divers, surfers, and a few tourists who ended up here by fortunate mistake.

There are world-class golf courses at Playa Conchal (designed by Robert Trent Jones II) and Hacienda Pinilla. The largest sport-fishing marina in Costa Rica is in Flamingo. Add terrific diving, beautiful national parks and private nature reserves, and it's easy to see what potential development interests see. Hurry – the tourism slump won't last forever.

The coastal area north of the peninsula is almost completely taken up by **Santa Rosa National Park**, and is isolated and hard to reach. The **Gulf of Papagayo towns** in the area of Coco are famous for diving – especially for opportunities to view manta ray, white tip and bull sharks up close. **Flamingo** is also a famous dive destination, but is best known for its large sportfishing fleet and nearby resort. **Playa Conchal** is one of the most luxurious beach and golf destinations in Costa Rica. The beach in front of the lodge has very white sand, in a country filled with stunning mocha and black beaches.

Tamarindo is a still-scruffy surfer town just now starting to succeed in turning itself into a proper tourist town. Pigs still occasionally wander through the streets. Farther south, **Sámara** and **Carrillo** are beach towns popular with Ticos. Both have great swimming beaches. South from Carrillo, toward the tip of the peninsula, are some of the wildest and most deserted beaches in Costa Rica. The four-wheel-drive-only road from Carrillo to Mal País is spectacular, with long stretches where driving on the beach itself is still the best route. This is one of my favorite drives in Costa Rica. If you have a good four-wheel-drive and a bit of an adventurous spirit, this is not to be missed.

Mal País is yet another surfer heaven, with little more than a one-lane dirt, a few bars and some surf shops. The surf spots go on for miles. **Montezuma**, although remote, is a small but clean and complete tourist town. It's a hip place, catering to young hippies and older bohemians. North Americans and Europeans flock there to hang out on the beach and slurp down cheap beer in the numerous bars and dance spots. It is much hipper than Jacó, and there is much more to do than in other cool towns to the south. The deluxe Flor Blanca lodge in Santa Teresa, just north of Mal País, is perhaps the hippest, and most luxurious resort, in all of Costa Rica. The older bohemians mentioned above (at least the ones with some bread), would think they have died and gone to heaven could they stay there.

There is good diving, fishing and snorkeling around Isla Tortuga.

Tambor and **Paquera** are quiet towns with a few upscale lodges, relatively uncrowded parks and nature reserves, and good swimming beaches.

The Nicoya area is not particularly well developed, but has a good airport and is really no farther from San José than some of the other resort areas up north.

Most people just think about the beaches, fishing, diving and surfing when they think of Nicoya, but the interior of the peninsula has its own rural beauty. The town of **Guaitíl**, just north of Santa Cruz, is famous for its pottery, and is definitely worth a stop. Although heavily agricultural, the peninsula has its share of tropical dry forests with national parks, and nature preserves with the inevitable canopy and zip line tours.

Climate

The Nicoya Peninsula is in Guanacaste, and is quite a bit drier than the rest of Costa Rica. It still rains plenty, but dust is more of an issue in the dry season than is mud. At times, a sweet-smelling molasses by-product is spread on the roads to keep the dust down to a minimum.

Dry season is from December through April, but expect the occasional afternoon shower throughout the year. Expect torrential downpours during the wet season. The area is rightfully famous for never-ending sunshine and blue skies, despite the frenquent rain.

Getting Here

There are three main routes to the area. Most visitors come right down from San José, or from Arenal and Monteverde. The main road, **Route 21**, runs from Liberia on the Interamerican Highway, through the middle of the peninsula to Nicoya and south.

By Ferry

Until recently, there were two ferries that ran from the mainland across the Gulf of Nicoya. The Tempisque ferry has been replaced by a bridge, vastly shortening the drive time from San José to the resort area beaches. Ferries from **Puntarenas** leave from the very end of the town. To find the ferry dock, drive all the way through town, looking carefully for the occasional signs. From the Puntarenas terminus, ferries run to Playa Naranjo and to Paquera. The waits can be very long, since the boats are small and can be easily filled by a couple of trucks or large tourist buses. When that happens everyone just continues to wait in line for three or four hours until the next ferry comes. The one to Playa Naranjo is usually less crowded and, since Naranjo is only about 25 km (15 miles) from Paquera, you can save time by taking it and simply driving the extra distance to Paquera.

It takes less time to drive across the new bridge at Tempisque, than to wait for the ferries in Puntarenas.

The main road through the peninsula is reasonably paved, but watch for enormous potholes, even on the best-paved stretches. Some of the them are big enough to hide a cow in.

The route that hugs the coast from Mal País through Sámara, and up to Tamarindo, is stunning.

By Air

There is an international airport in Liberia, but it was only handling charters in early 2002. Charter airlines, SANSA or Travelair, serve small airports in Tamarindo, Nosara, Tambor, Carrillo, Islita and Nicoya. Most hotels and resorts can arrange airport transfers for you.

Getting Around

Route 21 runs down the middle of the peninsula. The main roads are paved, but fields of potholes resembling battlegrounds can surprise you after miles of perfect pavement. Roads north of the peninsula, following the coast, are usually in bad shape or nonexistent.

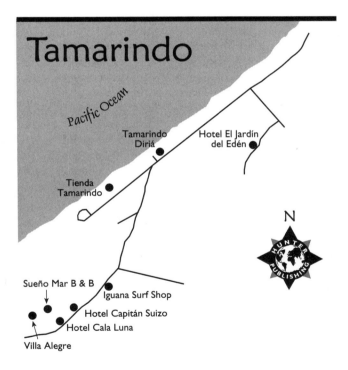

This means you have to drive back and forth from the main road, along the spine of the peninsula out to some of the beach areas. The road from Playa Naranjo to Paquera is rough, but passable in the rainy season. Roads to Montezuma and Mal País are interesting, and should be no problem for most vehicles.

Beach after beach after beautiful beach follow one another. Most are empty of people. The road pan is packed dirt and close to impassable in the rainy season, but is a great adventure for a four-wheel-drive vehicle when it is dry.

River crossings can be interesting. Be sure to roll up your windows before starting out across some of the rivers, or the wave your vehicle makes in passing may come in the car and soak everyone. Steep hills and meter-deep mud during the rainy season means you should have a strong winch and plenty of cable if you're going to try to drive this route. Flights within the peninsula are few, and the best way to get around is by car. Rental cars are available in major towns.

Practice rolling your windows up in a hurry – the dusty roads in the dry season generate impenetrable clouds of fine brown, gritty dust.

Car Rentals

It is prudent to rent four-wheel-drive vehicles unless you are only going to be on the main roads. The choice of car rental agencies near Liberia is almost as good as in San José, due to the international airport just outside town. Other towns have a very limited choice. Here are some choices.

BUDGET RENT A CAR
Gulf of Papagayo, Liberia
☎ 506-668-1024

TOYOTA RENT A CAR
Liberia, near the airport
☎ 506-258-6797

ECONOMY CAR RENTAL
Liberia, near the airport
☎ 506-666-2816

TRICOLOR CAR RENTAL
Liberia, near the airport
☎ 506-384-6000

ADOBE CAR RENTAL
Tamarindo, in the Cala Luna hotel
☎ 506-653-0214

BUDGET CAR RENTAL
Tamarindo, in the Best Western
☎ 506-653-0859

ECONOMY CAR RENTAL
Tamarindo, next to the Coconut Restaurant
☎ 506-653-0086

ELEGANTE/PAYLESS
Tamarindo, on the main road in town
☎ 506-653-0015

ECONOMY CAR RENTAL
Flamingo, in the Flamingo Shopping Center
☎ 506-654-4543

BUDGET
Sámara, in the Hotel Giada on the main street.
☎ 506-656-0132

Sunup to Sundown

Seven-Day Itinerary

Day 1 & 2

Stock up on cash at the ATM in Liberia (located in the Burger King building at the crossroads), as Flamingo is the only other place to do so. Drive south along Highway 21 to the area around Coco or Flamingo, and spend time **diving** or **fishing** from one of the resorts. **Bat Island** is the place to see rays. **Big Scare**, in the Islas Murcielagos, is where to go if you are inclined to dive with man-eating bull sharks (these are the ones that have been gobbling up swimmers in Florida). **Flamingo** is probably the best spot on the peninsula for fishing charters. Eat at **Camarón Dorado** (see page 240). If your tastes run to golf and all-inclusives, Playa Conchal would be a good base to explore the area. El Ocotal is not as fancy but has far superior views and is a good base for divers and anglers.

Day 3

Drive inland and go south on Highway 21, then turn right, just past Belen, to get to **Tamarindo**. Kayaking in the mangroves, diving, surfing, or checking out the bunnies in front of town are common activities for visitors. Don't miss eating at least one meal at the **Lazy Wave**, (page 244). Stay at the **Villa Alegre B&B** (page 224), and buy a cool shirt and grab a beer at the **Iguana Surf** (page 208). Dance, dance, dance the night away if you are so inclined.

Day 4 & 5

It's a long, half-day drive south along the coast to **Carrillo**. I recommend taking your time and stopping along the way at several of the deserted beaches for a stroll before checking into the **Hotel Punta Islita**, (page 229). One could easily spend several days there just chilling out and swimming.

Day 6

Continue the drive along the coast, being careful to drive on the sand between Punta Coyote and Ario only at low tide. Observe the cool surf scene in **Mal País** or **Montezuma**, and check into one of the beachfront lodges, such as **Tango Mar** (page 235) near Tambor. Be sure to make the scene in Montezuma and have a meal at the *Sano Banano* (healthy banana).

Day 7

Except for a few early-morning Tai Chi aficionados strutting their stuff on the beach, nothing much happens in Mal País or Montezuma before late afternoon. Laze around on the beach, or take a half-day fishing trip before heading back to San José via the Paquera ferry or the new bridge at Tempisque.

Beaches

The beautiful beaches of the Nicoya Peninsula are a major attraction. My advice is to avoid the big ones near the hotels (unless you really like to people watch), and search out one of the hundreds of more remote, deserted beaches.

Nicoya Peninsula

Gulf of Papagayo

Playa Conchal is the most classically beautiful beach in the country.

◉ **Playa Conchal** consists of an arc of white sand, backed with dry forest and the beautiful golf course at Melía Playa Conchal. The beach is made up of tiny bits of broken shells (and so the name), and is gleaming white and kind to the feet. I've heard it described as being a vanilla beach; if it is, it's definitely Häagen-Dazs. You can get to it by going into the little village of Puerto Viejo and turning left. You end up under the trees in front of the fancy Hotel Melía Playa Conchal. There always seem to be a few shady characters near the hotel beach entrance, but they are easily discouraged.

◉ Playa Conchal may be pretty and white, but **Pan de Azúcar** has more character. There is driftwood and looming bluffs, and the surf is not usually too high. Pelicans actively swoop down to scoop up baitfish and ride the uplift of air in front of the breaking waves.

◉ **Playa Brasilito**, in front of the Camarón Dorado, is just about one mile (0.6 km) past the turn to Flamingo. It's really a nicer beach than Flamingo (see below), with some shade. You can get drinks and snacks from a couple of little places along the top of the beach.

◉ **Playa Flamingo** is a gray sand beach you get to by turning left as you enter the town. There is a dirt road along the top of the beach. It's hot with little shade.

⊚ **Playa Potrero** is just a bit farther on, is also gray, and is perhaps the prettiest of the three beaches in the area.

⊚ **Playa Pan de Azúcar** (Sugar Bread Beach), is in front of Hotel Sugar Beach, and is hard to get to except by going through the hotel grounds. It is the best of the beaches in the area precisely because it is hard to get to and relatively deserted.

Tamarindo

⊚ **Playa Tamarindo** is a gray sand stretch running from right in front of the village and to the south. There is good surfing action in front of town. It is mushy in front of the lodges, just south of town. Most of the hard-core surfers stay in or near town, but move out for the day to other beaches with better breaks. Parts of it are good for swimming, and there are lifeguards on the beach in the village. Beautiful bodies cram the beach on weekends.

⊚ If Playa Conchal with its white sand is vanilla ice cream, **Playa Langosta** is Rocky Road (Ben & Jerry's). This is a beach with real character. The surf at the south end, near the inlet, is world-class, although the best spots may be crowded when the waves are at their best. It is a bit rocky (but, has interesting rocks), but the light brown sand is agreeable. Turtles do their thing in season. The estuary at the south end is a great

Playa Tamarindo is a good place to stroll along and admire the surfers in action – the surf breaks fairly close in, so you can really get a good look.

place to bird-watch. Take a fishing pole down there when the tide is going out and bring back a snook for dinner. The tiderips are tough and, even though there is a lifeguard at the south end in front of the Hotel Barceló Playa Langosta, you should be very careful.

◎ **Playas Sámara** and **Carrillo** are two of the best swimming beaches in the area, and are popular with Ticos down from San José on the weekends. They can be quite crowded. Just north of Sámara, **Playa Ostional** is famous for vast armadas of nesting turtles.

South to Cabo Blanco

The beaches along this stretch of the coast are some of the most deserted in Costa Rica.

◎ **Playas Bejuco**, **San Miguel**, **Coyote** and **Ario** are rarely visited by anyone other than a few intrepid surfers. Some are famous for turtles, and all are beautiful, stark and tropically hypnotizing.

◎ **Playa Santa Teresa** is a popular surfing beach covering several miles before you get to Mal País.

Montezuma & Mal País

◎ **Playa Montezuma** is famous for sunsets and surfers. **Mal País** is famous for sunrises and hippies. Most of the beaches in the area are a bit rough for swimming. Say no more. Take your pick.

Cabo Blanco
Absolute Nature Reserve

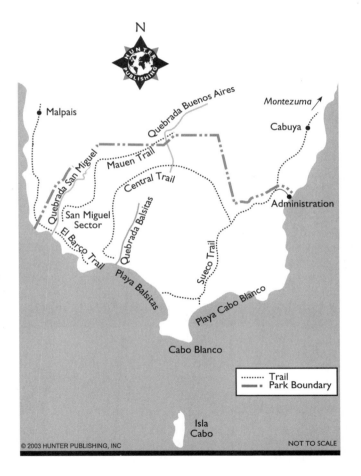

N

Malpais

Quebrada Buenos Aires

Montezuma

Cabuya

Quebrada San Miguel

Mauen Trail

Central Trail

San Miguel
Sector

Quebrada Balsitas

El Barco Trail

Administration

Sueco Trail

Playa Balsitas

Playa Cabo Blanco

Cabo Blanco

.... Trail
━ ━ ■ Park Boundary

Isla
Cabo

© 2003 HUNTER PUBLISHING, INC

NOT TO SCALE

Nicoya Peninsula

Tambor & Paquera Area

Most of the coast in this area is rocky but several nice sand beaches are popular with locals and visitors.

- ◎ There is a tropically stunning waterfall near **Playa Tango Mar** (this is where the television production *Temptation Island 2* was produced) that drops down directly into the sea. The surf is rough for swimming – be careful.

- ◎ **Playa Tambor**, in front of the town of Tambor, is long, wide and gentle. The surf never gets very high and you'll see lots of families splashing around with small children. It is a popular beach for horseback riding – you can gallop for a mile or so if the horse (and your muscles) are up to it.

- ◎ There are several other beaches nearby that are similarly good for swimming. **Playa Bahía Luminosa** and the beach at **Curú** are both worth a look.

Diving

Most of the diving is concentrated around the Gulf of Papagayo and for some distance south. The Papagayo area is most famous for encounters with manta rays and schools of devil and spotted rays, as well as shark dives.

Diving and snorkeling around Tortuga Island near Paquera and sites near Montezuma are also popular. The **Big Scare** site is well named – you can dive with man-eating bull sharks if that gets you going.

The operators in the south part of the peninsula offer pretty basic help, but dive shops in Coco, Ocotal, Flamingo and Tamarindo are well-equipped and fairly sophisticated. Prices for two-tank dives run around $70 with equipment, drinks and snacks.

Gulf of Papagayo

VIRGIN DIVING
Hotel La Costa, Playa Hermosa
☎ 506-670-0472; fax 506-670-0403

BILL BEARD'S DIVING SAFARIS DE COSTA RICA PLAYA HERMOSA
☎ 506-672-0012
www.billbeardcostarica.com

Nitrox, night diving, Bat Island, Catalina Island, resort, open water scuba instructor, staff instructor, open water, advanced open water.

DIVING SAFARIS DE COSTA RICA
Playas del Coco
Apdo. 121-5019, Playas del Coco, Guanacaste
☎ 506-670-0321; fax 506-670-0083

Diving and certification packages are offered. Trips off Catalina and Bat Islands.

MARIO VARGAS EXPEDITIONS
Apdo. 194, Playas del Coco, Guanacaste
☎ /fax 506-670-0351
www.diveexpeditions.com

Mario's gone, but the diving goes on.

OCOTAL BEACH MARINA
Apdo. 1, Playas Del Coco, Guanacaste
☎ 506-670-0321; fax 506-670-0083
www.ocotalresort.com

RESORT DIVERS DE COSTA RICA
In the Hotel El Nakuti and Hotel Giardini di Papagayo, Guanacaste
☎ 506-672-0106; fax 506-670-0421
www.resort-divers-cr.com; beckers@sol.racsa.co.cr

Bat and Catalina islands, night dives, snorkeling.

RICH COAST DIVING CO
Playas del Coco, Guanacaste
☎ 506-670-0176; fax 506-670-0176
www.richcoastdiving.com

Bat Island and Catalina Island, night dives, ask for Carol.

Tamarindo

AGUA RICA DIVING CENTER
Tamarindo
☎ 506-653-0094
www.tamarindo.com/agua/; agricadv@racsa.co.cr

SSI certification, Catalina Island, night dives, snorkeling.

Playas Sámara & Carrillo

TOM'S ADVENTURE DIVING
Playa Carrillo
☎ 506-656-0061
PADI-certified instruction

Montezuma & Mal País

CABO BLANCO DIVERS
Montezuma
☎ 506-642-0409
www.caboblancodivers.com
PADI certification and training

Trips to Tortuga, wrecks, night dives.

Tambor & Paquera Area

TROPIC WORLD
Playa Tambor
☎ /fax 506-220-4402

Fishing

There are a wide variety of fishing opportunities in the Nicoya Peninsula. All the lodges and hotels are able to set visitors up with guides and charter captains.

Sailfish are caught year-round, with the best season being May through August. **Marlin** are more active when the water is warmer, August through September (November to March can also be productive). Small **tuna** "footballs" are caught year-round, but the big boys are usually landed in the warmer months, August through October. **Wahoo** can be an almost daily catch at any time of the year, but are most frequent from June through August. **Roosterfish** are caught at almost any time of the year, but seem to be most abundant October through March. **Snapper** are dependable year-round. Prices run from $350 a half-day to $600 for a full day, with all equipment, lunch and drinks.

Flamingo is famous for its charter fleet. Small launches, complete with guides, can be hired almost anywhere along the coast.

Gulf of Papagayo

PAPAGAYO SPORT FISHING
Playa del Coco
☎ 506-670-0354, 506-670-0374; fax 506-670-0446

AGUA RICA YACHT CHARTERS
☎ 506-670-0805
www.aguaricachaters.com; jimgray@racsa.co.cr

Nicoya Peninsula

Tamarindo

CAPULLO
Tamarindo
☎ 506-653-0048
From $900, full day; $500 half-day

LONE STAR
Tamarindo
☎ 506-653-0101, 653-0318
$700, full day; $450, half-day
Captain Gaylord Townley, 30-ft. Palm Beach

NACOME SPORTFISHING
Tamarindo
☎ 506-653-0068
nacomesf@racsa.co.cr
$475, full day; $325, half-day
Captain Frank Berrocal, 23-ft. Mako

TAMARINDO SPORTFISHING
Tamarindo
☎ 506-653-0090
From $600, full day; from $375, half-day
Captains Jose Lopez and Randy Wilson, 27-ft. Escapade or 38-ft. Topaz

Tambor & Paquera Area

MALA CHICA
Contact Hotel Bahía Luminosa
About half way between Playa Naranjo and Paquera
☎ 506-381-2296, 506-641-0386; fax 506-641-0387
$265, full day; $175, half-day

The 26-ft. center-console *Mala Chica* goes inshore and offshore with two fishermen. Manager Finn Jonasson recently guided a saltwater first-timer to catch the largest roosterfish (73 lbs.) ever caught in Costa Rica. He knows where the fish are and hangs around Islas Negritas and Tortugas. Prices include drinks and classic fisherman's lunch.

Trips of several days are also offered to destinations as far away as Caño Island, or even Panama. Prices for overnight charters run from $600 per day, up to six guests. Scuba divers need to bring their own basic equipment and can rent tanks and weights at the hotel. There are kayaks, inflatables and a variety of small powerboats available for rent. Guided two- or three-day fully catered sea kayaking trips to nearby Tortugas, Isla Cedros, and beyond are featured.

Golf

The Nicoya Peninsula has the two nicest courses in Costa Rica. **Playa Conchal** (☎ 506-232-5150) has a stunning, Robert Trent Jones II-designed course. Fees are $85. **Hacienda Pinilla** is the newest and, perhaps, the nicest course (☎ 506-680-7000; cost is $60-$100). There are two courses in the Tambor area. Both are nine holes, nicely maintained and associated with hotels that share their names. **Los Delfines** (☎ 506-683-0303; from $50) is located near the Tambor airport on the main road toward Cobano. **Tango Mar** (☎ 506-683-0001; $25; nine holes) is a bit farther along on a side road. Both have views of the sea.

Horseback Riding

COSTA RICA RIDING
Brasilito, Gulf of Papagayo
☎ 506-654-4106
$1,300 inclusive of guides, horses, meals, lodging

Can arrange all-inclusive five-day horseback riding tours of the best beaches in the area, with stops in the top resorts for the evenings. This is a great way to have some intensive horsey activity and stay in luxury at night.

TAMBOR TROPICAL HORSEBACK RIDING
Tambor, book through the hotel
☎ 506-683-0011
From $30

The hotel maintains a healthy string of horses and has good equipment. Oregonian Bill leads tours along the beach, through the forest, to waterfalls, or along the coast to the "Jesus" tree. Bill is used to visitors with a minimum of riding experience and is cheerful and patient. He has mounts suitable for all experience levels. The beach in front of the hotel is perfect for romantic gallops along the sand.

Kayaking

Tamarindo

IGUANA SURF
In the village of Tamarindo
☎ 506-653-0148

Kayaking in the estuary and combination kayak/snorkeling tours.

Tambor & Paquera Area

BAHIA LUMINOSA KAYAK TOURS
About half-way between Playa Naranjo and Paquera
Contact Hotel Bahía Luminosa
☎ 506-381-2296, 506-641-0386; fax 506-641-0387

Guided one-day trips to the mangroves, or two- and three-day sea kayaking trips to the gulf islands are arranged by the Hotel Bahía Luminosa. The itinerary includes stops at former penal colony Isla San

Lucas (ask to see the "interesting" drawings on the cell walls), Gitana, Cedros, Negritos and Tortugas islands. All food and equipment are supplied. The chase boat brings food for breakfast, and runs ahead of the group to prepare a full dinner ready for guests on arrival at their evening destination. Optionally, the last day can be spent at Curú Nature Preserve, with transportation back to the hotel at the end of the day. The tour leaders have cell phones for emergency use.

You don't need to be an experienced kayaker to enjoy these trips.

Nicoya Peninsula

The bay is relatively calm, and the daily runs are short. Be prepared for hot, direct sun with plenty of sunscreen. Mosquito repellent is essential.

Tennis

Hotel Punta Islita is about 20 km (12 miles) south of Sámara and has two nice courts open to hotel guests only. ☎ 506-656-0471.

There are two hotels with courts in the **Tambor** area. Both have two courts and are reasonably well maintained. **Los Delfines** (☎ 506-683-0303) is near Tambor airport on the main road toward Cobano. **Tango Mar** (☎ 506-683-0001) is a bit farther along on a side road. Both are open to guests only.

Tours

Most hotels and lodges can arrange for any tours offered in the area. Both **Costa Rica Expeditions** (☎ 506-257-0766, www.costaricaexpeditions.com) and **Costa Rica Nature Escape** (☎ 506-257-8064, www.crnature.com) can make all arrangements for tours in advance. **Casa Rio Tours**, in Nosara (☎ 506-682-0117), offers tours to the Río Nosara, mangroves, horseback, kayaking and canoe trips.

Cheeky Monkey

Everybody likes monkeys and whenever I get a chance to take their picture, I'm ready. So when I was driving into Curú Wildlife Refuge , I was pleased to see a spider monkey low in a tree beside the road. I hopped out of the car and got some great pictures – the monkey was really close. Finally, I got back in the car. The monkey jumped out of the tree and started loping along beside the car. I thought I'd get another shot, so I stopped again and rolled down the passenger side window. As I was getting my camera ready, the monkey jumped in the car, and perched on the dashboard chattering at me. Imagine my surprise! I got out of the car in a hurry remembering a sign by the entrance to the park that said: "Don't feed the monkeys. They bite!" I had no intention of feeding the #$%!&# thing. When the monkey started grabbing things, I started hollering at it and eventually had to bop it on the head with my camera to get it out of the car. I rolled up the window and the monkey expressed its dissatisfaction with my performance by smearing excrement all over the window.

When I got to the ranger station and reported being assaulted by a spider monkey, the ranger said, "Oh no! What did he do this time?" Apparently, the monkey likes to perch on a gatepost and, as tourists slow down to see him, he reaches in the window and snatches sunglasses right off the driver's face. Sure enough, when I was driving out, there was the monkey (or one of his pals), perched on the gatepost waiting to have his fun. I kept the window rolled up and gave him the finger as I went by.

Curú Wildlife Refuge (☎ 506-661-8236; $5 entry), near Paquera toward the end of the Nicoya Peninsula, is a private 3,685-acre nature preserve. It is a former farm. The bay is famous for olive ridley and hawksbill turtle nesting.

The numerous trails are some of the better ones in the area. I especially enjoy the trails along the coast through mangroves and low-lying swampy areas. During one visit, I watched a kinkajou irritate a group of howler monkeys through the treetops for about a half-hour before it disappeared.

Researchers maintain a couple of rustic cabins with bunks ($30 a night) for anyone interested. You can hire a guide for $15. The entry gate by the road is usually shut, but when you pull up someone from the nearby rancho will come collect the fee and let you in.

Turtle Tours

COOPERATIVA TAMARINDO
Tamarindo
☎ 506-653-0201
$25

Mangrove and turtle-watching tours.

PAPAGAYO EXCURSIONS
Tamarindo
☎ 506-653-0254
$40

Turtle and nature tours.

Watersports

IGUANA SURF
Tamarindo
☎ 506-653-0148

Offers kayaking, snorkeling, surf lessons and equipment rentals. They also rent powerboats, Hobie cats, and jet skis.

FLYING CROCODILE
Sámara
☎ 506-656-0483

No crocs, but piloted ultra-light tours when the weather allows. They also rent motorcycles.

Shop Till You Drop

Tamarindo

The beachwear selection here is vast for such a small emerging beach town.

There are a couple dozen small gift and craft shops on the main street in "downtown" Tamarindo.

Tienda Tamarindo, ☎ 506-653-0519, on Main Street across from Frutas Tropicales, has a skimpy selection of books, but has fairly up-to-date US magazines and newspapers. It's air conditioned and cool inside but, given the small selection, it's hard to work yourself up to a very long browse.

Iguana Surf, ☎ 506-653-0148, is a bit off the main street (follow the signs), and has a great selection of tropical shirts and beachwear. The surfer shirts are bitchin' (cool).

Playas Sámara & Carrillo

There are only a couple of shops in town that sell anything other than groceries and hardware. The few that do exist tend to come and go a bit. **Boutique Shanna** on the main street in town has a very good selection of swimwear for women. **Hotel Punta Islita**, about 20 km (12 miles) south of Sámara, has a nice gift shop, with some particularly interesting woodcarvings. They have a variety of watercolors and oil paintings by local and San José artists for sale.

Montezuma & Mal País

At the end of the main street through town, where the buses stop, you can usually find a few hairy people selling jewelry and pipes. There are a couple of T-shirt shops, but nothing like the selection of beach goodies found in Jacó or Tamarindo.

Tambor & Paquera Area

Tambor is still a bit small and sleepy for tourist shops. **Tienda Dayanna**, near the police station, sells T-shirts, swimwear, jewelry, and a few wood handicraft items. **Salsa Boutique**, on the main road, has a little bit better selection of bathing gear, postcards and some jewelry. **Iguana's Books** on the main road in Tambor has a good selection of used paperbacks to feed your reading habit. Two-for-one is the usual deal. The selection is well organized, and the largest on the peninsula. It's only open when the owner is in the country, during January, February and March.

After Dark

Some of the beach towns are loaded with small, throbbing bars, but most towns are simply quiet, sleepy villages invaded by a few gringos.

Although many bars and clubs are aimed at the surfing crowd, others are quieter and offer snacks (*bocas*) and meals.

Bars, Discos & Nightclubs

There are few regular spots for live music. Some of the bars and a few of the upscale restaurants have individual entertainers or duos.

Gulf of Papagayo

BANANA'S BAR & GARDEN RESTAURANT
Playa del Coco
☎ 506-670-0605

This is a young crowd. This don't get started until after 11 pm.

COCONUTS
Playa del Coco
☎ 506-670-0272

Dancing, dancing, dancing to a mostly techno sound. Latin nights during the week.

FATHER ROOSTER SPORTS BAR
On the grounds of Ocotal Beach Resort south of Coco.

Bar food by the beach, with blaring music and weekend crowds. They have a legendary New Year's Eve party, but the food is poor and the smiles are on the faces of the customers – not on the staff.

Expect to go to the bar and get your own beer, even when you are the only customer. The "Sports" part of the name means there is a TV tuned to CNN blasting out all the time.

MONKEY BAR
A bit off the beach road in Playa Hermosa
☎ 506-672-0267

Bar food and pool.

PUERTA DEL SOL
Near the Sol Playa Hermosa hotel

Typical beach bar.

TUCAN JUNGLE SPORTS BAR
Just past Brasilito
☎ 506-654-4014

Not very sporty and a bit on the seedy side.

VILLA DEL SUEÑO
Playa Hermosa

Live music, sometimes.

Tamarindo

BOCA DEL RIO
On the beach in Tamarindo
Open 24 hours a day

You can get a cold beer at five in the morning if that's your scene.

BARCELO PLAYA LANGOSTA
Just outside Tamarindo on Playa Langosta
☎ 506-653-0363

Rocks with reggae and other popular sounds, from early until early. Few people not staying in the hotel bother.

Nicoya Peninsula

COCODRILO HOTEL PASATIEMPO
☎ 506-653-0096

Live music twice a week, sports bar, open mike on Tuesdays.

NOAI
NOAI (no hay, meaning "there isn't any," get it?) is "the" dance place in Tamarindo. Ask a local for directions.

Playa Sámara & Carrillo

EL ACUARIO
Playa Sámara
☎ 506-656-0038

Live music on the weekends. Expect the local salsa, merengue and cumbia sounds.

DISCOTEQUE TUTTI FRUTTI
Playa Sámara, turn right at the beach and walk up.

Latin sounds, lots of bass, cold beer, on the beach.

Montezuma & Mal País

Montezuma is about the only place you are liable to find anything resembling "action" in the Nicoya area, and there is plenty of it. The town attracts a strange mix of young stoners and older bohemian/hippie types. Middle-agers who feel comfortable with tattoos, long hair and flip-flops love the area. There are lots of young ladies and dudes hanging around. This would be the place to meet someone for a holiday friendship, or who knows what?

Los Delfines, just past Tambor Airport, has American-style loud sounds throbbing until late (☎ 506-683-0303). The place seems a little cheesy to me, but then I'm a bit over the hill for the late night disco scene. Thirty years ago when I was the right age this would have been the kind of place where the women wore white plastic go-go boots. I would have thought it was cheesy then, too.

Luz de Mono in Montezuma, located in the hotel of the same name, is a popular bar with a bit older crowd than most of the beach bars. It features live music most weekends. Acts run from light jazz to pop and rock & roll covers. Happy hour is from 4-6 pm.

Tropicana in Mal País, is straight ahead as you get into town, toward the beach and has good drinks, good food, dancing to a Latin beat. Surfer crowd.

Playa del Coco is probably the most happening spot on the Pacific coast for nightlife.

Sunset/Dinner Cruises

Gulf of Papagayo

PAPAGAYO PETE
Flamingo
☎ 506-654-4911

SPANISH DANCER
Playa del Coco
☎ 506-385-2260
dancer@racsa.co.cr

A six-hour cruise on the catamaran *Spanish Dancer* runs $60 per person for lunch, drinks, etc.

Tamarindo

MANDINGO SAILING
Tamarindo
☎ 506-653-0276
Half-day and full-day charters.

Nicoya Peninsula

Tambor & Paquera Area

BRIGHT SPOT, CENTURION
Contact Hotel Bahía Luminosa
☎ 506-381-2296, 506-641-0386; fax 506-641-0387

Both the 43-ft. Islander ketch *Bright Spot* and the 42-ft. motor cruiser *Centurion* are available for afternoon sunset cruises with drinks and dinner, or for longer charters. Up to 18 guests can be accommodated for day cruises that travel to the islands between Playa Naranjo and Paquera, including Tortuga, Cedros and former penal colony Isal San Lucas. Both boats are roomy and well-maintained.

HOTEL TROPICAL BOAT TOURS
☎ 506-683-0011
www.tambortropical.com
From $55

Beach and forest tours, sportfishing, island and custom boat tours.

 # Best Places to Stay

Alive Prices
Prices are based on double occupancy during high season, and given in US $. Taxes and meals are not included, unless so noted. Hotels and lodges marked with a ✫ are my personal favorites. "The Best of the Best" choices earn their title by offering top-quality lodging and services.

Gulf of Papagayo

HOTEL SUGAR BEACH
Five km (three miles) north of Playa Potrero
☎ 506-654-4242; fax 506-654-4239
www.sugar-beach.com
$110

Hotel Sugar Beach is one of the most peaceful places I have stayed in Costa Rica. It's a bit worn, but Klaus, the manager, was overseeing a renovation when I was there in 2002. The rooms are quite large and, if you leave the air conditioning off, and the windows open, the sound of the surf will lull you to sleep at night. They have 27 rooms, including two beach houses that can sleep up to 10, priced to $2,450 per week in the high season. The hotel is a bit overpriced for the area and the staff is not what you would call friendly.

There are no TVs or phones in the rooms, but those are things best left in another world. The 24-acre (10 hectare) gardens are serene. The views from the restaurant and rooms over the gray sand Playa Pan de Azucar (Sugar Bread Beach) are brilliant. At sunset, the sun sinks into the sea with a sizzle – look for the Green Flash. White-throated magpie-jays and raccoons treat the grounds as their own.

If the quiet and solitude palls, you can easily get into nearby Flamingo, billed by locals as the "Acapulco of Costa Rica." With luck, it will be several decades before the area lives up to that name. The hotel's open-air restaurant is open to the public, and is a bit cheaper than town. Hotel Sugar Beach is a good base for diving the nearby Catalina Islands. The hotel has its own 27-footer ready for fishing charters. Flamingo probably has the largest sportfishing fleet in Costa Rica.

EL OCOTAL BEACH RESORT
Two km (1.2 miles) south of Playas del Coco
☎ 506-670-0321; fax 506-670-0083
www.ocotalresort.com
$97

El Ocotal, perched on a hill overlooking of the Gulf of Papagayo, is a haven for anglers, divers, and families wanting to sport about on the beach. Some of the rooms are practically on the beach. Most have an amazing view of Monkey Head, Witches Head and Bat Islands, as well as a stunning view of Rincón de la Vieja volcano. The sunsets from the bar and restaurant attract tourists and locals from all over the area for an evening drink. With a pool, Jacuzzis scattered around the grounds, lighted tennis courts, mini-gym, and free use of mountain bikes and kayaks, there is plenty to do, even if you don't come for the world-famous fishing and diving.

There are 59 rooms, including five suites and 12 bungalows, all with at least queen-size beds. Some of the rooms are designed for handicapped occupancy. The gentle, black sand Playa Ocotal is a good spot to relax with the kids. There is a bar and snack bar just back from the sand. They will bring your order to you on the beach. The snorkeling is easy at either end of the beach. The hotel staff can drop off honeymooners on a remote beach you can only get to by boat. They set you up with a picnic basket full of food and wine, and come back for you later. ¡Que romántico!

Diving and fishing in the area are world-class. The dive shop is the oldest in Papagayo and pioneered many of the most famous sites, such as The Big Scare and Monkey Head. Manager Sisineo arranges specialty dives to swim with the dolphins when they show up in the thousands every summer to chase tuna. Tuna, sailfish, marlin, roosterfish and dorado are the common catches. In the fall, boats may release as many as 20 sails in one day. If, like me, you've been on many expensive boat rides chasing the Hemingway-esque dream of landing a marlin, this is about the best chance you'll have anywhere in the world.

The restaurant serves decent food and is a bit overpriced, but has a hypnotizing view of the Pacific. I had no problems with the service, but other guests felt it was abysmal. A basic continental breakfast is included in the room price. Father Rooster is located by the beach on the hotel grounds. It definitely has a service problem, as well as lukewarm bar food.

☆ MELIA PLAYA CONCHAL
On the road from Belén to Brasilito
☎ 506-654-4123; fax 506-654-4181
www.meliaplayaconchal.com
$235, including breakfast and airport transfer from Liberia

If your idea of a good vacation is to be pampered in an isolated, tropical beach setting with no outside intrusions, Meliá Playa Conchal should fit the bill. It's the largest and most luxurious resort in the country, located on the beautiful white sand Playa Conchal.

The quiet beach is clean, the water is warm and there is rarely enough surf to make swimming dangerous, as it is on so many beaches.

It is a relaxing getaway from the hustle of San José. Imaginatively set on 978 acres (285 hectares) of manicured dry forest grounds, the development, even though quite large, is a reasonably unobtrusive presence in the environment. From the beach, it would be hard to believe such a large resort is just beyond the trees.

The Robert Trent Jones II golf course located here is world-class – no other course in Costa Rica comes close. All the 368 rooms are suites, except for two "master suites," and are configured in a series of low-rise bungalows cozied up around the stunning pool. The golf course wraps around them all. The rooms are all large and comfortably appointed, with raised sleeping areas, living room and dining area.

The pool is touted as the largest in Central America, and is big enough to get lost in. The grounds are planted with specimens from all over Costa Rica and Central America. Orchids cling to palm trunks and lily pad-filled ponds teem with bird life. The occasional monkey cavorts in the trees.

There are seven restaurants and numerous bars – by the pool, at the 19th hole, near the beach – anywhere you might conceivably desire a tropical beverage, sandwich or beer. All the beef is imported from the US – the hamburgers are excellent if that's what you're into. Pizza at the pizzeria is a demonstration that sometimes luxury is appearance only. The Italian restaurant and steak house serve fine food. The highly trained waitstaff is perhaps overattentive. Of the seven restaurants, I found the Italian to be the best by far, although a bit overpriced. The restaurants are not open to non-guests.

Other amenities include a pro shop, shopping center with travel agencies, gift shop, mini-mart and Internet Café. There are four lighted tennis courts, a spa and fitness center, with saunas, casino, disco and watersports center. The hotel offers a complete, included-in-the-price animation program that with Spanish lessons, dance classes, aerobics sessions, and children's activities. You can safely park the kids and chill out by the pool, fish, dive or go kayaking, and find them excited and worn out at the end of the day.

The beautiful convention center on the grounds overlooks the bay and is large enough to handle over 600 people, is equipped to international standards and has hosted corporate clients including Intel, Pfizer and Monroe (shock absorbers).

The resort, which was designed by Spanish architect Alvaro Sanz, and was selected for an award by Resorts & Great Hotels International in their Connoisseur's 2000 survey. Interval ownership units are available and nearby, within the resort grounds, an equally well-designed condominium development offers units from US $280,000 to $380,000.

Tamarindo

BARCELO PLAYA LANGOSTA
Near Tamarindo Beach
☎ 506-653-0363; fax 506-653-0415
www.barcelo.com
$150

The Barcelo has 135 rooms, and was not really intended as a surfer hotel, but has become one by default. World-famous Playa Langosta is right in front of the place. Although remodeled in recent years, the hotel seems rundown. The crowd is young and the place echoes with loud music from the beach bar all day and most of the night.

TAMARINDO DIRIA
Tamarindo
☎ 506-258-4224, 505-653-0031; fax 506-258-4226, 506-653-0208
www.tamarindodiria.co.cr
$150

Tamarindo Diriá has 124 rooms, tennis courts, pool, a casino, and sportfishing available. It's a bit long in the tooth in spite of a recent facelift. Service can be surly, and it certainly doesn't have the charm it may have once had. Locals are irritated with the Diriá management, who control the local airport, and are seemingly trying to keep tour operators from bringing in anyone who is not staying with them. It's right in the middle of the village and is not nearly as peaceful and quiet as some of the other resorts in the area. With 124 rooms, it is not intimate, and reminds me of a typical beach motel in any US beach town. If you're the gregarious sort, who wants to meet people and enjoy the bar late into the night, ignore everything I just said and have a good time.

VILLA ALEGRE B&B

BEST OF THE BEST

A half-block south of Hotel Capitan Suizo, on Playa Langosta
☎ 506-653-0270; fax 506-653-0287
www.villaalegrecostarica.com
$125

I felt comfortable as soon as I walked in the door of Villa Alegre. I'm not talking about the level of the air conditioning, or the softness of the beds (although all of that is comfortable). Owners Barry and Suzye Lawson are comfortable people, and have created a comfortable home for themselves and their guests. You feel like you are friends hanging out in a pal's house for a week, but you don't feel guilty about not helping with the dishes. There's none of the uneasiness often associated with B&Bs, where you may rub shoulders a bit more closely than you would like with strangers.

Catalan Sheepdogs Metches and Plata greet visitors at the gate of the Spanish-style villa with a wag, and that sets the tone for the whole visit. The sound of the surf permeates the place; it hypnotizes and lulls you into a routine of rising late in the morning, and taking long (or several short) afternoon naps. Howler monkeys visit early in the morning to raid Barry's papayas.

Above: A stunning view of Melía Playa Conchal on the Nicoya Peninsula.

Below: A colorful bar outside Golfito.

Above: A rice field near Zancudo.
Opposite: A scarlet macaw agreeably poses for a photo.
Below: Kick back at the Hotel Punta Islita.

Above: The Poás Volcano crater is revealed through the mist.
Opposite: A delightful waterfall at Matapalo beckons.
Below: A most unusual flower at the Corcovado National Park.

Above: A Capuchin monkey peeks through the trees.
Opposite: Beautiful flora abounds in Costa Rica.
Below: A ride on a zip-line won't be soon forgotten!

Above: A farmer's truck with no door is typical in the countryside.
Opposite: A classic view at Drake Bay.
Below: Star fruit is one of the more easily recognized regional fruits.

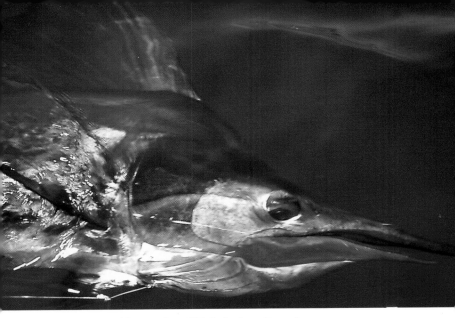

Above: A sailfish before its release.
Opposite: Giant ferns grow tall in the Monteverde Cloud Forest.
Below: Delicious Doka Estate coffees can be shipped home.

Above: Colorful birds aren't hard to spot.
Opposite: A fisherman about to release a roosterfish.
Below: Be sure to try some of Costa Rica's famous coffee.

Above: The Guanacaste countryside seems to go on forever.
Opposite: Caño Island Ranger Station is in an exotic setting.
Below: Beautiful and strange flowers are common sights.

Above: Butterfly at rest for a brief moment.

Below: Playa Conchal is an incomparably beautiful beach.

Villa Alegre fronts on Playa Langosta, first made famous by the movie *Endless Summer*. Surfers come from all over the world to surf the breaks just a five-minute walk down the beach.

A large library of books, games and videos are available in the living room. Tables groan with grand gourmet breakfasts, served on the shaded patio by the pool. It overlooks one of the most appealing beaches in Costa Rica. The seven air-conditioned rooms range from singles to private villas, each with a view of the sea or garden. All of the rooms and villas are decorated with bits and pieces from the many regions of the world Barry and Suzy have visited. Villas sleep up to five, and cost $175 in high season.

One of the best things about being friendly with the owners is that they know all the local tour operators, chefs, dive masters and fishing captains. They're not a tour agency, and they don't steer you to the operators who pay them commissions. They send you to their friends, and people they know who do a good job. Barry knows the pros at the golf courses in the area (Pinilla and Playa Conchal), and which captains are hot, and what fish are being caught and where. If you go fishing and catch something, bring it home and Barry will cook it up for you. This place is one of my favorites. I'll come back.

HOTEL Y VILLAS CALA LUNA
Tamarindo
☎ 506-653-0214; fax 506-653-0213
www.calaluna.com
$153, plus taxes

The Mediterranean-style Cala Luna, one block up from the beach, has 20 deluxe rooms, 15 two-bedroom villas, and three three-bedroom villas. Each room and villa is fronted by a completely private garden, but none have a view of the ocean. All

Nicoya Peninsula

the villas have their own full-size pool. Cala Luna is decorated in pastel shades, with heavy tropical wood furniture, and rooms have either one king, or two queen-size beds. Rooms have huge, free-form tubs.

There's a huge number and variety of earthenware jars scattered about the place. The villas are extravagantly equipped, with full kitchens that include a cappuccino machine, microwave and American-size refrigerator, as well as washing machines. Rooms are air-conditioned, with TVs and phones.

The Belgian-owned hotel has its own offshore fishing boat, and makes boogie boards, kayaks, surfboards, and other beach equipment available to guests. Every March the hotel is host to the Costa Rican leg of the world surfing championship tournament, and is well placed for surfers, located between Playa Tamarindo and Playa Langosta.

A basic continental breakfast is included in the price of the rooms (not the villas), and is served by the pool in the indoor-outdoor Cala Moresca restaurant. The restaurant serves local fish and the usual Costa Rican steaks. There is an extensive wine list.

Rooms and villas are stylish and luxuriously appointed, appealing to honeymooners and couples who don't demand immediate access to the beach (it's only a short walk away). It is probably the nicest hotel in Tamarindo, but is a bit overpriced, considering it is not beachfront.

☆ HOTEL CAPITAN SUIZO
Tamarindo
☎ 506-653-0075; fax 506-653-0292
www.hotelcapitansuizo.com
$125

This is a member of the Small Distinctive Hotels of Costa Rica, located on the beach, with 22 rooms and eight bungalows. There's a restaurant, bar, beach, kayaking, sailing, dive center, pool, wildlife and nature tour. It gets rave reviews from many guests.

EL JARDIN DEL EDEN
Tamarindo
☎ 506-653-0137; fax 506-653-0111
www.jardindeleden.com
$125

Jardín del Edén, perched on a hill above the bay, is Mediterranean-style. It accommodates upscale surfers and couples looking to enjoy the funky beach-town ambiance of Tamarindo, while enjoying a comfortable place to stay. It's a short walk to the beach and to the town's surferville attractions. With 18 rooms and two fully furnished apartments, the hotel has two lovely pools – one with swim-up bar. The grounds personify the magic of the tropics, and are a joy, lush with bougainvillea, heliconias, papayas, and the ever-present palms towering over everything. Weddings receptions are catered to from "lawyer to cake."

Owner Marcello Marongiu is an ever-smiling host in the European sense. He seems to be everywhere at once, waving his arms around, laughing, petting his cocker spaniel, and making sure everyone is happy. Try to corner him for a chat – his charm is infectious. He launched the hotel eight years ago and it is well known in Costa Rica for being one of the best places to stay in Tamarindo. Marcello's staff can arrange all types of area tours.

The restaurant is a blend of classical Italian, Costa Rican and North American styles, with a romantic ambiance (see *Best Places to Eat*, page 243).

Rooms all have a view of the grounds and the Pacific. You can lift your head slightly from your pillow and see at once if the surf is up. All rooms include air con-

Exercise restraint on your breakfast order, or you won't make it to the beach until after noon.

ditioning, ceiling fans, television, and phones. Breakfast is included in the room price, and consists of a good selection of breads, pastries, omelets, pancakes, and eggs with homefried potatoes, and on and on. When you sit down, out come coffee, fresh fruit juice, and an enormous plate of sliced fruit.

☆ **SUENO DEL MAR B & B**
Tamarindo
☎ 506-653-0284
$138, plus tax

You just can't get any closer to the beach in Tamarindo than Sueño del Mar (Dream of the Sea). If you don't mind stepping over Misha, an Australian shepherd/corgi mix on your way in, and being put to sleep every night by the sound of the surf, you might be right for the comfortable Sueño. The whole place looks like someone lives there.

There are dozens and dozens of free-form mobiles, made from shells, hanging up all over. Bits of flotsam and jetsam are perched on every conceivable shelf or ledge. Turtle skulls decorate the breakfast/hanging out area. This B & B has lots of character.

The upstairs honeymoon suite has a panoramic view of one of the best surf beaches in the world. The hotel appeals to couples – especially if at least half the couple is a surfer. When I visited I saw a couple arrive worn out from the drive from San José and, before they had even unloaded all their bags from the car, the husband was running down to the beach with a surfboard under his arm, leaving his surf widow to unpack and settle in. It's that kind of place. Upscale surfers love the place.

All the rooms are air-conditioned, but with ceiling fans and the alíseos trade wind blowing through the windows, few people use the AC. In many B & Bs, there are a few community paperbacks scattered about for the guests' enjoyment. At Sueño, each room has 50 to 100 well-worn books wedged in between shells and bits of driftwood. The outside showers (with hot water) are eccentrically decorated, with plaster imprints of sea creatures and paintings of tropical scenes.

This is not a hotel where the guests feel anonymous. Owners Gary and Susan Money are interesting characters and invite guests to share their laid-back, beachfront lifestyle. *Elle* magazine used Sueño for a shoot a few years ago, and the models keep coming back on their own to enjoy the beach setting and homey feel. I'll be coming back, too.

Nicoya Peninsula

Playas Sámara & Carrillo

Playa Sámara is a small town, right on a beautiful, light brown sand beach. The surf is gentle and good for swimming. The lack of surf means there are few North American budget travelers in the area, but it is quite popular with Ticos. **Punta Islita**, located several miles south on a terrible dirt road, is another lovely beach. There is really nothing there but the upscale Hotel Punta Islita.

HOTEL PUNTA ISLITA
10 km (six miles) southeast of Playa Carrillo
☎ 506-656-0471; fax 506-231-0715
www.hotelpuntaislita.com
$180, including breakfast

BEST OF THE BEST

When I first arrived at Hotel Punta Islita, I sat by the swim-up bar trying to decide which blue I liked better: the blue of the pool itself, or the blue of the Pacific. More than one guest has pondered this. One of the most isolated and undeveloped coastlines in Costa Rica is the Pacific side of the southern Nicoya

Peninsula. The blue of the sea and the light brown sand beaches seem to stretch to infinity, and are enjoyed by only a few locals, guests of the hotel, and the occasional turtle.

Built in 1994 by a Costa Rican consortium, Hotel Punta Islita is well situated to take advantage of this isolation and beauty. It's all by itself, overlooking one of the prettiest bays you'll find anywhere. The hotel's 32 very private rooms and five villas appeal to couples, and approximately half of the guests seem to be honeymooners. Activities include just relaxing on the beach, fishing, playing tennis, taking nature walks through the forest, bird-watching, horseback riding, laying around in hammocks, or swimming in the pool.

Transportation can be arranged directly to the hotel from San José, by car or air. Both SANSA and Travelair have scheduled flights. The hotel has its own airstrip and maintains a five-seat airplane available for the 45-minute flight from San José.

This is one of the finest luxury resorts in Costa Rica and a member of the Small Luxury Hotels of the World. The staff greets new arrivals not only with the clichéd welcome cocktail, but also with a warm, moist towel to refresh the road weary. Rooms are large and have everything: coffee makers, extra pillows and towels, refrigerators, TV, phone, air-conditioning, hammocks, and most of the rooms come with their own plunge pool or Jacuzzi. The casitas and suites are quite private, and are decorated in Mediterranean-style, with rough-hewn hardwood furniture and enormous tiled baths. The plunge pools are tightly surrounded by shrubbery, and are well-suited for even the most intimate honeymoon activities.

A large, tropical fruit breakfast is included in the room price served by the pool in the airy and tropical "1492" restaurant (see *Best Places to Eat*, page 246). The restaurant menu is a mix of delicious local and international dishes and includes local seafood specialties as well as tender, export-quality steaks. Surprisingly, for such a small and isolated resort, the wine list is one of the best I've seen in the country.

Even though the hotel caters mainly to couples, they have a 40-person meeting room, and play host to group tours, including bicycle tours organized by Backroads and Butterfield & Robinson. Politicians use the hotel for intimate conferences. The stunning beach and gardens are used for calendar photoshoots and swimsuit modeling sessions for fashion magazines. Several well-known movie stars (whose names shall not be mentioned for reasons of privacy), have standing reservations for the luxurious private villas.

The most difficult hotel reviews to write are for the hotels I like the most. It is easy to describe luxury appointments, but it is not easy to give a feeling for the personality and setting of a fine resort without sounding like a tour agency brochure. As I'm sure you can tell, I love the place. As soon as I walked in, I knew I would be placing it as one of my "Best of the Best" selections. Punta Islita is easily one of the top two or three hotels in Costa Rica.

MIRADOR DE SAMARA
Sámara
☎ 506-656-0044; fax 506-656-0046
www.miradordesamara.com
$80

With refreshing, fussy German attention to cleanliness, Mirador de Sámara ("Lookout") offers one-bedroom apartments, with kitchens on a short-term basis. If you plan on taking advantage of the fantastic fishing opportunities the area has to offer, this is a good base. There is a private pool, shared by the six apartments. A small restaurant in the Mirador features fresh local fish and export-quality steaks. The views of the bay are stunning, and the trade winds blow through the large doors to the terraces. It is just a few minutes walk to the beach, bars and restaurants of the town. The beach is a couple of miles long and is excellent for swimming, sunning or strutting your stuff, if you have it to strut.

German owners Max and Helen Mahlich keep the rooms spotless. The apartments are large and in reasonably good shape.

Montezuma & Mal País

SUNSET REEF MARINE HOTEL
At the south end of the beach road, Mal País
☎ 506-640-0012; fax 506-640-0036
www.sunsetreefhotel.com
$85

The well-named Sunset Reef is beautifully set at the edge of a reef-lined beach facing the Pacific, lined up perfectly for sunset viewing. The 14 rooms are arranged in a two-story, motel-style building, and are large, airy and air-conditioned. Although the hardwood-lined rooms are large and reasonably comfortable, the hotel is a victim of deferred maintenance and is in need of refurbishment. I never did figure out the source of the locker-room smell in my bathroom, and I kept the door shut on the largest cockroach I have seen yet in Costa Rica. All that said, Sunset Reef is still the nicest place to stay in the lovely Mal País area.

Popular with the more prosperous surfers and fishermen, it's a good place to base yourself to enjoy the laid-back atmosphere of the beach town. While more expensive than the budget accommodations on offer nearby, it is perhaps only slightly overpriced for the area.

The hotel has a focus on watersports, and offers a wide variety of ways to enjoy the reef and beach in front of the hotel. Snorkeling can be done directly from shore. Kayaks, water-skiing, banana boats, parasailing, boogie boards, and fishing and diving trips, are all offered. Diving is arranged through nearby PADI-certified Pacific Divers (see *Dawn to Dusk*, page 202), and both inshore and offshore fishing is done with the hotel's own 16-ft. rigid inflatable. Motorbikes are available for rent for those so inclined. Alberto, both manager and naturalist, leads tours through nearby trails and trips to Cabo Blanco Nature Reserve. Birders are delighted with the number of sea birds that can be observed while doing no more than sitting in the shade in front of their rooms. A restaurant of the same name is on the premises (see page 248).

Tambor & Paquera Area

BARCELO PLAYA TAMBOR
Tambor
☎ 506-683-0303; fax 506-683-0304
www.barcelo.com
$120, inclusive

There has been some controversy about the development of this hotel. Allegedly, environmental concerns were brushed aside (with local official connivance) during the development phase.

TAMBOR TROPICAL

On the beach, right in Tambor
☎ 506-683-0011; fax 506-371-2471
www.tambortropical.com
$150, plus tax

The American-owned Tambor Tropical, set just above the beach right in the village, is marketed as a relaxing resort for couples who want to get away from it all. To find it, look very closely for the tiny sign on the main road, or just turn down toward the Tambor police station, and then turn left. The 10 rooms are situated in five separate palm-tree shaded buildings surrounding the pool, Jacuzzi and bar. The beach is about a 30-second walk away, and is clean sand with a gentle slope – perfect for swimming, with very gentle surf.

The rooms are trimmed in tropical hardwoods, with wood floors, wooden slatted windows, wooden walls, wooden ceilings and even wooden toilet seats and wooden ashtrays. The trim carpentry is skillfully executed, and the beauty of the woods makes these very special rooms. They are large, spotlessly clean and well-equipped, with full kitchens, ceiling fans, broad porches and balconies. There are no TVs, phones or air conditioning, in keeping with the "get away from it all" approach to holiday relaxation. The upstairs rooms have superior views, but cost an additional $25 per night. A basic fruit and cereal breakfast is included in the price, which is the same for both high and low season.

"You can do anything or do nothing" is the hotel philosophy, and many recreational opportunities, as well as hammocks are offered. The hotel maintains its own stable of horses for trail or beach riding. Small boats and kayaks are also maintained for the guests' use. Diving, fishing, and nature tours to nearby Curú National Wildlife Refuge can be arranged. Adequate meals are served next to the pool.

The hotel was utilized in the production of the *Temptation Island* television show, and has a pleasant, tropical feel. With the idea of keeping things quiet for couples, children are not allowed, but the bar is popular with local expats, who hang out heehawing from early afternoon until late. Ask for a room well away from the bar.

The hotel's location at the edge of the village makes the scheme of tranquility and quiet a nice idea rather than a reality. The beach is often crowded with Ticos playing football, riding horses and simply having a good time with their families. There is constant movement in front of the rooms by delivery trucks and numerous locals, who somehow seem to be attached to the hotel staff or one of the other businesses run by the owner. The rooms are lovely, and the convenience of the village may be a plus for some, but the price is high. You can get much better service and more privacy at other hotels nearby.

☆ TANGO MAR
Just off the main road near Tambor,
on the way to Cobano
☎ 506-683-0001, 506-289-9328; fax 506-683-0003,
506-289-8218
www.tangomar.com
$165, plus tax

A long driveway lined with royal palms leads to the beachfront Tango Mar. The beach is lined with coconut palms and, since it is blocked by steep headlands at each end, is very private. The 150-acre resort is so private that it was used for the production of the television series *Temptation Island II*.

The romantic beach has a 40-foot waterfall cascading from the jungle-lined bluffs directly into the surf.

The Belgian owners have spent the last three years remodeling and upgrading the 35 rooms and public areas. It is well maintained, quiet and with discreet service. Weddings, honeymoons and quiet vacations for couples are the emphasis. Various vacationing celebrities are return guests.

There are several types of rooms – all beautiful. The best beach access, and some of the best views, are from the "ocean" rooms. These happen to be the cheapest, and are arranged on three floors (best views are from the middle floor). All are fully equipped with coffee maker, TV, phones, air-conditioning, king-size or two queen-size beds, walk-in showers; some have Jacuzzis. The surf sometimes reaches right to the base of the building, and can be quite loud at times. Most people find the sound of the surf soothing, but complain about being awakened in the mornings by the nearby howler monkeys doing their thing (they don't call them "howlers" for nothing), but this is all part of the Costa Rica experience. The Tropical Suites and Tiki Suites are more isolated and surrounded by tropical vegetation. The Mono Congo and Robinson Crusoe self-contained villas have two bedrooms, kitchen, and large living room. They are exotically and tastefully decorated. The Presidential Villa (see *Vacation Rentals*, page 239) has two extensive master suites, two junior suites, maid's or nanny's quarters, and is suitable for the most discriminating guests. It has its own pool, and waterfall flowing through the living room.

The resort has its own riding stables, two swimming pools, two lighted tennis courts and a nine-hole golf course.

The **Cristobal Restaurant** (see *Best Places to Eat*, page 249) features European and local seafood specialties. Views of the beach from the dining room and bar can hypnotize you if you are not already decompressed. The breakfast (included in the room price) is simple, but I was not the first one to be surprised checking out, by being charged $10 for a small scoop of rice and beans and an egg. The breakfast menu has no prices, and it is not clear which breakfast items are included in the price of the room. Make sure to ask.

Tango Mar is the resort all the others in the area envy and, although they may try to charge similar prices, none of the others have as much personality, or such a quiet, personal feeling. Nearby resorts Delfines and Playa Tambor are large, impersonal, package-tour luxury resorts, and simply not up to the same standard as Tango Mar.

HOTEL BAHIA LUMINOSA
20 km (12 miles) from Playa Naranjo;
eight km (five miles) from Paquera
☎ 506-641-0386, in US, 530-842-3322;
fax 506-641-0387
www.bahialuminosa.com
$55, not including taxes

Hotel Bahía Luminosa, tucked away under the trees in a bay all its own, is a pleasant escape. The hotel is not luxurious but is comfortable and, best of all, loaded with personality. Owner George Perrochet is definitely worth chatting with. He's got a sea story to tell about his years in the Merchant Marines and how he finally decided to build a retirement home for himself that eventually became the Hotel Bahía Luminosa.

While not primarily scuba- or fishing-oriented, the area is a good base for adventurous diving in the nearby Negritos and Tortuga islands and for fishing inshore and offshore for tuna, roosterfish, snapper and billfish.

Rooms are set in a nicely maintained tropical forest, with a pool and fantastic swimming beach. Some are a bit close to the road. Unfortunately, motorcycles grinding back and forth between Paquera and Playa Naranjo serenade you. The ambiance of the area and the main dining area is that of a tropical hideaway with a nautical theme. Room prices include a "Tico" breakfast. The restaurant serves good meals and wines, beer, and tropical drinks are available at the bar. You hear a lot of howler monkeys in Costa Rica, but I haven't been anywhere where they are so constantly loud and rambunctious.

The nautical theme extends to offering several boats for day-trips, or longer charters. Fishing, diving, sunset cruises or simply exploring the nearby islands are available on several boats (see *Sunup to Sundown*, page 205). The *Centurion*, a 42-ft. power cruiser, and the *Bright Spot*, a 43-ft. ketch motor sailer are available to charter. Although sea adventures are the main attraction, nature walks to Carú Nature Preserve, and golfing expeditions to Los Defines (nine hole course), are also possible. The hotel is popular with visiting yachtsmen. There are sometimes as many as 17 boats moored in the bay in front of the hotel. An isolated two-bedroom house called the Wood House, is available for vacation rental on the grounds (see *Vacation Rentals*, page 239).

Vacation Rentals

CASA LOS MANGOS
On the main road in Tambor
☎ 506-683-0259; in the US, 708-361-3859
Joan12003@yahoo.com
$65-$100

American Bernie and his partner rent two houses smackdab on the beach in Tambor. The beach is gentle and good for swimming. The houses are nicely shaded in the trees and are only a step or two from the sand. One nice thing about the location is that the houses are about a half-mile from the fishing docks. Since these are the closest houses in the village to the docks, the fishermen offer the very best of their catch every morning, as they start their rounds through town. They sell lobster, dorado, swordfish and tuna.

Los Mangos is a good place for kids, since the beach is calm.

Nicoya Peninsula

You can walk to stores, restaurants and drinking holes. The houses are both completely furnished, with full kitchens, linens, fans, etc. They are not air-conditioned, but do have hot water showers and electricity around the clock. They are simply but nicely furnished. The three-bedroom house is available all year for $65 to $100 per night, depending on the number of people staying. The other house has one bedroom downstairs and a large upstairs master suite suitable for kids. It is available from April to January, and rents $100 per day. As a bonus, you get the seventh day free, with either house.

WOOD HOUSE
Located on grounds of Bahía Luminosa Hotel
☎ 506-381-2296, 506-641-0386; fax 506-641-0387
www.bahialuminosa.com
$140 per night, four people

The two-bedroom Wood House is privately located on the grounds of the Bahía Luminosa Hotel (see page 237), which allows complete privacy, combined with use of the facilities of the hotel. Each bedroom has a double bed. Beds for extra guests can be provided. The kitchen is fully equipped, with electric range and refrigerator. The windows are screened and fans are provided. The house is not luxurious, but it is comfortable, with 24-hour electricity and hot water. The beach is calm and good for swimming (rare in Costa Rica), and is a five-minute walk away. Use of the pool and access to other hotel services is included. Small boat rentals can be arranged.

Best Places to Eat

Alive Prices

Prices are given in US $, and are the average price for an entrée or main course, per person, before taxes and service charges are added. Although Costa Rican law says restaurants must show prices on the menu with taxes included, many do not. Menus that include taxes almost always say so.

Gulf of Papagayo

AQUA SPORT
On the beach in Playa Hermosa
☎ 506-672-0050
$20

This is a funky beach restaurant attached to, well, an aquatic sports equipment store. Local specialties include lobster and, for small groups, paella.

☆ CAMARON DORADO
Brasilito just north of Flamingo
$8
Seafood

The word is out. Camarón Dorado can get crowded, but it's worth the wait.

This is a a good seafood place, with live music some evenings. There's lobster served several ways, all for $18, and lots of shrimp dishes. The service is a bit special: they bring around a bowl of cool water, filled with flowers, to wash your hands in before the meal. Servers are quite attentive. I would definitely make this a stop for lunch or dinner. The restaurant is located right in front of the beach in its own little compound. Parking is a bit tight, but the manager will come out, direct you to a good parking spot, and then guide you pleasantly to your table. If you have to wait for a table, order a tropical fruit drink, and stroll on the beach until your table is ready.

SUGAR BEACH
North of Flamingo, in the hotel of the same name
☎ 506-654-4242
$15
Seafood and local specialties

This is a delightful, peaceful place to eat dinner. It overlooks the whole bay facing Flamingo. The sun sets sizzling into the sea, if you get there in time for a drink before dinner. A bit cheaper than some of the restaurants in town, the seafood is fresh and well prepared. It's usually not crowded, and there is no blaring dance music to spoil the view and the mood. The jumbo shrimp are truly jumbo. They specialize in a creamy garlic sauce (*Camarones al Ajillo*) that is a bit different from what you would find in Spain, and even more interesting. Lobster is about $16.

MARIE'S RESTAURANT
In Flamingo
☎ 506-654-4136
$10
Seafood

Marie's is right in the village. It's in open air, but with no view of the beach or anything special, but that's okay, because Marie will take good care of you. Roasted chicken and seafood are the things to order. The fish burgers are great, if you like the kind of sandwich that oozes juice down your arm and drips off your elbow. I do. Happy hour is from 4 pm-6 pm, and the beer is cold. Call ahead and take a great meal back to eat in your room. Marie does breakfast, lunch and dinner with imagination. The place doesn't look like much, but don't worry. Just park, stroll on in you'll find yourself welcome.

PAPAGAYO SEAFOOD
On the main road in Playas del Coco
☎ 506-670-0882
$15
Seafood

Papagayo's has a good reputation for having the freshest of the fresh. If the fishermen didn't go out, they can cook up a perfectly good *lomito* (beef tenderloin) instead.

Tamarindo

Don't expect fancy linen tablecloths, crystal glasses or tuxedoed waiters; Tamarindo is the place for good seafood in a fun beach atmosphere.

Tamarindo has a variety of funky places to eat. Don't be discouraged by the appearance of some of the outdoor places, with dirt parking lots – the food is topnotch at many of them.

CAPITAN SUIZO
Restaurant in the hotel of the same name
☎ 506-653-0075
$15
Continental

The restaurant has an excellent reputaion and is set in tropically lush surroundings.

GECKO'S
Inside Iguana Surf, just a half-mile south of Tamarindo
☎ 506-653-0334
Open 8 am-2 pm, and 5 pm-9:30 pm
$10
Seafood

John Szilasi, previously chef at Capitán Suizo and Hotel Pasatiempo, is responsible for brilliant and imaginative breakfasts, lunches and dinners. Bocas are served at happy hour (5 pm-7 pm). Even though it's located inside a surf shop, the clientele is only about 50% surfers, as the prices area a bit high for the budget crowd. Garlic shrimp and ahi tuna with ginger sauce are great. Gecko's mixed salad has a bit of whatever the cook feels like is good that day, and with local chicken, beef tenderloin, a variety of fresh seafood or fruit tossed in, it can be a pleasant surprise. Ginger snapper is just what it sounds like, crispy with a ginger sauce, and delicious. Dorado and tuna are served in huge chunks, grilled to your taste. The room is open-sided, and the roof is one of the highest and grandest of any thatched-roof, palapa-style construction I have seen outside of Hawaii.

EL JARDIN DEL EDEN
In the hotel of the same name
☎ 506-653-0137
$15
Mediterranean/fusion

The restaurant is a blend of classical Italian, Costa Rican, and North American styles. The ambiance is romantic, with candlelit tables by the pool. It's tropical magic.

After kidding owner Marcello Marongiu about abandoning his "classical" roots, he prepared me a "fusion" pasta, with shrimp, crab, and lobster in a Thai sauce. It was very interesting and very good. The restaurant is usually about half full of locals and guests from other hotels, which is no surprise, considering he uses no frozen ingredients. Every serving is prepared from scratch. The pasta dishes take a little time since the pasta is cooked up fresh for each order. No steam table pasta here. Marcello is coy about naming his regular celebrity diners, but he greets his regular diners by name. Marcello is a delightful, arm-waving, exuberant host.

The wine list is basic including a selection of good Italian, French and Chilean labels. Characteristically, Spumante is a delightful wine list entry.

☆ LAZY WAVE
Next to Hotel Pasatiempo
☎ 506-653-0737
www.TheLazyWave.com
$14
Asian-influenced seafood and daily specials

You should make an effort to eat at the Lazy Wave more than once during your stay in town. With different menus every day (you have to look at the blackboard),they serve breakfast, lunch and dinner in a garden setting. A good sign at any restaurant: the place is always busy, and there are plenty of other, cheaper places to eat in town.

There are some tables covered by thatched roof in case it rains. Others are open to the sky. An energetic North American group runs the place. As it is more expensive than the many budget places in Tamarindo, the clientele tends toward middle-aged, non-surfer-types. My favorite seat is at the bar by the kitchen, where I can watch chefs Derek Furlani and Eddie Vargas do their stuff. Their inside-out sushi is a marvel of presentation and taste. Lobster patties resemble crab cakes, and are one of those vacation dishes you wish you could figure out how to make when you get back home. Peanut beef fried rice is representative of their fusion. The service is good, but the waitstaff is on the run, seemingly all night – they earn their pay. It doesn't hurt to come a bit early to make sure they don't run out of the best specials, like lobster at $12.

STELLA'S
Two blocks east of Hotel Pasatiempo
☎ 506-653-0127
Open 3 pm-11 pm; closed Sundays.
$10
Italian and international

Swiss chef Wally Unholz prepares local products with an Italian twist. The ever-present dorado, tuna and snapper are on the daily-changing menu, alongside Wiener schnitzel and pasta. This is one of the few places in Costa Rica where you might see lamb on the menu. There is a reasonable wine selection, from $15 on up. There's an open-air ambiance, with the wind blowing through. It can be a bit of a problem when the nearby road is particularly dusty.

Nicoya Peninsula

Playas Sámara & Carrillo

There are a variety of tourist-oriented places to eat in the area.

Playas Sámara & Carrillo are popular with Ticos and have plenty of típico offerings.

☆ **LAS BRASAS**
On the main street
$12
Spanish

A refreshing change from the common Costa Rican and Italian restaurants, Las Brasas ("The Coals"), offers some interesting Catalan dishes. There's the usual fish, but also well-prepared beef and pork. Gazpacho is on offer, along with several other starter items, such as ceviche, *ollas de carne* (meat soups), and hearts of palm salad. Of course, paella is on the menu but it, along with BBQ pork ribs, needs to be ordered for at least two people. Filet Catalonia consists of slices of beef loin grilled and topped with finely chopped garlic. Desserts include flan, fruit and ice cream. Beware of the "pajama," which is a huge concoction of peaches, flan, bananas and ice cream, topped with chocolate syrup. It is deadly.

The wine list is a skimpy selection of moderate Chilean reds and so-so whites. The Spanish (from Spain) bartender manufactures elaborate rum drinks if called upon to do so.

Las Brasas features a Latin sound, but it'susually kept low. The room is an open-sided, high-ceilinged affair, made of tropical hardwoods, with the breeze blowing through. You can sit on the balcony overlooking the street and watch passersby without being seen! This is a great place for lunch, but plan on a nap afterwards. It can get a bit crowded on weekends for dinner.

EL GAUCHO
On the edge of town near the main intersection
$8
Spanish

After many changes of ownership and name, El Gaucho remains a bit unfocused. I found the meat tough, and their fish uninspiring. They do have very cold beer.

☆ **1492**
Located in the Hotel Punta Islita, about 16 km (10 miles) south of Sámara
☎ 506-656-0471
$12
International/Costa Rican fusion

If you are tired of the medium-quality offerings around Sámara, and are ready for a really fine meal, the Hotel Punta Islita will be a refreshing change. Set by the pool in a large, open-air, thatched-roof tropical-style cabañuela, the luxurious hotel (see page 229) allows a few outsiders in for lunch and dinner. The view out over the Pacific bay is as spectacular as you are likely to find anywhere. The atmosphere is much more sedate than in the throbbing beach bars and restaurants in Sámara, or at one of the fishing lodges in the area. The honeymooners tend to sit quietly glued together. The service is smoothly professional. Latin music at lunch and smooth jazz at dinner sooth, rather than assault your senses.

The menu is a mix of local and international dishes, and includes local seafood specialties, as well as tender, export-quality steaks. Nightly specials are imaginative. For example, one night during my stay fresh mushroom soup and a lobster pasta was offered. The menu states that if you would like something you don't see on the menu, just ask, and they will see what they can do. The wine list is one of the best I've seen in the country. A refreshingly broad selection of reds and whites by the glass include cava (sparkling Spanish wine), and range from $5 to $8.

You must call in advance for reservations, not only to ensure there is space, but to make sure the river crossing on the road to the hotel is not too high.

⚠ WARNING

Don't attempt to drive the road to 1492 in anything less than a four-wheel-drive. In the rainy season, some of the uphill parts can require a winch. But don't let this caveat slow you down. The trip is worth it.

Nicoya Peninsula

Montezuma & Mal País

☆ EL SANO BANANO

Playa Montezuma, located right on the main street
☎ 506-642-0272
$8

You can sit outside and watch the parade of international groovy types, both young and old, troop by. Or, sit inside and watch the nightly movie, while you dine. El Sano Banano (The Healthy Banana) is just what the name implies: a healthy place to eat tropical specialties. Wild fruit smoothies, banana whole-wheat pancakes, cheese lasagna, and wonderful fish dishes make this by far the best place to eat in town.

They take great care that each plate that leaves the kitchen has only the best quality, well-prepared food on it. Everybody seems to like the place and everything on the menu is good. It would be hard to go wrong. The whole red snapper is wonderfully crusted with interesting spices, and the Mexican-ish casseroles are imaginative, tasty and filling. Service is usually snappy, except around 7:30 pm, when the nightly movies start in the inside dining room. Get there early for a good seat, as the place is popular with locals and the visiting gringo hip set.

HOTEL SUNSET REEF

Mal País
In the hotel of the same name
Seafood and international
$8

The restaurant menu is refreshingly imaginative and features Thai, Costa Rican and international dishes. Great view, sunsets, fresh fish and fair drinks. I will forgive them the loin steak with strawberry sauce, and praise the dorado with wonderful basil sauce. The bartender is North American and friendly, but could pour the rum with a heavier hand.

MILAREPA
About five km (three miles) out of Mal País, turn to the right along the beach once in town
French

They have reportedly the best food in the area, but the day I arrived, all worked up for a fine meal, I was informed the staff had all gone to town for a football game. Since it was well recommended, I'll give them another try the next time I'm in the area.

TROPICANA
Mal País, straight ahead as you come into town, toward the beach
$6
Local

This is a lively hangout for surfers and other gringos, with basic sandwiches, steaks and seafood.

Tambor & Paquera Area

CRISTOBAL
In Hotel Tango Mar, just off the main road
near Tambor on the way to Cobano
☎ 506-683-0001
www.tangomar.com
$18
Seafood and continental
Dinner only

The Cristobal Restaurant, in the beautiful Hotel Tango Mar, has a moderate wine list and features classical European dishes, steaks and local seafood specialties. The ubiquitous lobster dinner is smartly served, and the tails are large and fresh. The catch of the day runs from dorado to white marlin (a bit tougher than swordfish, but delicious). Steaks are export-quality and served with basil, pepper or mushroom sauces. The atmosphere is almost always serene, as few people outside the hotel come for dinner. This is rather surprising, considering this is really the only restaurant in the area up to international standards. The food is well-prepared and the quality is high. The prices reflect this.

PANCHO'S
In Tambor, south by the dock next to the "Yacht Club"
No phone
$16
Seafood

Pancho's is right on the waterfront. In fact, you can throw scraps from your table over the wall to fish in the bay, with only a flick of the wrist. It looks like just another roadside, Costa Rican family-run restaurant, and it is, but it aspires to be much more.

Pancho's is famous for its garlic bread, among other things. Delicious!

The seafood is as fresh as you are likely to find anywhere, the meals are very creatively prepared, well presented and, catering to North American tastes, the portions are large.

Specials run to swordfish, wahoo and yellowfin tuna. Dorado (mahi-mahi) and lobster are regular menu items. Dinners come with enormous, creative salads that are not the standard lettuce-and-tomato offering many restaurants send out. The cook (Mamí) knows her stuff. I've never heard anyone say anything but wonderful things about the food.

The service, although provided by a callow teenage Tica in T-shirt, shorts and flip-flops, is excellent. She stands by wielding a squirt bottle of water while you eat, in a partially successful attempt to keep the cats away from under your table. The building is rundown, made of unfinished concrete block, with a tin roof and a gravel floor. The tables are plastic-covered. You have to step over a sleeping dog to get inside. But the food makes the setting unimportant.

Now comes the hard part. The restaurant is way overpriced. I forgive the Third-World ambiance, since the food is so good, but the prices are almost double what you find in nearby five-star hotels. It's triple what you pay at local Tico places. A lobster dinner (one, good-sized lobster tail, with trimmings) is $38. You can get a lobster dinner anywhere else in the area for $12 to $24.

At the Camino Real in San José (probably the fanciest hotel in the country), on lobster night, you can have a full buffet with all-you-can-eat lobster served seven different ways, with steak on the side, a groaning buffet of salads and side dishes 30 feet long, and all the fancy desserts you can choke down for $36.

What gives? Did I get ripped off? As far as I can tell the menu and prices are the same for everyone. The food at Pancho's is a bit better than at those other places, and the portions are larger. I really do like Pancho's, but sometimes overpriced is simply overpriced.

Pancho's prices are over the top.

A to Z

Banks

Liberia has the only ATM that accepts international cards. It is a small booth located next to the Burger King at the main intersection by the turnoff to Nicoya.

Nicoya Peninsula

Emergency Medical

Call 911 in all areas. If you need a local clinic, ask at your hotels for details.

Police

Call 911 in all areas.

Post Office

If you must, have your hotel mail things for you. However, the postal service is slow and unreliable. Tiocs usually use faxes and couriers.

Tourist Information

Your best best is to go to the official tourist office in San José. The Costa Rican Tourist Board (ICT) has an office at Avenida 4, Calles 5/7 in downtown San José and one at the airport. They offer some basic tourist maps and books. ☎ 506-223-1733, fax 506-223-5452; In the US, 800-343-6332; www.tourism-costarica.com. Hotels can provide you with most of the info you need, though.

Quepos &
the Central Pacific

Overview

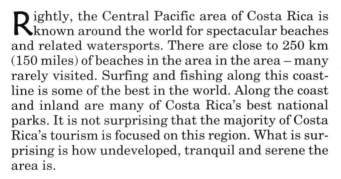

Rightly, the Central Pacific area of Costa Rica is known around the world for spectacular beaches and related watersports. There are close to 250 km (150 miles) of beaches in the area in the area – many rarely visited. Surfing and fishing along this coastline is some of the best in the world. Along the coast and inland are many of Costa Rica's best national parks. It is not surprising that the majority of Costa Rica's tourism is focused on this region. What is surprising is how undeveloped, tranquil and serene the area is.

Puntarenas is a rather unpleasant, hot and dusty port town. It is spread out along a small peninsula, crowded with fish packing houses, bars and rundown residential areas. Freighters and a few ill-advised cruise ships stop here, and it is the terminus for the ferry that runs to Naranjo and Paquera on the Nicoya Peninsula. Few tourists do more in Puntarenas than catch the ferry.

Jacó is famous for surf, surf, and surf. There are literally dozens of bars, restaurants and places to boogie at night. Not all of those making the scene are young surfers, either. The beaches in and around town are some of the more dangerous for swimming in the country, but fill up with Ticos and gringos in the high season and on weekends.

As the closest beach town to San José, Jacó fills up quickly on weekends.

Quepos is a rundown banana port town, but it is improving. However, it still seems a bit ratty, especially when compared to nearby upscale **Manuel Antonio**. Most, but not all, of the action in the area, is on the four-mile-long winding road that leads from Quepos, past restaurants, hotels, bars and tourist shops, all the way to the entrance of **Manuel Antonio National Park**. Along this strip, hotels run from budget to the quiet luxury of La Mansion, where celebrities such as Arnold Schwarzenegger rent the whole place for a month at a time. About half-way down this stretch, for some obscure reason, there is an enormous airplane perched at the edge of the road. The airplane serves as a handy landmark. People refer to a place as being located before or after the airplane. The park gets crowded quickly, but is a no-brainer as a way to spend a morning in peace, after a night whooping it up in town.

Most hotels offer a shuttle service to the public beach near the park.

Manuel Antonio beach is great – long and wide, with gentle surf, and a few bars and restaurants to refresh yourself. It is very popular with Ticos, but has few surfers, since the waves are too small.

Farther along the coast, **Dominical** is a scruffy surfer town with little of interest, except lovely beaches. If you have plenty of time, and the inclination to sink into the scene, it's a nice place to hang out. On the surface, there is not much to offer besides surfing. The bars and restaurants are aimed at a budget crowd with low standards. The few gift shops in town all sell rolling papers and small pipes, if that tells you anything. The beaches to the north and south are some of the prettiest in Costa Rica, but I suggest finding lodgings somewhere a bit more salubrious than the town of Dominical itself.

Quepos
& the Central Pacific

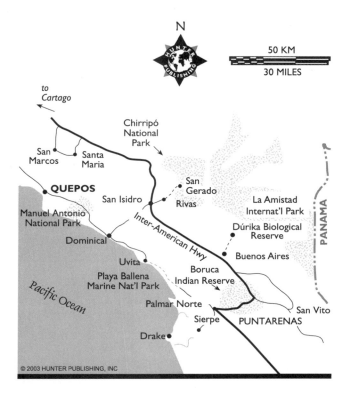

N

50 KM

30 MILES

to Cartago

Chirripó National Park

San Marcos

Santa Maria

QUEPOS

San Isidro

San Gerado

Rivas

La Amistad Internat'l Park

Manuel Antonio National Park

Dúrika Biological Reserve

Dominical

Inter-American Hwy

Buenos Aires

Uvita

Boruca Indian Reserve

Playa Ballena Marine Nat'l Park

Pacific Ocean

Palmar Norte

San Vito

Sierpe

PUNTARENAS

Drake

PANAMA

© 2003 HUNTER PUBLISHING, INC

© 2003 HUNTER PUBLISHING, INC

Quepos & the Central Pacific

The drive along the coast past deserted beaches is stunning. I've read guidebooks proclaiming the area ruined and overbuilt now that the Pacific Coast Highway has been completed, but I don't know what they are talking about. There are very few busi-

*The **Pacific Coast Highway** between Dominical and Palmar Norte is wide, paved and fast, with few potholes.*

nesses or residences of any sort in the area. In fact, I had trouble finding hotels and resorts to review. The beaches are simply spectacular, and it is one of the most unspoiled yet accessible areas in the country. I suggest choosing one of the few lodges near Uvita or Turtle Beach, and exploring the area by car.

Climate

The mid-Pacific region is truly tropical, with temperatures averaging in the 80s° (F). "Green" season runs from May through November, but it is relatively sunny the rest of the year. Humidity can be high, but afternoon showers tend to cool things down. Blue skies are regular, although rain never seems too far away. The name for Quepos comes from the Bribri Indian word for "rainy place."

Getting Here

By Car

It's an easy drive down to the coast from San José. The route out of San José, past the international airport (Route 1), is the best one to take. Watch the signs carefully around Orotina and San Pablo, where you need to turn toward Jacó.

An alternate route is the road toward Cartago and San Isidro de El General (Route 2), which is very busy and slow. Getting through San José to start on this road can take a headache-inducing hour or two by itself. It is easy to get turned around, since a couple of the signs point in completely the wrong direction. Always look back over your shoulder at the signs behind you as you drive away from an intersection. This may help you realize if you've taken a wrong turn.

The road southwest from San José to San Isidro de El General is known as "The Highway of Death," not for its horrendous traffic and associated accidents, but for a freezing death march by indigenous groups. Even so, the road is well named. It is paved, but with numerous potholes and the traffic is truly a nightmare. There seems to be a never-ending stream of fuming buses, and enormous, smoke-belching, overloaded trucks running bumper-to-bumper, in both directions all the way from San José, to the border of Panama. Getting out of San José to reach the highway is a nightmare in itself. I avoid this route like a visit to the dentist.

Even if you think it will take longer, you should always take Route 1 out of San José to the coast areas.

If you're coming from the north (Nicoya, Arenal, Monteverde), along the Inter-American Highway, be extra alert. There is only one very small sign pointing toward Jacó – you have to head for Puntarenas, while being careful to not actually go into the town itself. It's as if the sign makers expected everyone to be coming only from San José.

Route 1 is no grand boulevard, but is a much prettier route than the alternatives, and you will arrive in a much better frame of mind.

By Air

There are small airports serviced by **SANSA** (☎ 506-233-2714; www.flysansa.com), **Travelair** (☎ 506-232-7883, www.travelair-costarica.com), and charters at Puntarenas, Quepos, San Isidro de El General, and Uvita. Be sure to ask about the luggage weight limits on these flights. It is usually only 25 pounds.

Quepos & the Central Pacific

Getting Around

Roads along the coast are excellent, except for the occasional potholes. The Pacific Coast Highway just before Quepos is missing a few bridges, but new ones were under construction in 2002, and they may be done.

Some Costa Rica bridges are still of the variety locals call "Oh My God" bridges because they are made from old railroad tracks. The bridges seem safe but some have no side rails whatsoever. Just look straight ahead and don't look down as you cross.

The road from Quepos to Dominical is graveled and in good condition. It is very dusty in the dry season, and the vibrations induced by driving along it can irritate even the most patient passenger. A frequent debate is whether the ride is smoother by driving very fast, bouncing over the tops of the washboard-like bumps, or by driving very slowly.

For the most part though, the road is quite passable year-round. Considering that just a very short section of the coast road is not yet paved, a weeklong drive along the dramatic coast would be a spectacular and comfortable trip in almost any car.

Rental Cars

There are rental agencies in only the larger towns along the coast. Here are some to choose from.

Agencies

AMERICAN RENT A CAR
Puntarenas, in the Fiesta Hotel
☎ 506-663-5717

BUDGET CAR RENTAL
Jacó, in front of the Best Western Hotel
☎ 506-643-2665

ECONOMY CAR RENTAL
Jacó, next to the Best Western Hotel
☎ 506-643-1719

ELEGANTE/PAYLESS RENT A CAR
Jacó, on the main street
☎ 506-643-3224

ELEGANTE/PAYLESS RENT A CAR
Manuel Antonio, on the main road
☎ 506-777-0115

Sunup to Sundown

Seven-Day Itinerary

Day 1

From San José, get out of town quickly on the road past the airport. You have to take an off-ramp from the main highway. There are signs for **Jacó**, so it's hard to miss the turn. When you get to the coast, park at the end of the Tárcoles bridge a few miles before you get to Jacó. Walk out on the bridge with the rest of the crowd to marvel at the **crocodiles** bask-

Quepos & the Central Pacific

ing on the river banks. They are almost always there on display. The river drains San José, which is actually only a few miles upstream, and contains all sorts of delightful tidbits that appeal to crocodile tastes. This is not a healthy river to swim in for several reasons. It's only about a three-hour drive to Jacó from San José, so you should get there in time for **lunch**. Enjoy the beach and nightlife and sleep late in the morning.

Day 2

After a late breakfast, go to the beach or laze by the pool, before heading down the coast. Just south of Jacó there are a couple of great **lookout spots**, with plenty of parking. Take your time and stop along the way to Quepos to enjoy the beaches and amazing scenery. When you get to **Quepos**, you have to go almost to the end of town before turning left to find the road to **Manuel Antonio**. There is no sign actually at the turn, but if you get lost you can just wander around town a bit. There are a few signs with arrows in town, just not where you need them the most. Arrive in Manuel Antonio without bothering to stop in Quepos. I suggest driving all the way through to the end of the road before checking into your hotel, just to get a feel for the area.

Day 3

The two big things to do (besides hanging out at the beach or bars) are visiting **Manuel Antonio National Park** and **fishing**. The park is one of the most crowded in Costa Rica, but is still worth a visit. If you try, you can stretch a park visit out into a whole day. There are two nice beaches in the park and, of course, a bunch of monkeys.

Day 4

Going to the Quepos/Manuel Antonio area without fishing would be like going to Las Vegas and not visiting a casino. Need I say more? Even if you are not an avid angler, this is one of the most famous sportfishing centers in the world, and you should wet a line. The odds of catching a billfish are actually quite good.

Day 5

If you haven't had your fill of fishing, do it again, or take a scuba diving trip to Caño Island or one of the nearby dive sites. Every conceivable type of tropical tour can be arranged in the area, including kayaking, horseback riding, canopy zip-lines, waterfall rappelling, visits to butterfly farms and the list goes on and on. See *Sunup to Sundown* for operators, page 272.

Day 6

Get up late and head **south**. The road just out of Manuel Antonio is dirt for a few miles, but in pretty good condition (keep a good grip on your false teeth or they may vibrate out). Keep the windows rolled up and the air conditioning on, so you don't get splattered with mud or choked on dust. This road runs a bit inland, but if you look sharp you can find dirt roads. These lead through the oil palm plantations to sandy roads that run along the beaches for miles. My favorite is a small turn to the right 10.5 km (six miles) south of the Quepos airport that leads to **Playa Rey**. This is a great beach to loaf around on, but beware of crocodiles if you swim in the river mouths at either end of the beach.

Quepos & the Central Pacific

After this beach stop, keep going south right on through Dominical. Select a lodge almost anywhere past the town along perhaps the most beautiful and least developed coastline in Costa Rica. **Uvita** and **Playa Tortuga** are quiet, stunningly beautiful, and not at all crowded. At the southern end of this drive, the beaches give way to **mangrove swamps**, which are great for kayaking.

Day 7

Groove on the beaches and area wildlife before heading back to San José. The road back through San Isidro de El General may be a little bit shorter than the route back along the coast, but the traffic is notorious. It's guaranteed to give you a headache from bus and truck exhaust fumes. You also arrive in San José at the wrong end of town and, unless you are lucky, you will spend an extra hour or two trying to figure out how to get through the urban sprawl to your hotel.

The international airport is on the opposite side of town. Drive back along the coast road and spend the night near the airport. Stay at one of the lovely, quiet hotels in Alajuela, like **Hotel Martino Spa & Resort**, ☎ 506-433-8382 (see *Best Places to Stay*, page 139). If you have any time (and energy) left when you get to San José, or if you have time in the morning before your flight, visit **Zoo Ave** on La Garita Road in Alajuela (near the airport across the street from Hotel San Martino). It's a good chance to see the wildlife you missed in the national parks you visited. You can get really close to toucans and monkeys. No one will know the pictures you take here were not taken deep in the rainforest.

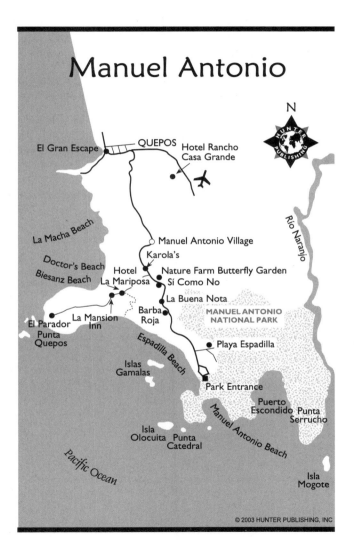

Manuel Antonio

N

El Gran Escape

QUEPOS

Hotel Rancho Casa Grande

La Macha Beach

Río Naranjo

Manuel Antonio Village

Karola's

Doctor's Beach

Biesanz Beach

Hotel La Mariposa

Nature Farm Butterfly Garden

Sí Como No

La Buena Nota

El Parador

La Mansion Inn

Barba Roja

MANUEL ANTONIO NATIONAL PARK

Punta Quepos

Espadilla Beach

Playa Espadilla

Islas Gamalas

Park Entrance

Puerto Escondido Punta Serrucho

Isla Olocuita Punta Catedral

Manuel Antonio Beach

Pacific Ocean

Isla Mogote

© 2003 HUNTER PUBLISHING, INC

Quepos & the Central Pacific

Beaches

In a country full of magnificent beaches, the central Pacific coast has some of the best. The choice is wide. You can select from busy, touristy beach towns, funky surfer hangouts, fishing centers, upscale luxurious beach resorts, or miles of deserted, rarely visited beaches, with tropical forest spilling down to the water's edge. Pick the color of sand you like: white, black, light gray, dark gray, mocha, brown, or any shade in between. You can choose beaches with rocks, without rocks, with waterfalls, with palm trees, with monkeys, or with all of the above. Along most of the coast, there are sandy roads that run just along the top of the beach for miles and miles until interrupted by inlets. If you look closely as you drive along the main highway, you can find dirt roads heading off to the coast. Try a couple of them until you find one that leads to the beach and one of the sandy roads that runs along the coast.

Keep an eye out for crocodiles if you decide to take a dip in any of the river mouths.

A few stories go around about people being gobbled up by crocodiles. The crocs are there. In 2002, there were reports of a three-meter (10-foot) crocodile hanging around Playa Espadilla. Local wildlife officials say the croc (affectionately named "Juancho" by locals), will need to be relocated farther south to Playa Rey, as they have done in similar cases.

Playa Herradura is gentle and famous for luxury resorts. **Playa de Jacó** and nearby **Playa Hermosa** are world-famous, not only for the party scene, but for surfing. They also have a deserved reputation for dangerous undertows and rip tides. **Playa Bejuco** is perhaps safer and is also a surf destination. **Playa Espadilla**, in Manuel Antonio, is gentle, wide and long. The public access areas can be crowded on weekends, but the other end is more private and quiet. There are dozens of stalls selling bathing gear, drinks and food. Personal watercraft, boogie boards, kayaks and banana boats abound.

Playa Baesanz is a small beach off the road that leads to Hotel Parador. Walk down the hill to the right off the road at the low spot, just before you get to the Parador. Most tourists won't know about this beach. It is a much more private place to hang out. There are four beaches in Manuel Antonio National Park: **Playa Espadilla Sur**, **Playa Manuel Antonio**, **Playa Escondido** and **Playa Playita** (Little Beach Beach). Enjoying them is included in the price of entrance to the park.

Several beaches carry the name Playa Hermosa. Be sure you know which one you are heading for before starting out.

Out-of-the-Way Beaches

South of Quepos the road is dirt (but quite good), and parallels the coast, but runs inland a bit. If you look sharp, you'll find a couple of turnoffs that lead to lovely, deserted beaches.

About 10½ km (six miles) from the Quepos airport, just past the little agricultural town of Finca Mona, there is a turn to the right through the palm oil plantation that leads to **Playa Rey**. The turn looks like just another farm road but, if you keep to the right, it leads to a sand road. It runs for about 16 km (10 miles) along the top of the beach through the coco palm trees. There's not much here but a few squatters' houses, and the occasional turtle.

Just past Rió Savegre, there is a rutted dirt road that leads to **Playa Savegre** and the river mouth. This is a good fishing spot and the beach seems to go on for endless miles. Be advised that there is a crocodile colony in the rivers in this area. Wildlife officials use the river at the north end of Playa Rey to relocate crocs that make a nuisance of themselves on popular swimming beaches.

Quepos & the Central Pacific

A few miles farther south there is a turn at the small town of Matapalo (just past the police post) that leads to one of my favorites: **Playa Matapalo**. It is pretty much deserted, even though there are a couple of small bars and restaurants at the end of the road. I spent a wonderful afternoon there watching four horses playing by themselves on the wide sand beach and in the surf itself. The sand is the color and consistency of Nestle's cocoa mix. You have to run from the top of the beach to the wet part of the sand. The water is usually very clear.

Playa Dominical is thick with surfers, and can be dangerous for swimming. Nearby Playa Hermosa is also a surf destination, but is much less crowded. Beaches around Uvita, such as **Playa Ballena** and **Playa Tortuga**, are usually relatively deserted and some of the most visually exciting beaches anywhere. Rocky headlands separate stretches of sand in this area, making for a variety of beach types within a short distance. Some are protected by offshore reefs and islands, and are therefore great for swimming. Others have dangerous riptides. There are no lifeguards in the area, so you should be very careful about where you swim.

The area is famous for nesting turtles & whales cavorting about in the bays.

Playa Ballena is part of **Ballena Marine National Park** (see page 279) and has a small park headquarters at the end of the access road. You have to look very close to figure out where to turn. The only sign on the main road in 2002 advertised some cabinas near the beach, and looked like it would be falling down in the next month or so.

These southern beaches are probably the most beautiful and deserted easily accessible beaches in the country. The Pacific Coast Highway in this area is wide and well-paved. There are not many restaurants, bars or hotels in the area, but you could easily stay in Manuel Antonio and make day-trips to the southern beaches to enjoy their incredicle, remote beauty.

Diving

The Central Pacific area is not well known for dive spots, but you can certainly find some good dives. From Quepos and Manuel Antonio, some dive operators run to **Isla del Caño**, which is one of the best dive locations in Costa Rica. About 25 km (15 miles) offshore from Quepos is **La Forruno**, which is a sea mound in the middle of nowhere. It is for advanced divers only – if you can find someone to take you there.

JD'S WATERSPORTS
Punta Leona, Jacó
☎ 506-257-3857; fax 506-256-6391
PHoyman@aol.com
jdwatersports.com

JD's has night dives, a resort course, and open water dives.

COSTA RICA ADVENTURE DIVERS
Quepos, Manuel Antonio
☎ 506-777-0234
www.costaricadiving.com

A variety of programs include PADI certification, Discover Scuba (Resort Course), Open Water, Open Water Referral, Advanced Open Water, Dive Master, night dives, Caño Island dives, Wild Dolphin Encounters and snorkeling. Each is limited to six divers max. Greg is the main man.

FIESTA DIVE CENTER
Hotel Fiesta, Puntarenas
☎ 506-663-0808, ext 462; fax 663-1516

Quepos & the Central Pacific

PADI, night dives, resort course, open water, 3 32-ft. diesel-powered boats.

Fishing

Quepos is one of the most famous sportfishing centers in the world. If catching a marlin is your dream, this is the place to make it come true. Quepos is definitely billfish territory, but roosterfish, dorado, yellowfin tuna, and the occasional wahoo are also part of the deal.

Sailfish season runs December through April and June through September. **Marlin** season peaks in October, and runs from September through November. Small **tuna** "footballs" are caught year-round, but the big boys are usually landed June through September. **Dorado** are most frequent from May through October. **Wahoo** are rare in this area. **Roosterfish** are caught most often from June through September. Listed below are outfitters.

Jacó

CAPTAIN TOM'S SPORT FISHING
Herradura
☎ 506-643-3995
www.captaintoms.com
$900

Based in the marina at Los Sueños, Captain Tom Carton takes guests out for sailfish, dorado, tuna and marlin on his 37-ft. custom-built Defender. He is well known to be one of the most successful captains on the coast, having tagged over 1,500 sailfish in 2001 (he only tags about a quarter of those he releases). His hit rate pushes 100%. He fishes with circle hooks, which makes for healthy releases.

Directly offshore from the marina are some of the very best fishing grounds in Central America: **Herradura Bank** and an unnamed series of mounds farther out, in about 1,000 feet of water. On special request, Carton will take guests 40 km (25 miles) farther south to the rarely fished **La Forruno**. Although he makes no guarantees, he is almost never skunked.

The morning I went with him we caught and released 15 sails, a dorado and a marlin all before lunch. The sails ran from approximately 90 to 125 lbs. Carton says that such a day is not unusual, and that the fishing is even better in the afternoon when the water warms up. Book as early as you can, since he is a popular captain.

Quepos & Manuel Antonio

You could go fishing in this area, with a different captain and boat every day for months at the right time of year. Prices depend on the size and quality of the boat, as well as the reputation of the captain. Trips run anywhere from $300 for a half-day and from $450 to $1,000 for a full day. Your hotel can make the arrangements. Most of the boats leave from the marina around 7 am.

BOBCAT
Quepos

Captain Daniel is perhaps the most successful captain fishing out of Quepos. Book early.

BLUEFIN SPORTFISHING CHARTERS
Quepos
☎ 506-777-2222

BLUE WATER SPORT FISHING
Quepos
☎ 506-777-1596

FLOUNDER SPORT FISHING OUTFITTER
Quepos
☎ 506-777-3432

J.P. SPORT FISHING
Quepos
☎ 506-777-1613

LUNA TOURS SPORT FISHING
Quepos
☎ 506-777-0725

Golf

The only golf course along the coast is the wonderful one at **Los Sueños Marriott** in Playa Herradura, just before Jacó (☎ 506-630-9000; www.lossuenos-resort.com). It's about $65 for 18 holes.

Horseback Riding

JACO EQUESTRIAN CENTER
Near the bridge in Jacó
☎ 506-643-1569
Call for prices.

You'll see signs for the Jacó Equestrian Center all over the area. For some reason, the signs include a picture of a jockey in full get-up, blasting along at a million miles an hour, rather than a peaceful tourist ambling along on the beach astride a quiet horse. The American-owned stables offer English and Western saddles, BBQ, sunset, jungle, beach or mountain tours.

EQUUS STABLES
Manuel Antonio
☎ 506-777-0001
Call for prices.

They have horseback tours to the mountains and beach.

HORSE TOURS MANUEL ANTONIO
Manuel Antonio
☎ 506-777-1108
Call for prices.

Kayaking

IGUANA TOURS
Manuel Antonio
☎ 506-777-1262

Iguana has sea kayaking, whitewater rafting, and horseback tours.

KAYAK JOE
Office in the Zona Libre bar on the main highway above Dominical
☎ 506-787-0121
$50 per half-day

Kayak Joe caters to all levels of expertise and includes snorkeling equipment if desired.

KAYAK EL TERRABA
Playa Tortuga

They offer mangrove tours where you see plenty of wildlife, including three types of monkeys, amazing bird life, raccoons and coatimundis. El Terraba caters to all levels of expertise. They also offer sea kayaking. The owner speaks French and English.

Quepos & the Central Pacific

Surfing

Dominical is one of the most famous and active surf destinations in Central America. The town pretty much centers on the budget surfer scene.

Perhaps more of a party town than a surf town, **Jacó** sometimes has good surf directly in front of town. Better beaches are nearby up and down the coast.

In **Quepos** and **Manuel Antonio**, the best surfing is on nearby beaches, although some surfing does happen right at the main public beach by the park. **Punta Dominical** and **Uvita** is fairly unexplored surfer heaven.

⊚ GO TO CAMP!

Wild Waters Surf Camp, runs 10-day surf camps in the summer for teenagers. They also have skateboarding and kayaking. You can just drop the kids off and forget about them (for awhile). In the US, ☎ 970-923-1317; fax 970-923-0648, www.surfcamp@aol.com, www.wildwaters.com.

Tours

Every conceivable type of nature and ocean tour is available along the Central Pacific coast and inland. Dolphin and whale-watching trips and horseback rides through the hills and along the beach are two of the most popular. Most hotels and lodges can arrange for any tours offered in the area. Both **Costa**

Rica Expeditions (☎ 506-257-0766, www.costa-ricaexpeditions.com) and **Costa Rica Nature Escape** (☎ 506-257-8064, www.crnature.com) can make all arrangements for tours in advance.

In the Jacó area, you can take canopy tours, horseback rides on the beach, sunset cruises, and more. It's all here. Don't forget there are some wonderful, deserted beaches within a half-hour drive south of Quepos. Few people seem to know about them, and they are almost always completely deserted. If you have a car, you should make a self-guided visit to the beaches between Quepos and Dominical or even farther south. Below are a few of the tours you can take.

OCEAN ADVENTURES
Jacó
☎ 506-643-1885
Call for prices.

Go snorkeling with a picnic lunch to Tortuga Island.

JORGE'S MANGROVE TOURS
Quepos
☎ 506-777-1050
$60 per person

This is one of the most enjoyable tours I have taken in the area. Jorge runs four boats and picks guests up at their hotels in air-conditioned vans for the short trip to Damas Estuary, where his boats are docked. To get into the mangroves they have to go near high tide, so the pickup times vary from day to day. The boat trip lasts about three hours and is in a covered launch with seats for 10 people. The water is very calm all the way and the cover keeps everyone in the shade.

Laura, the guide I went with, speaks excellent English, and is very knowledgeable about the area and the ecology of the mangrove estuary. On the ride to the boat dock she kept up a constant, informative commentary about the local area and the people who live there. During the boat tour she instantly identified each type of bird we encountered. She used her eagle eyes to spot wildlife back in the mangroves we would have never noticed on our own.

Monkey Business

We got as close as anyone can get to a troupe of friendly white-faced monkeys at one point. The boat pulled into a small indent in the mangroves and our guide made a few whooping noises to call the monkeys out for a visit. And they came. Within a couple of minutes about 10 monkeys were all over the boat, cadging sips of water from plastic cups the passengers held.

They held the cups in their greedy little hands and seemed to pose for pictures. Our guide says they refuse to allow feeding or giving the monkeys anything other than water. I'm not sure how ecologically ethical this interaction was, but the passengers on the tour loved every minute of it. The monkeys didn't seem to mind the constant clicking and whirring of still and video cameras. Even flash bulbs didn't seem to faze them. They were wild monkeys, but seemed to be experienced at visiting with tourists. One man almost lost his hat to what the guide described as the "unruly teenager" of the troupe.

This was a bird-watcher's dream trip for viewing water birds. We crept up on a variety of sea birds perched in the trees. Roseate spoonbills can be seen

The Barú River Falls, probably the most stunning waterfalls in Costa Rica, are set in a tropical rainforest. They cascade more than 100 feet into a large pool. Tour operator Don Lulo takes guests through the forest to the falls for photography, swimming and exploring. A meal is provided and the tour generally takes about six hours.

Ballena Marine National Park

Ballena Marine National Park (Parque Nacional Marino Ballena), located southwest of Quepos/Manuel Antonio and Dominical near Uvita, was created in 1989 to protect a bay and nearby shoreline. It is home to migrating and calving whales, dolphins, turtles (primarily olive ridleys) and a wide variety of other marine life. The park is small, with only 300 acres (120 hectares), but protects important habitats such as sandy beaches (turtle nesting grounds), rocky beaches, estuaries, mangrove swamps, islands, rocky shoals and, of course, the bay itself. Punta Uvita, Whale Rock and their associated coral reefs are part of the park and are important nesting sites for brown boobies and frigate birds. The mangroves behind the beach are important for reproduction cycles of multiple marine species, including snook, snapper and other game fish.

Facilities at the park are minimal. An entrance fee is voluntary. The park permits camping, swimming, fishing with hook and line, walking along the beach and horseback riding.

Fishing, scuba diving, and snorkeling trips can be arranged at the small entrance booth. Boat rides to see dolphins and whales are a major reason visitors to come. Divers, snorkelers, and even swimmers may be fortunate enough to hear the mysterious and

Quepos & the Central Pacific

enchanting singing of the humpbacks for hours on end. With a bit of luck, visitors can see humpback whales doing their thing from the shore. Whale Bay (Bahía Ballena) is small, and whales are often packed in, swimming around, breaching and waving their tails in the air. The beach is a great place for long walks. At low tide, you can walk way out to the farthest arm of the sand spit and reef enclosing the bay. The beach is wide and clean. The surf is gentle, making the beach good for swimming.

The park was created primarily to protect the area, which has been used for thousands of years by humpback whales as a calving ground. From August through October, whales from the Southern Hemisphere visit the bay for calving. December through April, whales from the Northern Hemisphere visit for the same reason.

Shop Till You Drop

Jacó

There is a vast selection of cheesy souvenir shops and surfboard repair stores in Jacó. Most carry the same stuff you can buy anywhere in the country, including the inevitable toucans carved from every conceivable material. I list a few of the more interesting shops here.

LA CORNUCOPIA
In Hotel Los Sueños, Playa Herradura
☎ 506-630-9000

This is a notable exception to other area gift shops. La Cornucopia carries high-quality merchandise, with a good selection of clothes and better-than-usual woodcarvings and souvenirs. Jewelry is noticeably superior to what the beachfront gift shops have, and includes gold and diamond creations kept in locked glass cases. Coffee, books, a good variety of international newspapers, and a broad range of sunscreen and after-beach ointments are available.

EUGENIO CHAVARRIA DISTINCTIVE FURNITURE

About two km (1.2 miles) south of Jacó, on the left heading south
☎ 506-643-2132

About two years ago Eugenio gave up his home-building business to concentrate on creating some of the most interesting tropical furniture I have seen anywhere. He built a home for himself and his family by the main highway past Jacó. Once people began to see the fabulous furniture he had created for his home, the orders started pouring in. His creations can now be seen in some of the finest hotels and restaurants in Costa Rica, in particular in La Mansion in Manuel Antonio.

Most of his furniture is free-form, incorporating the natural shapes and colors of the wood he works with. He travels all over the Pacific region looking for old-growth trees that have fallen. He makes slices of the trunks and stump sections, which he turns into tables, chairs, hutches, bureaus and a variety of other useful items. After seeing his work in several different hotels, I paid a visit to his workshop to see how he works his magic. When I was there, he was just finishing up a group of barstools for a bar in Jacó. The bar owner simply told Eugenio he wanted something "crazy." Although they were quite stable and useable, they were quite strange, incorporating twisting vines for legs and tree trunk sections for seats.

Quepos & the Central Pacific

I'm not sure how easy it would be to ship some of his creations to North America but, even if you can't figure out how to get his furniture home, you should stop by his workshop to see a real artist at work.

GUACAMOLE BATIK
On the main street in Jacó

All of the clothes sold in Guacamole Batik are made in Jacó. The selection includes dresses, shirts, pants for men and women, not just bathing suits. The workmanship and quality are high, as are the prices. This is not your usual beachwear shop.

HOT SEXY SHOP
On the main street in Jacó

Get teeny-weeny bikinis and navel piercing here. I admit I did not go into this shop to do my review — looking through the window was enough for me. No toucans sold here.

TIENDA NICOLE
On the main street in Jacó

The inventory includes some regular clothes, but is mostly beach stuff, postcards and the usual small souvenir shop items.

SOUVENIR PADANG PADANG
On the main street in Jacó

Padang Padang buys, sells and rents surfboards, and has the usual collection of beach clothes, jewelry made from seeds and rocks, little pipes and sandals.

HUMMINGBIRD SHOP & SOUVENIR
On the main street in Jacó

This ia another regular beach souvenir shop with T-shirts, beach stuff and toucans.

Quepos and Manuel Antonio

There are probably more little tourist shops in Manuel Antonio than in all of the other beach towns in Costa Rica put together. Unfortunately, they still offer only a few basic local crafts worth considering. There are probably a hundred shops and stalls selling bathing suits and wraps, dozens selling cheap necklaces and anklets made from seeds and things found on the beach, and even more places selling toucans, carved out of everything from bamboo to coconut to lava rock. At the end of the road near Manuel Antonio National Park, you will find dozens of stalls selling this stuff. If you want to buy bathing attire or souvenir toucans, prowl through more stalls, in the space of two or three hundred feet, than you can shake a carved toucan at.

There are only a few full-fledged crafts or art stores in the area.

There are two standouts. **Regálame**, next to Hotel Si Como No in Manuel Antonio, has another branch in Quepos. There are only a few dozen toucans and no bathing suits. They have a large selection of cute, wooden jewelry boxes and carved animals. A good selection of imitation gold pre-Columbian jewelry and stone figures are kept in a glass case. The large selection of framed artwork ranges from realistic to primitive, with a few dolphin/whale pictures. The owner has gone out of the way to locate talented local artists and artisans. It's a big store and nicely arranged.

La Buena Nota (☎ 506-777-1002), farther down the road (past the big airplane), has the best selection of US newspapers you'll see outside San José. There are many used and new books, including nature and travel guides. They also have beachwear, T-shirts, jewelry made from seeds and flotsam, and a wide selection of sunscreen and skin/beauty products.

Quepos & the Central Pacific

An interesting shop in Quepos that specializes in custom-made bikinis: **Ummará Bikini Shop** (☎ 506-777-3617) promises a 24-hour turnaround.

Dominical, Uvita

This is not really an area for shopping, but Dominical actually has better giftshops than bars or restaurants. Past Dominical, there are really no shopping opportunities unless you see a T-shirt or two you like in a lodge gift shop.

BANANA BAY GALLERY & GIFTS
Across the highway from the turn-off to Dominical

The usual surfwear, jewelry, rolling papers and postcards are on offer. Poke around and you can find some nice things, but there is not really much on hand from local artists or craftsmen. It's air conditioned and not a bad spot for a browse.

FUNKY ORCHID
In Dominical, near the police station
☎ 506-787-0061

Specializing in funky surf and beachware with souvenirs and artwork, the store sells all the necessary surfer gear and wild Hawaiian shirts. They also have local handicrafts and jewelry, as well hammocks. Closed on Sundays.

KINGSLEY SURFBOARDS
Near Roca Verde
☎ 506-787-0116

This shop sells only custom-made surfboards. Most of them are for the stars of surfing, but there are also inexpensive models available. If you're a big-time surfer, you've heard of Australian Kingsley Kemovske, and this is where he works his magic.

NEW QUAY SHOP

New Quay opened in 2002, with a nice selection of jewelry, exotic paper, cute carvings of fish and such, and beachwear.

After Dark

Casinos

Most of the area casinos are shabby and not really up to international standards. In Jacó, there is a quiet, but elegant casino at the **Los Sueños Marriott**, (see page 291). The few casinos in the Quepos and Manuel Antonio area are not that exctiting, but if you must, you have a couple of options.

Hotel Kamuk Casino (☎ 506-777-0379), a small hotel casino, is located in the Best Western Hotel, on the main street in Quepos. The hotel appeals to package fishing tour operators. It's usually full of good-time Charlies, and the associated female barflies who always seem to surround them.

Casino Byblos, in Manuel Antonio, is as close as you will get to an upscale casino in the area. It is in the Byblos hotel. If you get to an enormous airplane on the side of the road, you have come too far.

Bars, Discos & Nightclubs

Jacó

Jacó probably has the largest selection of places for youth-oriented evening entertainment in the country. For this reason, and because it is close to San José, the town gets crowded on the weekends.

DISCO LA CENTRAL
On the beach
☎ 506-643-3076
Disco ball-type place. Packed.

LA HACIENDA
On the main street
☎ 506-643-3191
Surfer dudes.

HOLLYWOOD NIGHTCLUB
Just north of Jacó
☎ 506-643-1703
Girls, girls, girls and expensive drinks.

SPORTS BAR
Hotel Copacabana

A couple of TVs and beer make this a "sports bar." Great, if you're in the mood.

Quepos & Manuel Antonio

There is no shortage of places to bend an elbow or shake a tail feather in this popular beach town. Distances are short, and the road is narrow and dangerous. The whole Quepos/Manuel Antonio strip is stretched out on one very twisting and turning road about six km long (four miles), starting at Quepos and running to the park.

Maybe one day someone will open a place that serves milk and cookies at 9 pm for an older crowd.

It's a good idea, and economical, to simply take a taxi to and from the scene. The dance places are aimed at a young crowd and, unless you are under 30, or too drunk to care, not only will you be embarrassed hanging around, but you won't be able to fathom the, uh, "music."

ARCO IRIS
Manuel Antonio
Just on the edge of town
☎ 506-777-0449

On the water, with dancing to DJ music.

EL BANCO BAR
Quepos
☎ 506-777-0478

US expats sportsbar; sometimes with live music.

BARBA ROJA
Manuel Antonio
☎ 506-777-0331

Happy hour runs from 4:30 to 5:30 pm. The place empties out pretty quickly after that, leaving only serious diners and middle-aged tourists downing margaritas at the bar.

BILLY BEACH'S
Between Quepos and Manuel Antonio. The driveway is just before the turnoff to the Mariposa, La Mansion and the Parador hotels.
☎ 506-777-1557

Billy Beach's is the bar at **Karola's** (a great restaurant, see page 308), and is a cheeky, informal, open-sided bamboo jungle bar. Billy Beach modestly claims to have the "best margaritas on earth." I'm not really sure about that claim, but they certainly are good and strong. They also specialize in what they call "Hard Lemonade – an excellent source of vodka." They will call a taxi for you when it's time to go. If you have more than two of their margaritas, you might need one.

Quepos & the Central Pacific

LA BODEGUITA
Quepos, behind the bus station

Loud, young, reggae, typical beach town shouting bar. Need I say more?

LA CANTINA
Past the airplane in Manuel Antonio

Features wood-roasted chicken, ribs and steaks, sports and CNN on TV, plus live music from the house band, "The Jungle Boys."

EPI CENTRO
Next to the Gran Escape in Quepos

DJ dance hall for the under-30 crowd. Nothing happens until well after 11 pm.

MAR Y SOMBRA
On the beach in Manuel Antonio
☎ 506-777-0510

Food and dancing.

MARACAS
On the dock just outside Quepos
☎ 506-777-0707

Big dance floor with Latin music.

VELA BAR
Manuel Antonio
☎ 506-777-0413

Popular place for the gay crowd.

Dominical, Uvita

Dominical has a couple of crummy surfer-tourist bars, and the feeling is run-down and cheap. None of them is worth a visit, unless you don't mind noise, dirt and poor food. Hangouts in Manuel Antonio and Jacó are vastly superior.

THRUSTERS
Near the beach and soccer field
☎ 506-787-0150

This place has little to recommend it other than surfers, pool and darts, but drink enough beer and it may just be your scene.

SAN CLEMENTE BAR & GRILL
Dominical on the main street

Multiple TVs blaring US football games and not-worth-it burgers and burritos. Skip San Clemente. It seems to be well-known as a surfer hangout, but it's scruffy and depressing. Keep going to Puerto Jiménez, or go back to Manuel Antonio. If these comments don't put you off, ask about their disco night.

Sunset & Dinner Cruises

The coast between Quepos and Manuel Antonio National Park is well worth a leisurely sail. The ocean is usually calm, but can get rough in the rainy season.

FREEDOM CRUISES
Marina Los Sueños, in the Los Sueños resort on Playa Herradura, Jacó
☎ 506-291-0191
freedomcruises@racsa.co.cr

The 96-foot *Breeze* offers full-day cruises to Tortuga Island, and sunset cruises with beach activities, cocktails, food and music.

PURA VIDA
Quepos/Manuel Antonio
☎ 506-777-0909
Call for price.

Cruise with snorkeling (and dolphins, if you're lucky), dinner, drinks and, of course, the sunset.

SUNSET SAILS
Quepos/Manuel Antonio
☎ 506-777-1304
Call for price.

Everything from sunset and moonlight sails, turtles, dolphin encounters, and occasional whale sightings, combined with dinner and drinks, make for a romantic alternative to a night in the disco.

Sunset Sails also offers sunrise cruises and is available for honeymoon or other private charters. The coastline around Manuel Antonio is spectacular, with rocky islands, jungle beaches and blue, blue water.

 # Best Places to Stay

Hotels and lodges in the Central Pacific region are among the most expensive in Costa Rica, although some of the luxury jungle lodges in Nicoya or Osa Peninsula are right up there with them. All the upscale hotels have air-conditioning and hot water, although a few may not have phones or TV in the rooms.

Alive Prices

Prices are based on double occupancy during high season, and given in US $. Taxes and meals are not included, unless so noted. Hotels and lodges marked with a ☆ are my personal favorites. "The Best of the Best" choices earn their title by offering top-quality lodging and services.

Jacó

☆ **LOS SUENOS MARRIOTT**
Playa Herradura, a bit north of Jacó
☎ 506-630-9000; fax 506-630-9090
www.lossuenosresort.com
$250

Los Sueños has by far the most luxurious accommodations in the area. The 201-room resort has everything expected for this type of property: beachfront with bar, restaurants, casino, conference facilities for up to 250 people, marina, yacht club, gymnasium, Jacuzzi, pool, lighted tennis courts, 24-hour room service, and all the extras. Rooms are large and completely appointed, down to hair dryers, extra fluffy pillows, and coffee maker. The pool is a kid's dream pool. There are channels, bridges, waterfalls, deep areas, shallow areas, tunnels and, for the adults, a swim-up bar. Unfortunately, the beach in front of the hotel (Playa Herradura), is gravel and gritty. About a half-mile down, it becomes sandy, and is popular with Ticos visiting up from San José.

The hotel is in the middle of a lush and luxurious walled condominium development, with a Ted Robinson-designed 18-hole golf course. The course is considered one of the best in Costa Rica, despite monkeys who occasionally lope onto the greens to grab balls and run off into the forest. It loops through a mountain valley, tropical forest and along the beach. Birds and iguanas compete for the attention of golfers. Caddies are called "green guides" and are fully trained naturalists who can give a running commentary on the wildlife and tropical greenery adjacent to the course. The hotel hosts the Costa Rica Open and the Tour de Los Angeles.

Quepos & the Central Pacific

There are six restaurants in the hotel, including fine dining, hamburgers by the pool and fancy coffee shop (see *Best Place to Eat*, page 304). La Vista is probably the best restaurant on this stretch of the coast and features buffet specials three times a week. Lobster night (I ate six) was a big hit with me. Breakfast is not included in the room price.

The adjacent marina is the nicest in Costa Rica. Gigantic yachts, some with helicopters, are kept here by the rich and famous, including a beauty owned by country music star George Strait. The hotel arranges fishing charters for all budgets to maybe the richest sailfishing grounds in the world. On a trip they organized for me with Captain Tom Carton (☎ 506-643-3995) we caught and released 15 sailfish before lunch. This also is one of the best places to catch billfish in the world. The hotel hosts several world-class billfish tournaments, including the hotel's own Pro-Am Billfish Tournament each February. The casino has seven tables, slot machines, roulette, craps, and even canasta.

Be aware that Los Sueños is a walled resort with armed guards. You get very little taste of Costa Rica, but if you want luxury, tranquility and full service, this is the place.

Quepos & Manuel Antonio

HOTEL RANCHO CASA GRANDE
North of Quepos airport near
Manuel Antonio National Park
☎ 506-777-0330, 506-777-1646; fax 506-777-1575
www.hotelranchocasagrande.com
$130

The Rancho Casa Grande is a rarely seen jewel. It's located a bit out of town, near the airport (don't worry, the airport is not at all busy). The owners, the Costa Rican Artiñano family, keep the extensively gardened grounds and facilities immaculately clean and manicured. The charming staff seems genuinely delighted to have you there. The air-conditioned rooms are in individual *casitas* and are very large, airy and clean, clean, clean. If you have a car and don't want to be right in the middle of Quepos, or on the Manuel Antonio strip, this is a great place to stay. It is only about a five-minute ride into town and is exceptionally tranquil.

The hotel is next to one of the premier canopy tours in Costa Rica. The same family which owns the hotel owns the **Titi Canopy Tour**, that runs through over a mile of primary and secondary forest (see *Tours*, page 277). The particularly lovely pool is right on the edge of the forest and seems about to be gobbled up by the nearby jungle. The hotel is set on over 500 acres (200 hectares) of gardened area and forest. There are over five km (three miles) of maintained trails through the forest.

Although not as luxurious as some of the fancy hotels in Manuel Antonio, and missing the views of the ocean, Rancho Casa Grande is quite comfortable and charming. Upscale hotel owners in Manuel Antonio told me the Rancho Casa Grande should not be considered in the same category as their hotels, but I beg to differ. The rooms are easily as nice as the standard rooms in the Mariposa, are much quieter, and are much better maintained. The Artiñano family also owns and manages the Quepos airport, and can arrange package deals for room and flight from San José.

The restaurant features the same combination of seafood, steaks and Costa Rican dishes found in all the area restaurants, but is priced a bit higher – a bit too high in my opinion. However, the service is excellent.

☆ HOTEL SI COMO NO

Manuel Antonio
☎ 506-777-0777, 506-777-1250; fax 506-777-1093
www.sicomono.com
$160

The unusual name roughly translates as "Yes, why not?" – which gives you a good idea of the level of service offered at this very special hotel. It's a member of the Small Distinctive Hotels of Costa Rica, with 58 rooms and suites, bar, two restaurants, Jacuzzis, two pools (one is adults only), one with water slide and waterfalls. Si Como No is highly recommended for honeymooners. There is a definite "Jimmy Buffett" feel to the place; in fact, Jimmy Buffett's book, *A Pirate Looks at Fifty,* devotes three chapters to the hotel.

Facilities include a small movie theater and conference rooms. There is a hotel shuttle to the black sand beach at the base of the hill. While the black sand may not be to everyone's liking, the beach is unquestionably picturesque. The view from the hotel over the beach and out to sea offers spectacular sunsets. The hotel is surrounded by lush gardens, is quiet and private, even though surrounded by the bustle (compared to other Costa Rica beach towns) of Manuel Antonio.

Local activities offered through the hotel include guided excursions into Manuel Antonio National Park, mangrove and ocean kayaking, horseback riding, tours of the nearby butterfly-nature farm, world-class sportfishing and whitewater rafting excursions. Interesting special packages include a unique yoga course conducted by Ganga White and Tracey Rich of the world-renowned White Lotus

Foundation in Santa Barbara, California and, of course, deluxe honeymoon specials.

The almost overdone Disney-esque architecture of the hotel includes bamboo railings and palm trees made from iron and concrete, and artificial streams and waterfalls. The hotel has won awards for being an eco-friendly combination of livability and unobtrusive closeness to nature. The rooms all offer balcony views of the jungle or ocean, with kitchens and king or queen-size beds. There is a swim-up bar, as well as an excellent gourmet restaurant. It says a lot that guests from the surrounding hotels make a practice of coming by Si Como No's **Claro Que** seafood restaurant (see *Best Places to Eat*, page 305). The breakfast buffet by the pool is included in the room price.

HOTEL LA MARIPOSA
Manuel Antonio
☎ 506-777-0355, 506-777-0456; fax 506-777-0050; In US, 800-416-2747
www.hotelmariposa.com
$200

Although most travel magazines speak well of it, and it has won many awards for excellence, the Mariposa seems to be getting a bit long in the tooth. The awards were presented in the mid-90s and the hotel seems to have gone downhill since. It is still nice, with perhaps the best view in the area, but the décor and infrastructure is certainly dated. The plumbing is quirky. Rooms are large and sunny, and most have a good view, but not all have the fantastic, broad view out over the Pacific. Be sure to specify a room with a view directly out to sea if that is important to you. There is no easy access to the beach below the hotel (it is quite a walk up and down the hill), but they run a shuttle to Manuel Antonio beach. Monkeys hop around in the trees in front of the rooms.

Be careful not to leave bathing suits or other things to dry on your balcony: I saw some squirrel monkeys having a high old time with a bikini left on the balcony of the room below mine.

The restaurant has a spectacular view out to sea and along the coast, and has a North American menu. Dinner service was good when I was there, but the restaurant staff seemed completely overwhelmed by breakfast (included in the room price). Both mornings I tried it, the buffet was depleted by 7:15, and the importance of coffee did not seem to be understood. The tables overlook the shoreline both toward Quepos and Manuel Antonio. The view is certainly the high point of both the hotel and the restaurant.

Considering the quality and views of other hotels nearby, the Mariposa is overpriced. Once considered to be the best in the area, the hotel no longer rates top ranking.

☆ EL PARADOR HOTEL AND RESORT
At the end of Punta Quepos in Manuel Antonio
☎ 506-777-1414; fax 506-777-1437
www.hotelparador.com
$280

The hotel, based on the architecture and tradition of a Spanish parador (a historic inn) is set high near the end of Punta Quepos. The views cover the coastline to the north, out to sea over the point, and southwest over Playa Espadilla to Manuel Antonio National Park. With a total of 80 rooms, the Parador is the largest luxury hotel in the area. In spite of its size, the service is attentive and thorough. Only 10 of the rooms are standard. The focus is on luxury and personal service. The Presidential Suite is supposed to be one of the most luxurious hotel rooms in the country. At least one of Costa Rica's presidents has actually stayed there.

Rooms have air conditioning, coffee maker, iron, queen or king-size bed, and hair dryer. Room service is available. Facilities include two restaurants, pool, putting green and driving box, tennis court, gym, beauty services, and heliport. Local and regional tours can be arranged through the hotel desk. There is a large conference room and gift shop. The hotel has hosted a variety of high-profile guests, including the Miss Costa Rica pageant and has appropriate, unobtrusive security. You don't just drive in casually – the gates are kept closed and guarded 24 hours.

The Parador is located on 400 acres (160 hectares) quite close to Playa Biensanz and is in one of the quietest and most tranquil spots in Manuel Antonio. The hotel itself only occupies a small portion of the land on Punta Quepos. It keeps the remainder in reserve for wildlife and simply to keep the tranquil atmosphere. Mono Titi monkeys are also residents of the lush grounds.

The formal, international-quality **La Galería** restaurant (see *Best Places to Eat*, page 306) is grand in Mediterranean-style and serves the most beautifully prepared and presented seafood, beef and international dishes in Manuel Antonio. The **El Quijote Restaurant and Bar** is the place to have lunch, or a casual sandwich or steak for dinner. The view is at least as good as in the main restaurant.

The breakfast buffet ($12, not included in the room price), is served outside in the main restaurant. On offer is a complete selection of international breakfast choices, along with traditional Costa Rican items like *gallo pinto.* The inevitable omelet specialist is standing by. Linen-covered tables are by the pool, or overlooking the Pacific. Service is snappy, with coffee brought promptly. This is an elegant breakfast scene.

Even though I usually prefer a smaller and more intimate hotel, the Parador is one of my favorites in the area. The complete service, well-appointed rooms, and fantastic views over the Pacific make it a stand out.

LA MANSION INN

BEST OF THE BEST

On the way toward Manuel Antonio National Park, before you get to the airplane, look for the signs on the right.
☎ 506-777-0002; fax 506-777-3489
www.lamansioninn.com
$250

La Mansion is more like owner Harry Bodaan's own home than a hotel, offering luxury, home-style privacy and elegance, with the best view of Playa Espalda and out to sea anywhere in the area. The inn caters to an upscale clientele of connoisseurs of fine living, including international celebrities, entertainers, diplomats and others whose privacy must be respected. The security is discreet but tight. The gates are manned 24 hours.

The front room (not really a "lobby") of the inn is homey and comfortable, but no one simply wanders in. Manager Harrison or one of the other staff mysteriously appears whenever anyone arrives. Owner Harry Bodaan is the former general manager and CEO of the National Press Club in Washington DC and the International Press Center and Club in Moscow. He's experienced at hosting high-profile guests. The halls of the inn are lined with pictures of Mr. Bodaan greeting heads of state and internationally recognized personalities.

The pool has a view of Playa Espalda and is bordered by heliconias, ylang-ylang and other tropical plantings. The pool and swim-up bar (only four underwater stools at the bar) are intimate and quiet, with rarely more than three or four people enjoying a soak.

Recently featured in *Estilos & Casas Costa Rica* (Costa Rica's *Architectural Digest*), the inn is arranged on two floors. Each room has a private balcony facing Manuel Antonio National Park and Playa Espadilla. The walls facing the sea are floor-to-ceiling glass, making it unnecessary to raise your head up off the pillow to enjoy the ever-changing seascape of clouds, sea and rainforest-covered hills. You don't need to get out of bed for breakfast either, since room service is available. This is rare in such a small, intimate inn.

The service is personalized and individual. With never more than 20 guests, the inn employs 20 staff members. Breakfast (included in the room rate) is tailored to each guest: if you're from the US you are likely to be served toasted bagels, cream cheese and home fries; if you're from France, expect croissants; if you're from Holland expect a boiled egg, bread and cheese. Packages including all meals and beverages are offered. Breakfast is served by the pool. No one comes by asking you to sign dinner checks during your stay. The staff quietly makes sure each guest has anything they want to eat or drink at any time of day or night.

Dinner is served in a dining room (not a restaurant and not open to the public) that resembles an elegant dining room in someone's home. Guests have kitchen privileges. If you feel the need to cook something at 3 am in the morning, the kitchen is not locked. Harry's chef, American Bob Williams, was formerly chef at the Hilton Lake Charles and Baton Rouge Country Club in Louisiana. He prepares a blend of local ingredients, Cajun traditions, and his own ideas, into an international cuisine he calls "Jungle Food." Dorado, snapper and steaks served with spicy or sweet tamarind sauces are typical selections. Everything is fresh. The freezer in the kitchen is used only to store drinks, ice and ice cream. Guests discuss dinner with the chef in the morning before setting out for any activities. Wines are from Harry's personal cellar.

Tours and activities in the area are arranged, and tend toward one-on-one guided nature expeditions and fishing trips with the most successful and experienced captains. Personal scuba instruction is offered in the inn's pool. Small (no more than four people) diving and snorkeling trips are arranged. Guests are not sent on package tours with large groups. The inn's spa and exercise facility offers extensive spa services, including morpho-lympho drainage, aromatherapy, tui-na, sport and shiatsu massages; exfoliation; herbal, coffee and sea-salt scrubs; and facials.

Rooms are furnished with wrought-iron king or queen-size beds, oversized showers, and air-conditioning. They are luxurious, with all the amenities you would expect in the world's finest hotels. There are three deluxe rooms, six suites, and the 2,300 sq. ft. Presidential Suite, with two king-size beds, 24-karat gold bathroom fixtures, jacuzzi, is almost always booked at rates up to $1,250 per night. Things are kept very low-key and quiet. There is a no- children policy, although the hotel is dog-friendly. Buffy, Harry's cocker spaniel, quietly pads about the place cadging pats on the head.

It is tempting to describe the inn as being a B&B, but it goes beyond what you would expect from even the best B&Bs. It offers guests the option of being private and very much on their own if mixing with other guests is not to their taste.

Luxury, personal service, fine dining and a tranquil tropical setting make La Mansion not only my "Best of the Best" for the Central Pacific area, but my favorite selection for all of Costa Rica.

Vacation Rentals

TRES AMIGOS
Isla Palo Seco, about 17 km (10 miles) north of Quepos
☎ 506-382-2904; In US, 800-683-1233
www.tres-amigos.com

Tres Amigos has three, two-bedroom vacation rental houses about 200 feet from the light chocolate sand Playa Mar y Sol and about 100 feet from the Damas estuary. The houses are sandwiched between the beach and an inlet leading to the extensive area of mangroves. They give guests the choice of beach activities or snook and snapper fishing. Go out the front door for the beach and out the back for snook. Look up to see the Costa Rican Air Force (flocks of graceful pelicans).

To get to the houses, turn off the main road at Parritas and go toward the beach until the road T's off. Turn left and follow the sand road between the palm trees for about five km (three miles). The beach is long, wide and usually deserted. There are a few other vacation homes in the area, most owned by North Americans who come down for a few months every year. The area is quiet, with not much of anything going on but the beach, the sun and the stars. It is about a 30-minute drive into the bright lights of

Quepos & the Central Pacific

Quepos or Manuel Antonio if you feel the need for fine dining, sportfishing or beach bars.

The three homes are private and nicely situated, under palm trees with a BBQ, pool and all the water toys you could ask for, including snorkeling equipment, boogie boards, surfboards, a small zodiac and bicycles. The houses are fully furnished with queen-size beds, hammocks, air-conditioning, TV, VCR (and massive video collection), stereo with Bose speakers, teak furniture and fully equipped kitchens. The AC works great; there is plenty of hot water and a full-size washer and dryer are available. Cleaning and maid service is included in the rental price. The well-maintained houses are American-owned and there is a Canadian manager with his own home on the grounds. Three friendly dogs useful for walks on the beach are also included.

Best Places to Eat

Alive Prices

Prices are given in US $, and are the average price for an entrée or main course, per person, before taxes and service charges are added. Although Costa Rican law says restaurants must show prices on the menu with taxes included, many do not. Menus that include taxes almost always say so.

Jacó

There are piles and piles of places to eat in and around Jacó, but there is nothing that can be called fine dining, except for the two wonderful restaurants at Los Sueños (see below). Fish, fish and more fish is the deal. Dorado, snapper and tuna are seen on almost every menu. There is a Pizza Hut in Jacó.

Ceviche (raw fish marinated in lime juice with spices) is a common appetizer all over Costa Rica.

BAMBOOSA
Playa Hermosa
$15
Sushi

Bamboosa, with a view of the beach action, is the only proper sushi place on the coast. It's friendly and informal. Spicy tuna roll is the crowd favorite.

CALICHE'S WISHBONE CAFE
On the main street in Jacó
☎ 506-643-3406
$10

Mexican, pizza and seafood with a surfer clientele.

CUSCO BAR
On the main street in Jacó
$8
Peruvian and seafood

A few Peruvian items flesh out the usual menu of steak, shrimp and fish. The service is a bit frantic as the owner tries to do everything himself, from shilling for customers on the sidewalk, to waiting and clearing tables. Strolling musicians line up outside on the sidewalk to come in and do their thing. The food is good, although the ambiance is a bit lacking.

MONICA'S
Playa Jacó
$10
Italian

The pasta is made fresh on site and covers the range of the usual Italian sauces.

Quepos & the Central Pacific

RIO OASIS
On the main street in Jacó
☎ 506-643-3354
$14
Mexican and Italian

LA VISTA
In the Los Sueños Marriott, just north of Jacó
☎ 506-630-9000
$25
International

Be sure to call for reservations, and to see what the buffet special is at elegant La Vista. The nightly buffets can be completely booked – especially on lobster night. Complete buffets run about $38, but include a huge selection of salads, meats, fish, shellfish, desserts, and all the trimmings.

This is a big hotel buffet done well. The lobster does not run out on lobster night. The wine list includes the usual Chilean, French and a few Spanish entries. For some reason, American wines are limited to Robert Mondavi. The dining room is by the pool with a good view of the distant hills and the ocean. You can eat inside or out. Service is excellent.

Quepos & Manuel Antonio

Restaurant prices in Quepos and Manuel Antonio are certainly not cheap. For a dinner in one of the "nice" restaurants, with an appetizer, or "starter," main course, and two glasses of house wine, you can count on spending at least $30 per person, with no dessert or coffee. Remember, 25% for service and taxes will be added on to the price of your meal. Few menus list prices with these extra charges included. so don't be surprised when you see your bill.

CLARO QUE SEAFOOD

In the Hotel Si Como No, Manuel Antonio
☎ 506-777-0777
www.sicomono.com
Seafood
$20

The open-air restaurant at Hotel Si Como No is one of the nicest in Manuel Antonio. It's a nice place with linen napkins. You probably wouldn't feel comfortable here in a bathing suit, like you would at almost any other restaurant in the area. A very civilized acoustic combo quietly plays local tunes adapted for a mature dining environment. There's no booming Latino or bass-thumping reggae here.

The seafood menu is a cross between North American and Costa Rican, and runs to ceviche, shrimp cocktail and calamari for starters, and seafood ravioli and grilled fish and gnocchi for mains. Lobster and jumbo shrimp are prominent. On my visit the ingredients were fresh and it was a pleasure to find myself in a more or less formal restaurant for a change.

My waiter quickly told me they had a few snapper available that day only (not on the menu, so be sure to ask), and it was served lightly grilled with herb butter and lemon. The herb butter was delicate and did not overpower the fish, as is so often the case, and the accompanying vegetables were very lightly sautéed. Sure enough, the next night there was no more snapper, but another fish special, dorado, was almost as good.

The wine list is limited, but includes a sampling from both the Old and New World. The ever-present Chilean wines are featured. For a nice change, menu prices include taxes (but not service), so you have a good idea of what your meal will cost without using a calculator.

LA GALERIA

In the Hotel Parador, at the end of Punta Quepos
☎ 506-777-1414; www.hotelparador.com
Dinner only, reservations essential.
$18
Seafood, international

The formal, international-quality La Galería restaurant is grand in a Mediterranean-style. It serves the most beautifully prepared and presented seafood, beef and international dishes in Manuel Antonio. The tenderloins, lobster, jumbo shrimp, *langoustines,* and fresh local fish are prepared and served as well here as anywhere in the area. I particularly recommend the *pargo entero* (whole red snapper) accompanied by a Cáceres Gran Reserva (I prefer red wine even with fish). Special evening menus include seafood buffet grills and grilled steaks and ribs. The steaks are export quality.

The wine list is comprehensive and offers basic reds and whites from $15, to fine Gran Reservas from Spain and vintage champagnes. The Chilean list includes several reserves if you're getting tired of the bland Concho y Toro served almost everywhere. Spanish wines include riojas and tempranillos from DOC, crianzas and reserves, to Cáceres Gran Reserva.

Balconies surround the high-ceilinged dining room, with art on display by local artists. Antiques collected in Spain by the Dutch owners include suits of armor, massive armoires and wrought iron chandeliers. The exquisitely decorated Reina Isabel dining room is decorated with similar antiques and isavailable for private, intimate dinner parties. The views overlooking the Pacific and coast toward Quepos and Manuel Antonio feature seemingly millions of stars and the lights of Quepos and Manuel Antonio during the evening dining hours.

While almost all the restaurants in the area serve fresh, wonderful seafood at lower prices than La Galería, none offer the same setting, service and elegance. If you want fine dining and all that implies – great food, well-presented with fine table settings, and first-class service – La Galería is the best place in Manuel Antonio for that experience.

☆ **EL GRAN ESCAPE**
On the main waterfront road in Quepos
☎ 506-777-0395
Closed Tuesdays.
$18
Seafood

This place has probably the best eats in Quepos. The bar and restaurant are always crowded. You may have to wait for a table, but that's a sign of a good restaurant, isn't it? The menu covers seafood well and has a few token Mexican items, as well as burgers, crab cakes, and a few Italian dishes. The ambiance is fishing.

This is where the big-time charter fishing crowd hangs out, but don't let that put you off. Many visitors to the area who have never picked up a rod eat here and love it. The walls are covered with pictures of guys with big beer guts standing proudly beside big fish. The TVs over the bar run fishing videos constantly (with the volume turned down). All the local fishing tournaments seem to be headquartered here and you may find yourself in the middle of an award presentation or tournament kick-off meeting. For some reason, the younger crowd stays away (probably the prices), but that doesn't lower the volume any. Things can get interesting after about 9 or so.

The food is good and the service quick and friendly. Drinks are strong and come in "yards," in case you're particularly thirsty. I like the place and have lunch here whenever I can.

☆ KAROLA'S

Entrance is just before turn off to La Mansión, Mariposa and the Parador hotels in Manuel Antonio.
☎ 506-777-1557
$12
Seafood, international

The menu features, ribs, Mexican food, shrimp and, (modestly) "without doubt the freshest tuna any-where," and very cold beer. I can't say anything about the freshness of the tuna since I had dorado, but it was the nicest piece of fish I'd had in a long time. I also sampled the baby back ribs and found them meaty with plenty of sauce – not quite like back home in Tennessee, but good. The roasted garlic heads are a great way to clear the palate between courses. Avoid the *chile relleños*. They simply aren't up to snuff. They don't have the right peppers (they use regular green peppers instead of poblano), don't put in enough cheese, and don't deep-fry them. I will excuse them this lapse. The Chilean wines are reasonably priced and the music is calm and soothing American rock and roll. The prices are not high, but high enough to keep the rowdy crowd out. For rowdiness try La Bodeguita in Quepos.

The entrance is a steep drive off the main road and the restaurant is the usual thatched roof, open-air kind of place set in a tropical beauty spot. There's no doors, no windows, no walls, and no need for them. The waitstaff is North American, very professional and comfortable. Billy Beach's bar makes up the front part of the restaurant, but rarely gets rowdy. Karola's is a quiet place for a meal. Visitors tend to come back during their stay in the area because they know it will be good.

BARBA ROJA
Just before the airplane on the Manuela Antonio strip
$16
Seafood and nachos

After the happy hour crowd thins out around 6 pm or 6:30 pm, and the decibel level drops, Barba Roja (Red Beard) becomes civilized. Fish portions are large and the service is snappy. The nachos servings are gigantic and meant for two or four people. For some strange reason one interesting way nachos are served in Manuel Antonio is with the toppings melted together in a little bowl set in the middle of a plate of bare tortilla chips. You either dip the chips in the goo or just dump it out on top of the chips yourself. Barba Roja also offer their nachos in the more common style with the toppings already on top of the chips.

Dominical & Uvita

Dominical has only a few scruffy surfer bars and no restaurants of note. Farther down the coast there are some standouts, so keep on driving past Dominical and have a nice meal a few miles along.

LA CAMPANA
Dominical, on your right just as soon as you turn into town from the main road.
$12
Italian

La Campana has probably the worst food I've had in Costa Rica. The pizzas have a strange taste of soap and the salads are drenched in vinegar. Others have confirmed my own bad experience, but some local

La Campana was dirty when I was there and the same surfer song played loudly over and over.

Quepos & the Central Pacific

expats seem taken with the place. Maybe I was there on a bad day.

SAN CLEMENTE BAR & GRILL
Dominical, on the left

Unless you like multiple TVs blaring US football games and not-worth-it food, you should skip San Clemente. It seems to be well known as a surfer hangout, but is scruffy and depressing. Keep going south or go back to Manuel Antonio.

RESTAURANTE EL VIAJERO
Uvita, on the main highway
$7
Seafood, in typical Tico style

The Viajero's fruit drinks and fresh fish are hard to beat. Closed Mondays.

EL BALCON DE UVITA
Just off the highway near Uvita
Indonesian
$12

Run by a Dutch and Indonesian couple, Bart and Gabriela, this is probably the most innovative restaurant in the south of Costa Rica. Whether you are pining for a Nasi Goring, Loempia or chicken satay (peanut butter kebabs), you can expect a creative version to be served up with flair. Chicken with white wine sauce and other European dishes also grace the constantly changing menu.

RESTAURANTE EXO-TICA
Located in the Hotel Complejo Diquis, Playa Tortuga
French/Caribbean with Thai tendencies
$10

Run by a Belgian chef, ceviche, banana-curried shrimp and fish, or tenderloin steaks are all expertly prepared. This is one of those places you should stop at for a meal when you're driving by even if you're not hungry – you will be when you enter and smell what's cooking.

A to Z

Banks

There are plenty of banks in Quepos. Puerto Jiménez has a few banks but no international ATM machine.

Emergency Medical

Call 911 in all areas.

Police

911 in all areas.

Post Office

If you must, have your hotel mail things for you. However, the postal service is slow and unreliable. Tiocs usually use faxes and couriers.

Tourist Information

Your best best is to go to to the official tourist office in San José. The **Costa Rican Tourist Board** (ICT) has an office at Avenida 4, Calles 5/7 in downtown San José and one at the airport. They offer some basic tourist maps and books. ☎ 506-223-1733, fax 506-223-5452; In the US, 800-343-6332; www.tourism-costarica.com. Hotels can provide you with most of the info you need.

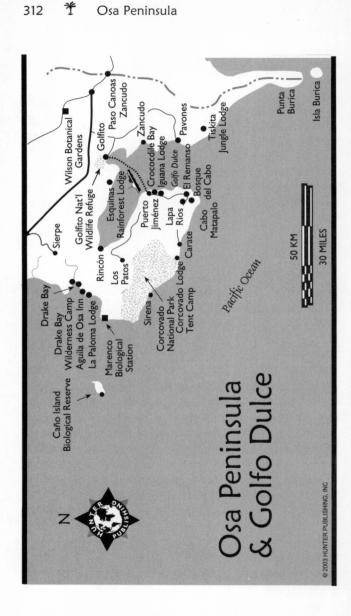

Osa Peninsula & Golfo Dulce

© 2003 HUNTER PUBLISHING, INC

Osa Peninsula & Golfo Dulce

Overview

Osa Peninsula (locally called *Osa de Península*), is one of the most remote and wildlife-rich parts of the country, located in the extreme south of Costa Rica on the Pacific side. It is tropically lush and green and less developed for tourism than the rest of the country. Osa is a bit hard to get to, but is worth the effort. There are several excellent and luxurious lodges and the remoteness is part of their charm. The Osa Peninsula is now similar to what the Nicoya Peninsula must have been like 10 or 15 years ago. Hurry up and enjoy it before it becomes over-commercialized. The remoteness of the area, and the fact that there is so much to do, means you should allow at least a week to enjoy it.

Some remote lodges may not have 24-hour electricity or hot water; if these comforts are important to you, be sure to check before you make your reservation.

You could spend a week or two just in **Drake Bay**. It's a bit slow to get around in the Osa area and it's hard to do it all in only one week. Concentrate on only one or two areas that appeal to you the most if you are here a week or less.

Puerto Jiménez, near the end of the Osa Peninsula, is a sleepy, old gold rush town with lots of character and characters. It's the kind of place where you meet the stereotypical "white man going to seed in the tropics" made famous by Humphrey Bogart and others in so many Hollywood black & white films. It's a good place not to pry too deeply into the past of people you meet. You get the feeling some of the expats are probably not using the same name they used back home in their old life. There is still a whorehouse in town and things can get lively on Saturday nights.

Jiménez and the **Matapalo** area out at the end of the Osa Peninsula have beautiful beaches and easy access to **Corcovado National Park**. The fishing is superb and is a bit less expensive than at Golfito. Although there is good diving in the area, there are no dive operators. Matapalo is a legendary surfer destination. There is a wide choice of lodges ranging from tent camp to luxury.

Drake Bay (pronounced Drah-KAY) has no town to speak of. It is a very quiet and hard to get to tranquil place, with a group of nice lodges clustered around the small, crocodile-infested Rio Agujitas. There's a couple of tent camps and a small store. There is a bit of a beach, but most of it is rocky. Dense rainforest, both primary and secondary, surround the area. Enjoying walks through the forest and exploring nearby Corcovado National Park is what most people come for. First-class game fishing and some of the best diving in Costa Rica make Drake Bay a great, all-around destination.

From any of the lodges in Drake Bay you can fish, dive, snorkel or explore the rainforest at Caño Island, take a guided or self-guided tour to Corcovado National Park, and generally soak up the laid-back atmosphere of this remote paradise.

Quepos is an unattractive ex-banana port with a couple of interesting nearby lodges and fishing, fishing, fishing. There are some beautiful primary and secondary forest experiences to be had just outside Quepos, but the hotels in town are not particularly attractive.

Zancudo and the nearby beaches are laid-back and mostly surfer-oriented. There are a couple of serious sportfishing operators. If you have the time to sink into the scene, you can join the funky group of cheerful expats and surf, fish, or just feed your head. There are good dive spots nearby, but no dive operators. The surrounding area is very agricultural and, although there is a surprising amount of wildlife, serious trips to see rainforest and wildlife involve driving, taking the ferry or a plane to the nearby Osa Peninsula. The beach is long and wide, but is lined with private residences, small farms and the occasional store, bar or lodge. There are several public access paths to the beach, but no place to leave a car. If you are not staying in the area, it is difficult to get to and enjoy the beach.

There are not a lot of reasons to go to Pavones unless you are looking for the Best Wave in the World or are a very hardcore birder.

The Best Wave in the World takes lucky surfers on a ride that lasts almost a mile.

North American birders huddle around their fireplaces in the winter reading books about birds and fantasizing about a trip to Tiskita Lodge, just past Pavones in Punta Banco. The area is agricultural, but backs onto some relatively untouched forest. There are no places to stay or eat other than rather bare-bones budget joints and the comfortable Tiskita Lodge. This is really the end of the road. If you were to walk along the coast another 50 km (30 miles) or so, you would get to Panama or be eaten by a jaguar on the way.

Climate

Osa Peninsula

The climate in the Osa area is truly tropical. Rainfall averages up to 25 feet yearly. I said *feet*, not inches. The dry season runs from December through

Rainfall in the area averages about one inch per day.

April, and could be considered somewhat dry at times, although you can expect almost daily showers. Tropical rainforest covers much of the area and it can be quite humid, even when it is not raining.

There is a pleasant breeze for much of the year and, in the dry season, afternoon squalls blow through and cool things down. The weather is actually spectacular. The towering cloud formations and marvelous rainstorms can be awe-inspiring.

Getting Here

The roads from San José are paved with more than their fair share of potholes, and the traffic consists of a train-like series of overloaded trucks and chicken buses. It takes about six hours to get to the base of the peninsula from San José. It takes another two hours to get to Puerto Jiménez or another two hours to get to Golfito. It is at least a two-hour drive from Jiménez to Carate. The best route is to drop down to the coast and follow the Pacific Coast Highway from Dominical to Palmar Norte. Older maps show this as being an undeveloped road, but it has been recently transformed into one of the widest, fastest and best roads in Costa Rica.

In the Osa Peninsula itself, the road is paved from Chacarita to Rincón, where it then turns into a passable but rutted and muddy dirt track the rest of the way to Puerto Jiménez. From Jiménez to Matapalo and Carate, the road is pretty good, but there are numerous river crossings and some can be a challenge if there has been much rain. The road to Sierpe from Palmar Norte is solid, but potholed and resembles a large washboard rather than a road. Fortunately, it's only a short ride. You can drive right down to Golfito on paved roads the whole way. Past Golfito to

Zancudo and Pavones, the roads get "interesting." There are rivers to ford and few signs.

There is one river crossing that must be done on a two-car ferryboat. It's funky, but worth doing just for the picture to show less-adventurous pals back home.

Scheduled and charter flights go to Sierpe, Drake Bay, Sirena (in Corcovado National Park), Puerto Jiménez, Carate, Pavones and Golfito. Tour agencies will arrange vans and small tour buses from San José and other cities. I suggest calling Costa Rica Expeditions, ☎ 506-257-0766, or Costa Rica Nature Escape, ☎ 506-257-8064, and let them arrange the trip for you if you don't want to drive yourself. Most visitors to Drake Bay buy packages that include transportation by air or tourist bus from San José, tours, food, lodging and all the rest. This probably works out best, but remember, without a car, you'll be dependent on taxis to take you anywhere if you want to leave your lodge.

Getting Around

The best way to enjoy the area is to have a car. You can leave it in a guarded lot if you're going to one of the more remote lodges. Without a car of your own you are more or less stuck in the lodge you are staying in. Taxis can be expensive and, from most of the lodges, are the only way to get around. There are few rental cars available in the area. Most visitors fly in and use taxis or drive down in rental cars from San José

There are airports in or near Sierpe, Drake Bay, Sirena (in the middle of Corcovado National Park),

Jiménez and Carate. You can book scheduled flights from one to another.

If there are more than four in your party, it may be cheaper to hire a small plane.

Most of the flights within the Osa/Golfito area will be 15 minutes or less. If you drive, expect to average about 10 mph (6 kph) on the main roads in the Osa Peninsula, and 40 on the mainland around Golfito. Roads on the peninsula, even the main one, can be closed for days at a time for enormous mudslides to be cleared. Sometimes the mudslides block the road; at other times they simply slide the whole road down the mountainside. Back roads can be impassable even for four-wheel-drive vehicles during the rainy season. Dry season can be a bit better. The problem is often deep river crossings. Bridges are a novelty in remote areas.

Getting to the lodges in Drake Bay used to be possible only by launch from Sierpe. There are now flights from San José to Drake Bay. The drive from Rincón during the rainy season is almost impossible for even the most gung-ho four-wheeler – really. Once you get there you have to park your car just above the beach and radio for the lodges to come and get you by boat anyway. You may as well save yourself the trouble and leave the vehicle in Sierpe or fly in. The trip down the muddy River Sierpe in a launch is an adventure in itself and is a great way to get you in the mood for the remote lodges.

You can get to Sierpe in a regular car, but going to Puerto Jiménez without a four-wheel-drive is more of a challenge if the road hasn't been graded recently or if the rivers are high. There are good roads all the way to Golfito and you can take a ferry from there to Puerto Jiménez. The ferry carries only people, no vehicles.

⊚ RENTAL CAR TIP

Most people fly into the area or rent a car in San José and drive down. It is prudent to rent four-wheel-drive vehicles, unless you are only going to be on the main roads. For a fee, it is possible to have a rental car delivered and picked up at one of the regional airports.

Sunup to Sundown

Seven-Day Itinerary

Day 1 & 2 - Sierpe River and Drake Bay

Fly or drive to **Sierpe** and take a launch to one of the lodges in **Drake Bay**. The ride down the Rio Sierpe through the mangroves is great all by itself. From your lodge, be sure to take a trip out to **Caño Island** for fishing, diving or rainforest walks. Boats take visitors to Sirena in the middle of **Corcovado National Park**. Be sure to go on a night walk with Tracie the Bug Lady (see *Tours*, page 334).

Day 3 - Puerto Jiménez & Matapalo

Take the launch back to Sierpe on Day Three and fly or drive to **Puerto Jiménez**. Check into one of the rainforest lodges near Jiménez, or in nearby **Matapalo**, where you can surf, fish, kayak, or just enjoy the beach and funky gold rush-town atmosphere. Get ready for some serious rainforest walks. Jiménez is probably the best and most economical

Osa Peninsula

base to enjoy the area's big-time game fishing famous worldwide.

Day 4 & 5 - Corcovado National Park

On Day Four, drive or take a taxi to **Carate** to meet your escort to **Corcovado Lodge Tent Camp** (page 332). Walk along one of the most beautiful beaches in the world to your platform tent and then take guided tours of the surrounding **Corcovado National Park** (page 330). Stay here all day and soak up the wonders of the park and beach. Check the beach on your way in and out for jaguar, tapir and other exotic wildlife tracks.

Day 6 - Golfito

Get up early on Day Six, fly or drive to **Golfito** and go fishing for roosterfish, sailfish, tuna and marlin. If you still have energy, take a boat and visit the **Casa Orquídeas Botanical Garden** (page 338), just north of Golfito.

Day 7 - Zancudo & Pavones

Day Seven would be for beach activities near **Zancudo** and **Pavones**, or more fishing, birding, and nature walks. Check out the local watering holes and think about ditching your job back home, letting your hair grow, and going to seed in the tropics.

Beaches

Most of the beaches on the Osa Peninsula, and near Golfito, are gray or brown sand, some with plenty of rocks to make things interesting. I quickly run out of words to describe the beauty of the beaches in this area. Combine craggy mountains tumbling down to the palm-tree lined brown sand with heavy surf, monkeys, birdcalls, and you have tranquil, peaceful, better-than-the-movies beaches. Many travelers become dazed by the sound of the surf, call home to quit their jobs, and never go back. Don't laugh; it really happens.

No-see-ums are pure hell for many people. Avon's Skin-So-Soft is the best repellent.

The best all-around beaches in the area are **Playa Platanares**, outside Jiménez; **Playa Zancudo**, and **Playa Carate**. Surfers sell their souls and live on bread and water to surf the magic breaks at **Zancudo**, **Pavones** and **Matapalo**.

The movie Endless Summer *put this region firmly on the surfer map.*

Diving & Snorkeling

Some of the very best diving in Costa Rica is at **Caño Island** near Drake Bay. Manta rays, pelagics, white-tipped sharks, turtles, and enormous swarms of smaller fish are commonly seen. Lucky divers will encounter whale sharks, sailfish and the occasional sperm or humpback whale. Visibility is usually at least 60 feet, and can be up to over 100 in the dry season.

Dive sites near **Golfito** and **Puerto Jiménez** are also interesting, but the visibility is not as good. There are no dive operators, but if you can arrange a trip with a local, the diving can be superb. There are literally miles of rarely visited sites around **Matapalo** and toward the **Panamanian border**, past Pavones.

Snorkeling can be done at most of the beaches near the lodges, but the surf can be high and visibility low. Costa Rica in general is not especially good for inexperienced snorkelers.

Osa Peninsula

Drake Bay

Caño Island is a national park and diving is strictly limited to only four sites, with no more than 10 divers in the water at any one time.

Almost all diving in the Drake Bay area, and to Caño Island, is arranged through local lodges, although there are a couple of independent operators out of Sierpe. The main lodges are well equipped and some offer extensive certification programs. Dive operators from Sierpe take independent divers, but the ride down the Rio Sierpe adds another two hours or more to the trip in each direction. You also have to stay in one of the cheesy hotels in Sierpe, which all fall into the extreme "basic" category. Caño Island is like a mini-version of Isla de Cocos, but without the swarms of hammerhead sharks.

The best site is probably **Bajo del Diablo** and is worth several visits. The variety of marine life is extensive and changes as different pelagics roam by from day to day. One of my favorite dive sites is **Sassy's Bight**, a rocky point slightly to the north of Drake Bay.

One operator is **Aguila De Osa Inn** in Drake Bay (☎ 506-232-7722, fax 506-296-2190, www.Aguilade-OsaInn.com). Diving is done from a 30-foot Island Hopper, with daily visits to Caño Island, and a couple of "secret" spots only Bradd's dive masters know about. Advanced divers can also arrange to visit La Foruno, but it is a deep dive, starting at around 20 meters (75 feet), with sometimes stiff currents. You may see sailfish, amberjack, and huge, huge snappers. Night dives can be arranged on request. Dolphin interaction expeditions for snorkelers and scuba happen when conditions are right. The equipment is all Sherwood, and is replaced on a strict three-year rotation. There are two Bauer K14 compressors. Dive masters are friendly and helpful.

La Paloma Lodge in Drake Bay (☎ 506-239-2801; fax 239-0954; www.lapalomalodge.com), has a pontoon boat and two fishing boats available for diving. Manager Nicole is an enthusiastic PADI-certified diving instructor. You can take lessons or refreshers in the hotel pool and dive within a comfortable boat ride of the lodge's dock. The lodge has its own compressors and dive shop. Their large pontoon boat is by far the most comfortable diving platform in the area.

Puerto Jiménez

There are no organized dive operators in the Puerto Jiménez or Matapalo area, although the diving can be great if you can hook up with a local. Visibility in the gulf can be limited but the opportunity to see whales or pelagics on clear days can make for some memorable dives. **Surfer Mike** (see *Surfing*, page 329) may take you out himself, or help you get in touch with someone who can take you to the good dive sites. You would almost certainly need to have your own equipment. Some of the area lodges offer dive trips from around $250 per person, but they are just going to fly you to Drake Bay and arrange for one of the dive operators there to take you out to Caño Island.

Fishing

Golfito is probably the most serious fishing destination in Costa Rica, but Puerto Jiménez is less expensive and a bit closer to the action. Word of catching and releasing in the neighborhood of 20 sails and several marlin per day has made its way around the world. This has attracted hardcore anglers from as far away as Japan. Roosterfish in Golfo Dulce are a dream for most anglers. Drake Bay on the other side

Osa Peninsula

of the Osa Peninsula has several lodges well-equipped for fishing. It is an easy ride from there to nearby offshore fishing grounds, and the rarely visited La Foruno off Turtle Beach.

Dorado are a common catch at any time of the year, but particularly so from May to October.

Blue, black and striped marlin, sailfish, tuna, dorado and wahoo are the main targets of offshore anglers. Snook, roosterfish and snapper are fished for closer to shore.

Sailfish are caught year-round, with the best season being December through March. Marlin are more active when the water is warmer, August through December. Small tuna "footballs" are caught year-round, but the big boys are usually landed in the warmer months.

Roosterfish are caught at almost any time of the year. Snook are wily, tough to find, but the best luck seems to be during May through July, or in January and February.

Drake Bay

Most of the lodges in the area offer offshore and inshore fishing but Aguila de Osa is best equipped for the serious angler. More than 80 world records have been made within an 80-mile radius of Drake Bay.

At **Aguila De Osa Inn**, (☎ 506-232-7722; fax 506-296-2190; www.AguiladeOsaInn.com), anglers are well served with three, 31-foot Gamefishers. They are equipped with outriggers for sails and dorado, and planers necessary to get down where the 150-pound-plus yellowfin tuna hang out. The captains have been taking sport fishermen out in Drake Bay for over 20 years and know how to fill the boat with fish.

They are very experienced in catering to fly-fishermen hoping to catch-and-release sailfish and even marlin. Special trips to La Foruno, an unfrequented sea mound about 40 kilometers (25 miles) offshore, can be arranged for the hard-core.

"Gato" Fred, or **Club Fred**, is not strictly associated with any one lodge in particular. He has been fishing the area for years and offers a 26-ft. custom sport-fishing boat for offshore, and an 18-ft. skiff for in-shore. He caters to fly-fishermen. Any of the area lodges can contact him for you and help arrange charters, or you can try him on his cell phone ☎ 506-380-4763.

Golfito Area

Golfito is one of the most famous fishing destinations in the world. If you read fishing or outdoor sports magazines, or watch TV fishing shows on Saturday morning, you probably already know what it's all about. Golfito is considered the place to come for roosterfish, blue, black and striped marlin. Snook and snapper are also targets.

Golfito Sailfish Rancho, (☎ 800-450-9908, in the US; www.advmktl@juno.com; www.GolfitoSailfish.com), is the premier fishing lodge in Golfito. Most visitors purchase a package that includes lodging, meals, fishing, drinks and transportation from San José (around $350). The boats are roomy, new and very well equipped. Rumors of closing have been greatly exaggerated. The lodge is open and the fishing is first class.

You can also try the ***Perfect Hooker***, a luxury boat skippered by Jens Klaus, out of Banana Bay Marina (☎ 506-775-0225). Cost is $500/day for up to six people.

War Eagle, ☎ 506-750-0838, Luxurious, with air conditioning, microwave and more.

Osa Peninsula

Puerto Jiménez

Puerto Jiménez makes the most sense as a place to base yourself for serious fishing around the Golfo Dulce. It is less expensive than Golfito and there are a variety of great lodges to stay at. Any of them can arrange fishing trips with local captains and there is much to do in the area for any non-anglers.

Captain Mike Hennessey, famous for being the most productive captain in the area, is always in demand. He's usually booked up by the upscale resorts in the area. Originally from Newport Beach, he is friendly and helpful, offering gentle tips to beginners and old salts. It's a rare day he gets skunked – he claims a 98% success rate for billfish. Captain Mike is an avid proponent of using circle hooks, which virtually guarantee the ability to release a fish relatively unharmed to be caught again another day.

Although it is a bit harder to hook a fish using a circle hook, the design ensures that very few fish are lost during the fight after a hook-up.

He is adamant that you hook your own fish. He is expert at teaching you how to do it, so few rises do not result in a hook-up. Not only is it simply uncool to let the mate hook your fish for you and then hand you the pole, hooking the fish yourself guarantees that, if you do happen to land a world-record, you honestly qualify to be the record holder. He usually trolls only with hookless teasers and, when a sail or marlin makes an appearance, guests quickly drop in a live sardine (with circle hook). It's usually gobbled up immediately and quite an exciting and satisfying way to fish.

Captain Mike is the founder of the "Circle Rock" tournament that takes place every February out of Puerto Jiménez. The tournament, originally established to educate other fishermen and guides about the advantages of using the circle hook, attracts all the serious captains in the Golfo Dulce and fishermen from around the world.

Area lodges can hook you up with Captain Mike, or you can call him yourself on marine band 73. You can also e-mail him at bigbrisa@hotmail.com, info@laparios.com. Costs range from $400 to $580 for a half-day, and $850 to $925 for a full day. He operates a 25-ft. twin outboard, center-console Kinembe and a 30 ft.-Carolina Classic with twin turbo diesels.

Captain Mike also gives surfing lessons and, while thus engaged, changes his handle from "Captain Mike" to "Surfer Mike."

Crocodile Bay Lodge, (☎ 877-733-5146 in the US; www.crocodilebay.com), is a fairly new, modern lodge close to town and caters to groups of package tour fishermen from all over the world. They will arrange your whole trip, including a couple of nights in San José at the Del Rey, a famous spot for single males on the prowl for a quick, good time. Reports are that they are struggling to establish themselves in the area and have trouble keeping talented captains.

The lodge staff and management seem impersonal and poorly trained in guest relations. They did not have time to let me see their boats or talk to their captains when I made a visit for purposes of this review. The lodge has a reputation for serving as a training ground for guides, skippers, hotel staff and cooks who seem to move quickly on to other, more friendly lodges in the area once they have learned useful skills. Check their website for more detail.

Kayaking

Many of the lodges include the use of kayaks in the price of the rooms. Guided kayaking tours through the mangroves and up the various jungle rivers are usually arranged through the area lodges. For the more serious kayakers, sea kayaking around the Osa Peninsula can be arranged from Puerto

Osa Peninsula

Jiménez, through **Escondido Trex** (☎ 506-735-5210; osatrex@sol.racsa.co.cr). They offer two- to 10-day kayaking adventures around the Golfo Dulce and Corcovado National Park. They provide tents, food, and lodge accommodations from budget to deluxe trips.

Surfing

Few places in the world excite surfers as much as the beaches around **Zancudo**, **Pavones** and **Matapalo**. Each of those areas has an ever-shifting population of baggy-panted surf gods living cheap and enjoying the surfer lifestyle. **Drake Bay** is not known as a surfing destination. It could be a real challenge to work your way around the rocky beaches discovering unsurfed breaks.

Zancudo has a broad beach with famous waves and probably the most laid-back surf community anywhere. Torpor rivals surfing as the best way to spend your day. Pavones has one of the most famous waves in the world – reportedly almost one mile long. It also has a reputation for having some of the snottiest surfers demanding newcomers to get off "their" wave if they get in the way.

Some surfers camp on the beach and there are a few budget places to hang out. Some of the local upscale lodges refuse to rent to surfers. Even if surfing is not your scene, be sure to stop by the Buena Esperanza (locally known as "Martina's"), a bar on the left side of the road about three km (two miles) before you get to Matapalo. Martina is an interesting, tattooed German lady who cooks spectacular meals and baked goodies. The Matapalo surf community hangs out here and is very nice about tolerating unhip non-surfers.

⌾ LEARN TO SURF

Most Puerto Jiménez and Mata-palo area lodges can hook you up with **Surfer Mike** for surf lessons on Pan Dulce Beach in Matapalo. As he says: "You're movin', you're groovin', go-splash!" A get-up-the-first-day guarantee is offered for beginners. He is a wonderful guy and doesn't care if you're a hodaddy or sport a memorable beer gut – he'll get you up. He gives his lessons (including surfboard) on a gentle beach in waist-high water and charges $40 for a two-hour session. Reach him on Marine band Channel 73 "Surfer Mike."

Day-Trips & Tours

Most hotels and lodges can arrange for any tours offered in the area, but some tour operators operate independently. **Costa Rica Expeditions** (☎ 506-257-0766, www.costaricaexpeditions.com) or **Costa Rica Nature Escape** (☎ 506-257-8064, www.crnature.com) can arrange tours in advance.

Since transportation is often difficult unless you have a car, most tour guides will pick you up and drop you off at your hotel, or arrange for taxis. Local lodges and hotels will usually be able to give you good information about what to see in the area. The usual rainforest adventures, early morning bird walks and eco-hikes are offered by all the lodges. A

Osa Peninsula

few tours, like a night walk with Tracie the Bug Lady, are more or less unique to the area.

Corcovado National Park

Corcovado is not a place you can get to casually. Most people are taken in by boat from the lodges in Drake Bay or near Carate. A few people trek in along the beach or over the mountain from near Rincon, but it is a long and rough hike. There are no facilities for overnight stays within the park except for very basic wooden pallets for campers at Sirena. Small planes can be chartered to land on the grass strip at Sirena from Sierpe or Puerto Jiménez. Whichever part of the park you can get to, this is one trip you must not miss. The wildlife in Corcovado is legendary. You are more likely to see mammals, reptiles and exotic birds in Corcovado than in almost any other National Park in Costa Rica.

Visitors frequently see sloths, agoutis, and coatimundis, along with howler, squirrel, whiteface and spider monkeys. Crocs and Jesus Christ lizards are almost ordinary sights, as are toucans and scarlet macaws. It is essential to have a guide if you want to see very many animals. You will see 90% more wildlife and learn much more if someone trained to spot wildlife accompanies you. Serena is known to be the best area for wildlife viewing, but is also the hardest to get to. Most lodges charge a supplement for trips to Serena. Three- and four-day treks through the park can be done independently, or arranged by Costa Rica Expeditions, ☎ 506-257-0766. They offer a two- or four-night organized treks, with stops in Sirena and Corcovado Tent Camp. The trek involves several hours a day of moderately strenuous hiking carrying a 25-pound pack.

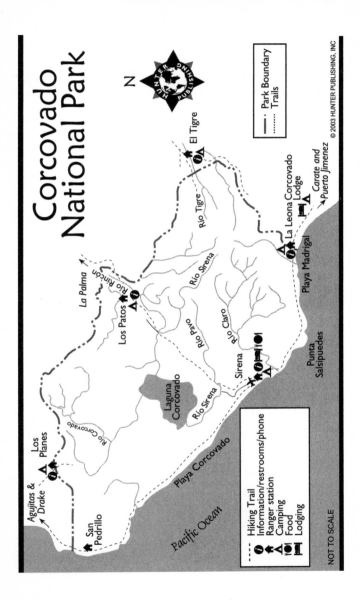

Corcovado National Park

N

Park Boundary
Trails

© 2003 HUNTER PUBLISHING, INC

El Tigre

La Palma

Los Patos

Río Rincón

Río Tigre

Río Sirena

Río Pavo

Río Claro

Río Sirena

Sirena

La Leona Corcovado
Lodge

Carate and
Puerto Jimenez

Playa Madrigal

Punta
Salsipuedes

Laguna
Corcovado

Río Corcovado

Los
Planes

Aguijitas &
Drake

San
Pedrillo

Playa Corcovado

Pacific Ocean

Hiking Trail
Information/restrooms/phone
Ranger station
Camping
Food
Lodging

NOT TO SCALE

Osa Peninsula

Corcovado National Park Treks

This is one of the best areas in Costa Rica for seeing wildlife. In five hours in Sirena in Corcovado National Park, I saw more wildlife than I had seen in the previous month taking tours in Nicoya, Monteverde, and the area around Arenal. The lodges arrange tours from Drake Bay. In Puerto Jiménez, lodges make arrangements with several operators. You can contact them yourself. Treks from Carate or Rincon through the park usually include stopovers at the ranger station in Sirena.

Corcovado Lodge Tent Camp, ☎ 506-257-0766, is located at the edge of the park. It is a great and comfortable place to enjoy the park in a series of day-long hikes.

☆ **COSTA RICA EXPEDITIONS**
Calle Central & Avenida 3, San José
☎ 506-257-0766, 506-222-0333; fax 506-257-1665
www.costaricaexpeditions.com

Guided treks from Los Patos through the park stop in Sirena and end up at Corcovado Tent Camp. It takes from three to five days. The trek involves several hours a day of moderately strenuous hiking.

Sirena ranger station is a bare-bones, but fascinating, place to spend a night or two and really get a feel for the park.

The treks through the park start at about $900 per person, with a two-person minimum, including transportation from San José, space and meals at Sirena ranger station, and one or more nights at Corcovado Tent Camp, and the services of a guide throughout.

Parts of the trip can be done by light plane to maximize the time spent actually in the park, enjoying the profuse wildlife and secondary and pristine primary forest areas. If you have a bit of energy and really want to experience the best wildlife and tropical forest viewing in Costa Rica, this is the best trip to take. Corcovado National Park is remote and, partly for that reason, has more wildlife than any other park in Costa Rica.

Corcovado Tent Camp is located almost at the edge of the park and is the best place to base yourself for day-trips into the park. It is quite comfortable, in a fantastic setting at the edge of the forest, on one of the most beautiful beaches in the world. The food is great. If I had only one week to spend in Costa Rica, I would be sure to spend at least two days at Corcovado Tent Camp. You can fly from San José directly to Carate, where a guide with a horse cart meets you to carry your baggage and lead you along the beach to the lodge. CRE is one of the oldest and most experienced tour operators in the country, with the most experienced guides. You don't have to worry about anything working with these guys. They have a friendly and efficient operation.

OSA AVENTURA
By the gas station at the south end of Puerto Jiménez
☎ 506-735-5431
www.osaaventura.com

Irish and French biologists arrange custom multi-day trips to Corcovado, including night walks. They arrange for all transportation, lodging and tours including diving, kayaking and nature walks.

OSA PENINSULA TOURS
Puerto Jiménez
☎ 506-735-5135

This locally run group offers hiking in Corcovado, horseback riding, kayaking, night hikes, canopy climbs, snorkeling and bird-watching.

Osa Peninsula

THE BUG LADY

Biologist Tracie Stice, or The Bug Lady (as she is known around the world), operates out of Drake Bay. She and her spotter Carlitos take no more than six people on after-dinner night walks. You go in the forest for the express purpose of finding and looking at bugs. Tracie graduated with a BS in biology from Auburn and has been doing entomological research and exploring the rainforests around Osa for over eight years. This lady really knows her bugs and has the ability to describe them in a way that makes their fascinating lives compellingly interesting. Although bugs may not be something you're interested in, after just a few minutes into the walk you'll realize you are working with a true expert. Bugs are much more intriguing than you ever thought they could be. You'll learn that the insects around us live lives of quiet (sometimes noisy, actually) desperation, as exciting as any Arnold Shwarzenager movie. Some praying mantis species cannot breed until their heads have been chewed off; female spiders often eat their mates after, and sometimes during, the reproduction act; the noise you hear crickets making is their loud love song, but once they attract a potential mate, they start a new serenade (quietly so as not to attract competitors); queen leaf-cutter ants mate with seven males within a few minutes, but only one gets to fertilize eggs, and they all die immediately afterward.

Tracie is currently writing a book, *Cultural Entomology*, describing how humans use insects and arachnids for their own purposes. She'll tell you how the US military field-tested a species of bed bug as an early warning sniper device during the Vietnam War. Did you know astronauts use a species of bioluminescent fungus to detect impurities in space capsule air supplies? She has dozens of buggy anecdotes and amusing stories. Tracie guarantees you will see more spiders on her tour than you have ever seen in your entire life – no idle boast.

Outfitting her guests with flashlights and night-vision scopes, she makes what might seem to be a casual stroll through the jungle into a cerebral adventure. A trip to her house in the forest to see at her displays and living insect zoo is a special treat. Carlitos, her spotter, quietly walks a hundred feet ahead of the group looking for interesting things to see, while Tracie leads the group behind enlightening them on the mating habits of various tarantulas, scorpions or other critters. Since 80% of forest creatures are nocturnal, the night vision scopes also offer the best opportunity to see bats, sloths, peccaries, or even elusive cats, as they go about their business. This is undoubtedly the most interesting wildlife tour I've been on and, although insects may seem boring, if you go to Drake Bay, you should not miss taking a walk with The Bug Lady. You can reach her at ☎ 506-382-1619. She monitors marine channel 14 and uses the handle "Tracie Tracie." Or, check out www.thenighttour.com.

Whale-Watching

Whales often spend weeks frolicking in Drake Bay and visitors can view them from the balcony of lodge rooms while sipping rum drinks. Most lodges will take boats out to hunt for them, and there is a good likelihood of seeing humpback whales on any particular outing. Sperm whales and killer whales are not as common, but are also seen. Tours can be arranged in Drake Bay by **Aguila de Osa**, ☎ 506-232-7722, or **La Paloma**, ☎ 506-239-2801, and in Puerto Jiménez by **Escondido Trex**, ☎ 506-735-5210.

Osa Peninsula

Wild Dolphin Encounters

Dolphin worship is a worldwide phenomena and growing. Swimming with captive dolphins in dolphin show parks can cost over $100 per hour, and is frowned upon by most environmentalists. Dolphin therapy centers seem to be a cheesy, high-priced way of justifying keeping these highly intelligent animals in captivity and draining money from the gullible.

Plopping in the water with a pod of wild dolphins and hoping they will hang around is another thing. They often take the opportunity to swim with you and check you out. They can leave if they want and are not coerced or intimidated. It can be a mystical experience.

Pods of dolphins numbering in the thousands are frequently seen off Drake Bay. They often will swim around snorkelers for hours.

On a trip in 2001, I snorkeled for over an hour with an uncountably large group of striped dolphins. Leaving from Aguila de Osa Inn in Drake Bay, my group went about 40 km (24 miles) offshore past Caño Island and, after seeing several whales and turtles, ran into a pod of well over one thousand striped dolphins. They were feeding on small blue runners, but seemed to have plenty of time to chase around our boat and swim with us when we jumped in with our masks and snorkels. They swirled around us about 20 feet away in a busy, squeaking crowd. They never came extremely close, and were always moving quickly, but seeing them in their element and experiencing the sounds they make was one of the most interesting wildlife encounters I have ever had.

Dolphin encounters are arranged from most of the lodges in the Osa Peninsula, and it is usually a supplement to the standard packages. Drake Bay seems to experience the most reliably large pods. Tours can be arranged in Drake Bay by **Aguila de Osa**, ☎ 506-232-7722 or **La Paloma**, ☎ 506-239-2801; and in Puerto Jiménez, by **Escondido Trex**, ☎ 506-735-5210.

Climb Up a Hollow Tree

Near Matapalo, an ancient strangler fig has encircled and killed a 200-foot-tall ficus tree called the "Cathedral." Visitors can climb up the wide hollow core, using steps built for that purpose. Once at the top you can hang around getting dizzy and then rappel down. Although it is a bit gimmicky, everyone I talked to that took the tour thought it was great.

Wildlife can be seen on the way to and from the tree, but expect the commotion of you and your companions' tree-climbing to scare off all but the most jaded birds and wildlife in the immediate vicinity. All the area lodges can arrange the trip, or contact **Everyday Adventures**, ☎ 506-735-5138, in Puerto Jiménez. Operated by wildlife biologist Andy Pruter and Theresa Huisman, the trip has you climbing the "Cathedral." The couple can also arrange other outings. Just ask.

Gold Mines

The Osa Peninsula used to be a real gold rush scene with claim jumpers, shootouts, rich, unshaven gringos, whorehouses, strings of pack mules, and the lot. Some of this atmosphere remains and can be enjoyed either by walking around Jiménez staring at the down and out gringos, or by visiting a working or abandoned gold mine. You may even strike it rich yourself and pan enough to pay for your entire vacation (yeah, right!). All the area lodges can arrange the trip, or contact **Escondido Trex**, ☎ 506-735-5210, in Puerto Jiménez.

Horseback Riding

Rainforest Pioneers has 18 horses and takes guests well into the more remote areas of the forest surrounding Agujas (Drake Bay area). Most of the lodges use this company. The office is on the main trail near Jinetes and they monitor marine channel 16. In Puerto Jiménez, rental horses are available about one block behind Carolina's. Ask anyone to point out the way.

Botanical Gardens

There are two botanical gardens in the Golfo Dulce area. One of the most extensive collections of orchids in Central America is the draw at **Casa Orquídeas Botanical Garden**, and a more general biosphere experience is found at **Wilson Botanical Garden**, both near Golfito.

CASA ORQUIDEAS BOTANICAL GARDEN

The gardens, remotely located east of Golfito, are only accessible by boat. It's open Monday through Thursday only. The entry fee is a mere $5, and is worth every penny. Tours start at 8:30 am (no phone).

The gardens offer a wide variety of plants, birds and butterflies, including tropical fruit trees, spices, flowering ginger, hundreds of orchid varieties, heliconias, bromeliads, palms, aroids and other unusual plants. If you've been wondering what some of those strange flowers and plants you've been seeing are, this is your chance to find out, and get some great close-up photos. A guided walk around the grounds takes about three hours, and is topped off with a refreshing glass of fruit juice squeezed from fruit grown in the gardens. Most area lodges can arrange trips or you can catch a boat from the main dock in Golfito.

WILSON BOTANICAL GARDEN

The gardens, near Golfito on the main highway between San Vito and Neily, cover 25 acres of grounds. It contains a broad collection of bromeliads, heliconias, lilies, gingers, ferns, bamboos and other exotics. The palm collection alone contains over 700 species. Birds and monkeys make the protected area their home, adding to the experience. There are basic guestrooms and a restaurant. ☎ 506-773-4004.

Shop Till You Drop

Other than the locally popular duty-free shopping in Golfito, there are very few shopping opportunities in the Osa/Golfito area. The duty-free concessions in Golfito are aimed at the Tico market. You are required to spend at least 24 hours staying in one of the local hotels before being allowed to make a purchase.

The emphasis in Golfito is on electronic goods and appliances and the prices are usually not any better than what you would expect at a Wal-Mart in the US.

Some of the lodges maintain small gift shops with a selection of local carvings and handmade jewelry. **Crocodile Bay** near the airport in Puerto Jiménez has the largest selection of gift items in the area, such as it is.

Osa Peninsula

After Dark

F ew towns in the area have much to offer in the way of nightlife. There is not even an identifiable small village in Drake Bay, and nothing to do at night outside of the lodges.

Puerto Jiménez has a selection of bars and local dance joints but they are not what you could call salubrious.

There is a whorehouse left over from gold rush days. There are a few restaurants, none of which can be described as being more than "interesting." Golfito is best avoided at night. It has little to offer in the way of restaurants or good nightlife.

Bars, Discos & Nightclubs

Most of the evening drinking is done in Tico bars by the side of the road, but there are a few colorful places to try. Ask in your lodge if there are any interesting watering holes nearby and you may be steered to a fun evening. Appearances of bars in rural Costa Rica can be deceiving. Some rough-looking places can be quite all right. There are not really any bars in the area that are not a bit rough-looking. Most tourists end up in their lodge bar, if they end up in a bar at all. Many visitors do early wake-ups for bird or other nature walks, and are not inclined to late-night carousing.

Many more remote lodges do not have much in the way of electricity, so early nights are the norm.

It is not unheard of to simply drop in at another lodge at night to check out what's happening around the bar. Try the **Aguila de Osa** in Drake Bay or **Lapa Rios** near Matapalo.

Drake Bay

Almost everyone who visits Drake Bay stays in one of the lodges or tent camps. The tiny village of Agujas has no restaurants, and only one bar worth the title. Occasional Saturday night dances are loud, but friendly affairs. The locals put on their finest and dance until the wee hours. The hanging out area (bar) at **Aguila de Osa** gets lively some evenings, and many times guests from nearby lodges will drop in for a drink, dinner and a chat. They have an absolutely great collection of rock, blues and Latin CDs.

Puerto Jiménez & Carate

There are a few gold rush-style bars in town and a leftover whorehouse. Seedy expats, backpackers and yuppies on one-week holidays hang out in **Carolinas**, a restaurant on the main road. Carolinas is the best place in town for lunch.

Buena Esperanza, also known as **Martina's**, is on the left side on the road from Jiménez to Matapalo, about 16 km (nine miles) from town. Colorful and pleasant, this is one of my favorite hangouts in the Osa. Martina is a cool-looking German lady who washed up in the area some years ago and was kind enough to open the only bar for miles around. Open-air and often quiet, things can get lively on Saturday night. New Year's Eve is legendary. Martina's also has a few things to eat, and the vegetable truck shows up on Sunday at 11 for locals to buy produce. She bakes incredible German breads. Toucans and monkeys frolic in the surrounding trees. Techno and new age music unobtrusively entertains the clients. The beer is cold, but if you ask for a complicated cocktail Martina may give you a fishy stare and ask you to select something easier to make. This place is one of my favorites.

Best Places to Stay

Practically all of the good places to stay in the area are eco- or fishing-oriented "jungle" lodges. Many of them are luxurious, or are at least moderately so. Most of the lodges are located in areas with no public electricity, phone service or public water. Generators and solar panels with banks of batteries power most of the lodges. Some of the lodges do not have electricity around the clock or hot showers, but can still be wonderful places to stay. If a hot shower is essential to your happiness you should be sure to check with the lodge about the availability of hot water before you book.

Part of the price you pay for being in a remote area close to wildlife and primary forest is a lack of some of the comforts of home.

Almost all of the lodges include three full meals, and sometimes alcoholic beverages, in their pricing. Since they are remote, there is usually little choice but to eat at the lodge. All the prices in this section are based on double occupancy during high season and include three meals a day. Lodges marked with a ☆ are my personal favorites. "The Best of the Best" choices earn their title by offering top-quality lodging and services.

It is impossible to drive to many of the lodges. Most people arrive in the area by small plane and then take a taxi or boat to their lodge. Without a car it is a bit difficult to get into town to loaf around or try a restaurant without taking a sometimes-expensive taxi. Some tour guides will pick you up at your hotel, or the hotel will include the price of a taxi in the cost of the tour.

Vacation rental houses are available, mostly near Puerto Jiménez, but be sure you know what the house offers in the way of electricity and hot water before you pay a deposit. Many of the locals renting vacation homes consider such things to be frills and don't mention their lack on their websites. There are cabins available in Puerto Jiménez, but anything outside town is hard to manage without a car. See page 369.

Drake Bay

The lodges in Drake Bay are mostly clustered around the crocodile-infested Agujas River. The best way to get to them is by river launch from Sierpe or small plane to the grass strip in Drake Bay. It's about a six-hour drive from San José to Sierpe. There is a road from Rincón to Drake Bay, but it is not passable even by four-wheel-drive much of the year.

When I tried the road in the early dry season, the local police told me the road was fine if I went slow. It was pretty rough for the first three km (two miles) and then I came to a river crossing that was about four feet deep. A couple of farmers hanging around nearby fell over themselves laughing when I told them where I intended to drive. They said there were about 10 more river crossings that were just as bad and that I should wait a couple of weeks before trying. So much for local police knowledge. I turned around, spent the night in Sierpe, and took the launch in the morning. The launch ride is great.

The hotel Oleaje Sereno (Serene Wave) in Sierpe, formerly known as, and referred to by all, as the

Pargo, is clean and adequate at $25 a night, but you should try to get there in time to catch the launch directly to the lodges.

The night I stayed there, the Pentecostal church across the street was having an all-night revival, complete with drums, electric guitars, tambourines and PA system. They whooped it up until dawn.

Scheduled and charter flights are available to Sierpe and to Drake Bay.

AGUILA DE OSA INN

Drake Bay
☎ 506-232-7722; fax 506-296-2190
www.AguiladeOsaInn.com
$150
The lodge is closed in October.

BEST OF THE BEST

Genuinely friendly Bradd Johnsond said he drove out of Honolulu one day, took a right, and the next thing he knew he was building a lodge in Drake Bay on the Osa Peninsula. Isolated and supremely comfortable, the Aguila de Osa Inn caters to a mix of visitors interested in exploring the nearby Corcovado National Park, anglers, divers and anyone who just want to chill out perched above the tropical beauty of Drake Bay.

Visitors usually arrive by launch from Sierpe and are greeted at the dock by long-time Manager Pedro Garro. They are greeted again as they enter the open-air dining room, bar, and hanging-out area by Aguila (the dog). Aguila is a guide dog, but not for the blind. He likes to take people on walks through the trails behind the Inn. If the group seems uncertain which way is back, or where they should go next, Aguila utters a low bark or growl and leads them down the right path. Unfortunately, he offers no spoken commentary on the birds and wildlife.

Speaking local guides retained by Bradd are experienced birders and naturalists. They lead full-day and half-day trips to Corcovado National Park and to Caño Island, which is just 20 km (12 miles) offshore. Horseback riding, night walks with The Bug Lady (see *Tours*, page 334), mangrove expeditions, whale-watching trips, dolphin interaction, and wildlife tours are all offered.

Corcovado National Park is probably the best place in Costa Rica to see wildlife. Visitors frequently see four types of monkeys, various toucans, trogons, sloths, and a wide variety of other rainforest creatures. The guides are specialists in several fields and speak good English. Kayaks and snorkeling equipment are included in the room prices, which also includes three family-style meals a day (excellent), and unlimited wine (decent) at meals.

The inn, with 11 rooms and four suites, is set just above Rio Agujitas facing Drake Bay. As you walk through the grounds on concrete pathways, the profusion of over 100 varieties of bromeliads, heliconias and seemingly thousands of orchids keeps your head turning at every step.

Aguila de Osa maintains a small orchid nursery that's well worth a visit. Photographers are able to take some great macro shots here.

Anglers are well served with three, 31-foot Gamefishers equipped with outriggers for sails and dorado, and planers necessary to get down where 150-pound-plus yellowfin tuna hang out. Special trips to La Foruno, a seldom-visited sea mound about 40 km (25 miles) offshore, can be arranged for the hardcore. More than 80 world records have been made within an 80-mile radius of Drake Bay. Dive trips and dolphin encounters can be arranged as well. See *Sunup to Sundown*, page 336.

When you wake up in the morning, you will find a thermos of coffee waiting for you on the balcony in front of your room. Rooms are furnished with bam-

Osa Peninsula

boo and native hardwood furniture, with ceiling fans and the best reading lights I've found in Costa Rica (very important). Laundry is a reasonable $10 per load. Wet hiking boots are taken from you when you return from your walks and dried out in front of the generator's cooling fan. The hot water is plentiful and hot (really), and there is 24-hour electricity.

Service is quiet, efficient and friendly. While many hotels tend to over-do the friendliness thing, Bradd's staff are locals and have learned the knack of being just as friendly as guests want them to be. If you prefer to hang out and chat with your travel companions or other gringo guests, the staff is unobtrusive. They seem to sense the people who want to get to know Ticos and are always ready for a chat. This is one of my favorites. I'll be back.

DRAKE BAY WILDERNESS CAMP
On the Rio Agujitas in Drake Bay
☎ 506-284-4107; fax 770-8012; In US, 561-371-3437
www.drakebay.com
$180 (call for specials)

Drake Bay Wilderness Inn has the best view of the bay. Its 20 comfortable rooms are well spread out over more than 30 acres of grounds. It's very comfortable, clean and friendly. Owner Herbert Michaud greets guests at the airport or dock when they arrive, and personally escorts them to the lodge and their rooms. Herbert, his wife Marleny, and their daughter Diane, make sure guests feel at home and have everything they need to enjoy their stay.

The lodge is strategically located on one side of Drake Bay on land that was formerly a family farm owned by Marleny's parents. It catches the breezes and sounds of the surf off the ocean. Toucans flit about eating plantains and tearing at coconuts. Hammocks are conveniently scattered about the grounds for enjoying the shade and sea views. You can sit in the pool with your chin on the edge and gaze out over the bay.

The lodge offers more than 15 different tours, including a couple that are a bit unusual, like nighttime phosphorescent walks in the forest, and on the beaches. Kayaks are free for guest use and the lodge backs on to the Rio Agujitas, which leads quickly into rainforest. A variety of monkeys are almost always seen on the kayak trips. There is a fully equipped dive shop and biologist, dive master Shawn Lin leads dolphin interaction and free diving tours aboard their 24-ft. twin-engine dive boat. Both offshore and inshore fishing trips are also available.

Drake Bay offers solar hot water, 24-hour electricity and free laundry service.

The food is an interesting mix of local Tico dishes and US-style favorites. It is served family-style, allowing you to meet other guests and find out about the best things to do in the area. Most of the fruits and vegetables served are grown on the owners' nearby farm. Herbert grows white pineapples and both red and yellow papayas, ensuring there is always fresh, sweet fruit on the table. Coffee is available free for guests all day long in the bar, which is the best place in Drake Bay to enjoy the views. In the spring, the bay is at times filled with breeding humpback whales for days at a time.

☆ LA PALOMA LODGE
Drake Bay
☎ 506-239-2801; fax 506-239-0954
www.lapalomalodge.com
$260

Fortunately for us, 10 years ago Americans Mike and Sue Kalmbach decided to give up on their commercial fishing venture and open a lodge in Drake Bay. Oriented toward eco-tourism, they cater to divers, anglers, and anyone wanting to explore the

Osa Peninsula

nearby Corcovado National Park or Caño Island Biological Reserve.

The lodge is small with four standard rooms and five bungalows. The Kalmbachs decided to focus on getting better, rather than getting bigger, and it shows. The hummingbird and butterfly-filled grounds are flourishing, the rooms are well-appointed and tropically luxurious; the winds and butterflies blow through the screenless windows. The view of the Pacific and Caño Island includes the occasional whale breaching. Mike, Sue and manager Nicole hang around barefoot in the open-air "clubhouse," where meals are served and cutthroat Scrabble is played, and make you feel at home. White-faced monkeys visit daily, making it almost impossible for the lodge to grow their own fruit. Extravagant begonias, heliconias, traveler palms and frangipani make a walk through the grounds or a lounge by the pool an experience for even the most jaded horticulturalist.

Kayaks, snorkeling and nature trails are included in the room price. There is 24-hour electricity and a cell phone if you feel the need to communicate with the outside world. This is a modestly luxurious lodge, but remote. No CNN. No phones in the rooms. Hot water is solar heated.

One of the bungalows has been remodeled into the sumptuous "Sunset Rancho." Sleeping up to six people, the Rancho is set by itself on a high point overlooking Drake Bay. The sun sets off the veranda, going down next to Caño Island. Sliding doors to the veranda and the upstairs bedroom open up an enormous view, so you feel like you're living in a tree house.

The food is included in the price of the rooms, and is imaginatively prepared fresh fish, shrimp, chicken, or vegetarian. Fresh loaves of bread, hot from the oven, are served at every meal.

Drake Bay is the best base to enjoy Caño Island whether you want to fish around it, dive around it, or walk through the virgin rainforest. La Paloma has two fishing boats and manager Nicole is an enthusiastic PADI-certified diving instructor. You can take lessons or refreshers in the hotel pool, and dive within a comfortable boat ride of the lodge's dock. The lodge has its own compressors and dive shop. Their large pontoon boat is by far the most comfortable diving platform in the area.

La Paloma is very comfortable, peaceful and highly recommended.

MARENCO BEACH & RAINFOREST LODGE
Just north of Corcovado on Punta San José
☎ 506-258-1919; fax 506-255-1346
www.marencolodge.com
$250

Marenco, the first lodge in the Drake Bay area, sits perched high on a hill, almost directly facing Caño Island. It's a bit away from the rest of the Drake Bay lodges, in a 1,250-acre (500 hectare) private nature reserve, mostly primary forest. There's really nothing between Marenco and Corcovado but a couple of miles of rainforest.

About 20 years ago, the land was set aside for research. Groups of researchers, including one from Pepperdine, still conduct projects in the preserve. The lodge has over five km (three miles) of shoreline and beaches. The howler monkeys are so loud at times it can get annoying, but they don't drown out the hypnotizing sound of the surf. The 25 rooms are in cabins scattered around the bar/restaurant/hanging out area, surrounded by dense rainforest. Owned and operated by a prominent Tico family from San José, the lodge is very professionally managed. The staff is quite attentive and eats with the guests during meals.

Osa Peninsula

The lodge is older and could use some refurbishment, although there is a continuous remodeling program. The public areas have been well maintained, but the rooms are a bit dingy. The well-seasoned mattresses insist you wallow in their valleys. There is no hot water and the electricity comes on at four each afternoon. Some of the rooms suffer from the noisy generator, so be sure you request one well away from it. Getting to the lodge involves taking a boat from either Sierpe or Drake Bay, and doing a wet landing on the beach below the lodge. This isn't as bad as it sounds, as parts of the beach are quite protected. Baggage is hauled up to the rooms in a trailer pulled by a tractor. The launch ride out to the lodge is a treat in itself.

Unlike some of the other area lodges, meals are served at tables set for four. There is some effort to keep guests who are traveling together at the same tables, with guides and staff members spread around equally. The food is good and plentiful, with coffee available at any time.

All the expected tours are offered, including night walks (ask for the Bug Lady) and mangrove explorations. Corcovado is almost next door, and you can spend plenty of time exploring the park, since so little time is spent getting to and from the entrances. Bird walks for the enthusiastic start every morning at 5:30 before breakfast.

Puerto Jiménez & Nearby

Some of the best lodges in Costa Rica are located in this area of rich wildlife and fantastic beaches. One of the most luxurious lodges in Costa Rica, Lap Rios, is here. It's an upscale, luxurious lodge, with exotic food, and jungle showers outside the cabins. Iguana

Lodge is small, friendly and smack-dab on one of the best beaches you'll find in Costa Rica. The food is superb and the ambiance is laid-back.

☆ **CORCOVADO LODGE TENT CAMP**
Near Carate. You walk along the beach to get to it.
Costa Rica Expeditions, Apdo. 6941-1000, San José
☎ 506-257-0766; fax 506-257-1665
www.costaricaexpeditions.com
$134

If you only have a few days or a week to enjoy Costa Rica, and want to combine a relaxing beach holiday with the best of wildlife observation, Corcovado Lodge Tent Camp has it all. But don't worry, just because the words "tent" and "camp" are in the name, don't think the lodge has anything to do with camping, although rooms are actually tents.

The accommodations are unique. Costa Rica Expeditions owner Michael Kaye has built low wooden platforms scattered around the grounds and covered them with large, airy tents. Inside they are roomy and fitted with beds and nightstands. They are just like in any hotel room, but the warm tropical breeze blows through, and the sound of the surf permeates everything. Macaws and monkeys are all around.

It's a short walk to the shower rooms and dining room, and another short walk to the "hammock house" where you do what comes naturally in hammocks. You snooze, relax, read a book, swing back and forth in the breeze, enjoy a tropical cocktail or local beer. Even though it is way out in the jungle, the infrastructure is modern and clean. Water is purified beyond US standards for drinking water, and all fruits, vegetables, meat and fish are compatible with North American tummies. Meals are served at a long table, family-style. and include jumbo shrimp,

Osa Peninsula

fish, steak, typical Costa Rican and vegetarian dishes. The piña coladas are superb.

The lodge is built on the edge of the forest on a slight rise above one of the most beautiful beaches in the world. It's right next to Corcovado National Park, the best park in Costa Rica to view wildlife. To get there, you have to either fly or drive to the tiny town (it consists of only one small "store") of Carate, and walk for about 45 minutes along the beach to the lodge. Baggage is carried for you on a horse-drawn cart. What an entrance!

The beach is one of the finest I've enjoyed anywhere. One of the challenges of being a travel writer is coming up with superlatives to describe beautiful beaches. Describing the beach in front of Corcovado Lodge Tent Camp could exhaust my thesaurus quickly. The sand is the color of hot chocolate and the jungle tumbles down to meet it. Coco palms lean over, shading driftwood and crab holes. Macaws and monkeys twitter and scamper about. The water is warm and the swimming is great. And it is just a few feet from your room (tent). This convenience led me to take several short dips during each day I was there. I would wake up about 6 am, grab a quick cup of coffee, and plop down in the shallows. I let the waves wash me gently back and forth along the sand. I would gaze back to the forest, listen to the howler monkeys carry on, and watch the macaws fly by. I would repeat this several times through the day, and finish the day with a longer soak.

There are 20 hardwood-floored rooms set slightly more than 100 feet from the high-tide mark. Each one is furnished with two, moderately comfortable, single, bamboo-frame beds, a nightstand and curtains that can be raised to catch the ocean breeze or lowered for privacy. There is no electricity or water in the rooms. The lodge has no phone, no TVs, and nothing to do but enjoy nature and relax. Hot water and electricity in the rooms are irrelevant luxuries in this context and are not featured.

There is probably no better place to enjoy Corcovado National Park. The lodge is surrounded by primary and secondary forest. A wide variety of tours are offered, including a visit to Michael Kaye's tree house, a platform built just above the forest canopy over 100 feet up in a guapinol (hymenaea courbaril) tree. The only way to get to the platform is by being winched up on a cable. Once there you can spend hours enjoying a bird's-eye view of the rainforest canopy and its inhabitants. I spent several hours there watching a nearby sloth move a total of perhaps two feet and saw a variety of monkeys and seemingly hundreds of bird species. I learned several new Spanish words for "cool" and "beautiful" from the guides who accompanied me as they marveled at the natural life around us. Some of the guests I spoke with thought the platform was a bit boring, but I enjoyed the solitude and view.

Although it is a bit hard to pin down the nesting seasons, Ridley, green and leatherback turtle action takes place on the beach and, even though there is no guarantee, many guests do get to see them.

Costa Rica Expeditions also offers accompanied or unaccompanied treks through Corcovado National Park, which include stops in the middle of the park at Sirena (see *Sunup to Sundown*, page 332).

If you have a little stamina, and don't mind a few days without hot water and CNN, there is simply no better way to see the wildlife.

Osa Peninsula

CROCODILE BAY LODGE
Just outside Jiménez by the airport
☎ 877-733-5146 (US)
www.crocodilebay.com
$300

Crocodile Bay, the only lodge in the area with phones in the rooms, air conditioning, TV, and doors with keys, is aimed squarely at package tour sport fishermen. The lodge needs the A/C, since it's located a bit off the water in a breezeless area by a mangrove swamp.

The lodge, relatively new (built in 1999), is on the site of a former cattle ranch. There is little in the way of trees or plants to offer shade from the sun. The rooms are attractive with carved doors featuring fish, and all have Jacuzzis and two queen-size beds. The pool has a swim-up bar that is the most elaborately stocked of any in Jiménez. The staff is a bit tense and any friendliness seems purchased. Although I am a hard-core fisherman, I did not find the amenities or atmosphere at Crocodile Bay very appealing.

Groups of fishermen from North America, Europe and Japan on weeklong package tours visit. The management did not have time to introduce me to any of their captains, or show me the boats and fishing equipment. There is a large, well-stocked gift shop.

If I were going to spend a week fishing in southern Costa Rica, I'd stay at one of the other lodges and let them arrange all my fishing through "Surfer" Mike. Mike's boat is well equipped for serious offshore or inshore fishing. He's a wonderful guy and puts you on the fish. His rates are much lower than those at Crocodile Bay. See page 326.

IGUANA LODGE

Puerto Jiménez, past the airport, on the left after the turn to the beach road
☎ 506-735-5205; fax 506-735-5436
www.iguanalodge.com
$200

**BEST OF
THE BEST**

A six-mile-long beach with gentle surf, kinkajous, and scarlet macaws make the Iguana Lodge a unique place to relax and decompress from life in the fast lane. Many lodges in Costa Rica are near the beach, or are on a rocky, dangerous beach, but the Iguana Lodge is about 200 feet from the magnificent, dark sand, deserted Platanares Beach on the Golfo Dulce. It is also next to the Refugio de Vida Silvestre Preciosa-Platanares, and convenient to Corcovado National Park. Lauren and Toby Cleaver, former defense attorneys from Colorado, have owned the lodge for three years, and have expanded it to eight rooms. They have made it into a tropically comfortable refuge from the pressures of civilization. Most visitors come for a week or more, and spend their time reading, walking on the beach and experiencing wildlife and nature tours in what is probably the most biologically diverse region of Costa Rica.

The food at the lodge is legendary. Chef José was an Osa Peninsula gold miner until the government sent him to cooking school in a program to minimize mining in the region. It was a perfect career change. After several years paying his dues in minor positions, he became head cook at the nearby Lapa Rios Lodge, which is world famous for fine dining. Lauren and Toby somehow managed to lure him away. Breakfasts run from mango scones and banana crêpes to exotic omelets. Lunches are usually traditional Costa Rican selections. Dinner is served upstairs in the main "rancho," at a candlelit table that easily

Osa Peninsula

sits 30 people. The menu is fixed daily and is inventive, with dishes such as North African chicken with chutney de albericoques ceviche, dorado with ginger and chile, and steak kebabs with guava, pineapple, chilies and onions. Special diets are accommodated. Good quality, complimentary wine is offered with dinner. Toby sometimes whips up interesting rum drinks using fresh squeezed fruit juices.

All five types of turtles have been seen nesting on the beach in front of the lodge. Iguana Lodge is the main supporter of the Association to Save the Turtles of Costa Rica. The hatchery is just down the beach. Researchers patrol the beaches looking for nests, and bring eggs to the hatchery for protection. In 2001 they released over 7,000 baby turtles to the wild. This is down from 12,000 the year before, possibly due to a red tide. Guests at the lodge can contribute a helping hand to the effort or just observe.

The first afternoon I was there, Toby came by my room and said "Bruce, would you like to see a kinkajou?" Just outside my room, high in a cedro maría tree, a sleepy kinkajou raised his head to pose for pictures. The only decent pictures I have taken of trogons were captured within 200 feet of my room. Fiery-billed aracaris flit about. An exotic collection of heliconias, bamboo, fragrant flowers and fruit trees has been planted around the seven-acre grounds.

Rooms are built in treehouse-like bungalows scattered around the grounds. They have bathrooms that are almost outdoors, with vines and plants in planters. They are completely private, but you feel as if you are taking a shower in the forest. Furniture tends toward bamboo and renewable native hardwoods. Rooms also feature good reading lights, open-air sleeping areas and hammocks. Mattresses and pillows are topnotch – none of the moldy, sagging bags found in some of the cheaper lodges.

One of the main advantages of Iguana Lodge is its location 6.5 km (four miles) from Puerto Jiménez, where big time fishing, wildlife and birding tours can be arranged. Lodge staff helps guests arrange tours to Corcovado National Park, Casa Orquídeas Botanical Garden, horseback rides and fishing.

Kayaks and boogie board use are free to guests, and the beach is just steps from the rooms. The Cleavers' 13-year-old son Rio will gladly give boogie board or surfing lessons. Chester, a kleptomaniac Labrador, lurks by the path to the beach, waiting for someone to walk with. You need to watch your sandals if you take them off because he thinks it is amusing to hide them. The wide, sand beach is a spectacular place to enjoy the sunrise over the Golfo Dulce.

Another gem is the Lodge's Japanese bathhouse. Kneel outside the tub and, using the paraphernalia provided, thoroughly wash yourself before taking a long, hot soak. You can enjoy your soak solo or with friends. A "Do Not Disturb" sign is handy if you need it. Just a couple hundred feet down the beach is the Pearl of the Osa, a bar and grill (with a few nice, and somewhat less expensive, rooms above the bar), also owned by Toby and Lauren. For a change of pace in the afternoon or evening, the bartender is a master at creating interesting tropical cocktails.

☆ LAPA RIOS

South of Puerto Jiménez, near Matapalo
☎ 506-735-5130; fax 506-735-5179
www.laparios.com
$408

If you don't want to give up your luxury, but want to get as close as possible to rainforest wildlife, Lapa

Rios is a good choice. The comfort, food quality, level of service, and views of the gulf and the legendary surfing beaches are unbeatable by any of the other lodges in the area.

All of the spacious, thatched-roof cabins, built from tropical hardwoods and bamboo, have 24-hour electricity and hot water. Once again, my travel writer's supply of superlatives is challenged. Lapa Rios is one of those special, remote tropical lodges in the world that somehow manages to combine luxury with a true rainforest adventure. You can sit on your deck after a hot shower watching toucans, squirrel monkeys, macaws and dozens of bird species as they strut their stuff only a few feet in front of you.

The food choice is extensive, delicious and imaginatively presented. The lodge is highly rated by *Condé Nast* and is aimed at upscale adventurous types.

The lodge was designed by eco-tourism architect David Andersen. It is built on a series of ridges high above Matapalo, the extreme end of the Osa Peninsula, overlooking the Golfo Dulce. The 14 bungalows are luxuriously spread out over five acres in the resort's own 1,000-acre reserve. World-famous surfing beaches Playa Carbonera and Playa Sombrero are at the bottom of the hill.

Rooms are individual cabins with two queen-size beds, ceiling fans and bamboo furniture. Paths wind through the forest from the main building to the cabins. Although it's a bit of an uphill hike to the restaurant and pool, I like cabins 12, 13 and 14, since they are the farthest away from the activity of the main buildings, and wildlife is seen more frequently up close.

At Lapa Rios, I was hard-pressed to find anything to complain about. The fact that there are no TVs, phones or air conditioning doesn't really count, since this is a remote, tropical lodge, and you don't come here to watch *Adventure Island* or call the office. A breeze blows through the walls made of netting and keeps the rooms cool. My only quibbles were that although the shower inside had hot water, the shower outside each cabin in the private gardens had only cold. Also, there were no electrical outlets by the desks to plug in a laptop. That's it. Oh yes, it's expensive. In fact, it's way overpriced. That's all I can come up with. There are extra fluffy pillows and towels in the closet in case you want them, coffee is delivered to your door at 6 am if you so desire, the individual reading lamps are excellent, and the mattresses and sheets are of the very highest quality. The staff is extremely sensitive to your needs and moods and fulfills your slightest whims so quickly you don't have time to feel guilty.

Lapa Rios offers all the usual tours: early morning bird walks, night walks, trips to botanical gardens, fishing, surfing and rainforest excursions. Corcovado National Park is a short ride away. One special guided tour is a medicine walk led by a local Biribiri Indian who is equally shaman and showman. Traditional Indian medicinal uses for leaves, bark and sap are explained as the friendly, loquacious and fascinating Augosto leads you on a three-hour walk through forest trails. Don't miss this one.

It should be no surprise that other lodges in the area are jealous of the success of Lapa Rios and you may hear comments about crass promotion of the lodge. Owners Karen and John Lewis are former Peace Corps volunteers, are undoubtedly experts at promoting the lodge, and present their efforts to gently incorporate it into the natural and social environment in a flattering, self-promotional light.

Osa Peninsula

The lodge is built only from trees that have fallen naturally. No living trees were cut for its construction. Effort is made to employ and educate local residents so they benefit as well from the lodge's success. While the local Carbonero school was built and is supported through the fundraising and hands-on efforts of many people, including other local lodge owners, the owners of Lapa Rios seem to use their involvement in the school project as a promotional tool. It is mentioned prominently in their advertising and brochures. Visitors are encouraged to bring pencils, books and other needed school supplies. I personally have no problem with this, and can only praise anyone who helps those with less than them, whether they talk about their charitable donations or help more quietly.

BOSQUE DEL CABO

22 km (13 miles) south of Puerto Jiménez,
at Cabo Matapalo
☎ 506-381-4847; phone/fax 506-735-5206
www.bosquedelcabo.com
$250

Phil Spier moved from Florida in 1987 to realize his dream of living a fulfilling life in the most ecologically pristine area of Costa Rica, the Osa Peninsula. With 425 acres (140-hectares) of grounds, Bosque del Cabo is more than just a collection of bungalows overlooking the Pacific at Matapalo, the most extreme point of the Osa Peninsula. Phil has allowed major portions of what was once farmland to revert naturally and by design to forest. He's cultivated hundreds of flowering shrubs, fruit trees, spices and native ornamentals in a highly manicured, yet natural, park-like setting.

The nine thatched-roof bungalows, bar, pool and restaurant are carefully placed around the grounds.

You'll find few lodges anywhere in Costa Rica set in such imaginatively and carefully maintained grounds. Because of its location near secondary rainforest and Corcovado National Park, the area seems to be swarming with scarlet macaws, monkeys, agoutis, and hundreds of bird species. Guests can lounge about on their front porches enjoying, not only the view of the ocean, but all this wildlife without stirring from their hammocks.

Considering the remoteness of the area (the electric power grid stops 16 km/10 miles from the lodge), the modest luxury of the rooms is surprising. Utilizing solar and hydro power, the rooms are large and airy with tile floors, beautiful teak woodwork and porches built for enjoying the breeze, view and wildlife. Each room is in its own cabin and is naturally isolated by landscaping on a bluff overlooking the sea. The views are stunning.

The deck from the Congo room has been the site of more than a few proposals and several weddings. The showers (cold water, sorry) are built outdoors with stucco walls, bamboo and heliconias providing some modesty. You hear the waterdrops falling on the heliconia leaves while showering; it's like taking a shower in the bushes. The king and queen-size beds are comfortable, with what have to be the fluffiest pillows in the Osa, and beautifully patterned sheet. It's refreshing after some of the even more basic lodges in the area. Electricity is offered in the deluxe cabins only, and is on only for a few hours in the evenings. Reading lights are weak and there are no lights over the mirrors in the bathrooms.

Meals are inventive and are served in the thatched-roof, open-air restaurant and, unlike many of the laid-back lodges in the area, offer a choice of dishes for breakfast and lunch. Banana pancakes for breakfast, pork chops for lunch, pasta and fish dinners are typical. Wine and beer selection is very basic. There are no other dining or evening entertainment choices in the area.

One of the best things about Bosque del Cabo is the setting, and the guides the lodge employs to bring the surrounding forest to life for guests. When I was there in late 2001, Henry Kantrowitz, one of the founders of the Birding Club of Costa Rica, was a resident guide and offered informative early-morning bird walks (a bargain at $15). His knowledge of birdcalls is astounding. He showed me much more than birds, including poison dart frogs, bats, monkeys, a tayra (weasel-like mammal), and taught me about the flowering trees and shrubs that fill the lodge grounds. Night walks conducted by Brummie Phillip reveal bats, snakes, rainforest frogs and the occasional cat.

The lodge has arrangements with some of the area's top guides and can arrange all the usual tours, include fishing, kayaking, trips into Corcovado and horseback riding. Guided or self-guided trips on the trails through the lodge preserve lead to the beach at Matapalo past two of the most spectacular waterfalls I have seen in Costa Rica. Most guests come for the hiking and bird-watching.

There are four standard and five deluxe bungalows, as well as two isolated houses, one originally built for the owner's mother. They are rented by the week or month (see below).

The lodge is very well-maintained and comfortable and the bungalows have great views, but it is a bit expensive. Considering the lack of hot water and very limited electricity, lodges nearby offer better value.

CASA BLANCA & MIRAMAR
Book through Bosque del Cabo (above)
☎ 506-381-4847
www.bosquedelcabo.com
$1,400 or $1,950/week

These two houses, located on the grounds of Bosque del Cabo Lodge, are unique, charming and beautifully situated. They resemble something out of the *Flintstones* cartoon, with painted snakes climbing columns, and wildlife scenes on the walls. They are isolated and private, and come completely furnished, ready for living, cooking and relaxing.

The houses are two and three bedrooms respectively, and are the nicest I have seen in Costa Rica. The views out to sea high above Cabo Matapalo are astounding. Both houses have hot water and solar panels with battery banks for electricity. The grounds are alive with wildlife. I saw more mammals in the few days I visited than I did over several trips to Corcovado National Park. The management at the lodge will help arrange tours and expeditions, and can make their excellent guides available.

EL REMANSO RAINFOREST BEACH LODGE
Matapalo
☎ 506-735-5569
www.elremanso.com
$190

El Remanso, situated on a bluff overlooking the open Pacific, offers proximity to the primary rainforest of the Osa National Wildlife Refuge, and easy access to the sea. If you happen to be into climbing things, you're in luck. Owner Joel Stewart climbs everything: trees, waterfalls, cliffs, you name it. He offers lessons in rappelling and draws guests interested in experiencing the very top of the rainforest, as well as those simply wishing to spend time relaxing close to nature. There is a zip line on the grounds spanning a picturesque rainforest valley for the adventurous.

With only three cabins, Joel and his Spanish-born wife Belén have the time to make each guest feel special. The cabins are very comfortable, with hot water, 24-hour electricity and fans. They have been designed with comfort in mind: even the hammocks have good-quality reading lights. The windows are screened and each cabin is surrounded by a narrow "ant channel" with gently running water designed to keep crawling insects outside in the forest where they belong.

Rates include a taxi ride to and from the airport in Puerto Jiménez and three meals. The food is prepared to suit the guests. If you have special dietary requirements or preferences you will be carefully catered to. The lodge offers good value for the area and, with only three cabins and numerous repeat visitors, it is not easy to get into. Be sure to reserve well in advance. The lodge is closed in October and November.

Golfito, Zancudo & Pavones

The town of Golfito is a huge draw for Ticos, who come here to indulge in the delights of duty-free shopping. The law requires them to stay overnight to be able to shop duty-free, so there are dozens of inexpensive and usually crowded hotels. The duty-free prices are good for Costa Rica, but no bargain for those used to USA prices. Consequently, the most attractive hotels are a bit out of town. It's not really a town with attractions for travelers, especially considering the amazing beaches and wilderness nearby. If you want to buy a refrigerator, however, Golfito is the place to come.

ESQUINAS RAINFOREST LODGE
In Piedras Blancas National Park, just outside Golfito
☎ /fax 506-775-0901
www.esquinaslodge.com
$180

About 10 years ago, the government of Austria, along with a group of local farmers, initiated a program to purchase land adjacent to Piedras Blancas National Park, donate most of it to the park, and develop a small, ecologically and socially advanced lodge. A 10-room lodge was built at the end of a three-mile-long road, deep in a valley of the forest. Nearby, the Gamba Biological Research Station was established as part of the program.

The lodge is on 19 acres (seven hectares) and is surrounded by the national park. The lodge employs local residents, with the idea of providing income to the area, and reducing illegal logging as a means of support for the local community. The mission of the project is to help the local area by educating and providing a sustainable source of income. Success has made it famous in eco-development circles around the world.

The lodge is not luxurious, but is in such a unique location that any lack of creature comforts can be overlooked. If you are a serious birder you probably already know that the area of Piedras Blancas National Park is a particularly rich area in exotic bird life. Walking around the grounds of the lodge and exploring the nearby forest trails is an eye-opening experience even for people who have no previous interest in birds. The air is alive with brightly colored hummingbirds, trogons, parrots and aricaris.

A pool is set at the edge of primary forest and is filled with naturally filtered water from a mountain stream. They use no chemicals to treat it and it is re-

Osa Peninsula

freshingly cool and much clearer than many fancy hotel pools I have seen. The rooms are large with ceiling fans and hot water and have bamboo rocking chairs on the porches. They are clustered loosely around the open-air dining room/bar/reception building.

Several trails are maintained around the lodge, varying from a mile to several miles in length. Guided tours are some of the most interesting and extensive of any Costa Rican lodge, and include trips to the nearby (and almost inaccessible) Casa Orquídeas, all-day horseback and mountain bike trips, and night hikes. The services of nearby biology researchers are available if you are really serious about learning more about what you are seeing. Some of the hikes are easy; others are long and arduous going over the primary-forested mountains and along the beaches of Golfo Dulce. The mostly Austrian regulars seem up to hiking for six to eight hours through the forest. As mentioned, the area is a special destination for birders, and trained ornithologists are available for educational talks and tours. Long-term researchers and students are accommodated at the nearby Austrian biological research field station.

The food is an unexpected delight. The chef is a Brazilian and serves Austrian, Brazilian, and local specialties presented in artful displays that are almost too beautiful to eat. You can watch parrots munching plantains and caimans lurking in a pond while you enjoy your meal. I had trouble staying focused on my breakfasts in the mornings, as dozens of exotic birds perching nearby had me reaching for my camera instead of my coffee cup.

As I said, this is not a fancy lodge but is quite comfortable and is in such a tranquil and special setting. It is a place I hope to come back to again and again.

GOLFITO SAILFISH RANCH

A boat ride from Golfito
☎ 506-381-4701; fax 506-775-0750
www.golfitosailfish.com

Pool, bar, tournament-quality fishing gear, new boats, waterfall.

ROY'S ZANCUDO LODGE

Zancudo
☎ 506-776-0008
www.royszancudolodge.com

Looks okay but very fishy clientele.

TISKITA JUNGLE LODGE

Near Pavones
☎ 506-296-8125; fax 506-296-8133
www.tiskita-lodge.co.cr
$240 (two walks also included)

The Tiskita Jungle Lodge, revered by birders and wildlife enthusiasts, and fascinating for anyone interested in tropical fruits, is set in over 550 acres (215 hectares) of forest reserve and an experimental fruit farm. About 30 years ago, Costa Rican Peter Aspinall moved back to the area from the US, and started converting a cattle ranch into a farm to grow and experiment with exotic tropical fruits. When he realized it was going to be difficult to make a living selling star fruit, mangosteens and Java plums, he decided to see if he could lure visitors to experience the local bird life and other wildlife. He has 14 cabins well spread out on ridges bordering his farm at the edge of an extensive primary forest.

Osa Peninsula

The lodge is comfortable and offers a unique chance for birders and wildlife enthusiasts to stay in one of the most remote areas of Costa Rica. Rooms are furnished with two single beds and have 24-hour electricity, fans and hot water. Bathrooms are outside the bedrooms (but private), and you can watch monkeys and toucans while showering or brushing your teeth. The occasional skink watches you as you go about your ablutions.

Food is served buffet-style and is wonderful, Costa Rican *tipico*. This is as good a chance as you'll get to sample authentic Tico *ollas* and *empanadas*. The refrigerator is always stocked with exotic fruit juices. Just help yourself.

Although remote, the lodge is only minutes away from one of the most dreamed about surfing spots in the world. Made famous by the movie *Endless Summer*, nearby Pavones draws serious surfers from around the world. There are no organized fishing or diving operators in the area, although the lodge can arrange tours. Tiskita is about a two-hour drive into Golfito. It's an hour to Zancudo and big-time fishing.

Because of its location, Tiskita offers some unique tours. If you like fruit, try a tasting walk through the experimental orchard. Fruits you can sample (in season) include star fruit, several varieties of mangoes, sugar apples, sapote, mangosteen, a wide selection of different guavas and, my favorite, unusual citrus crosses. I hauled away a huge sack of extra-large limes crossed with grapefruit. They are very good for daiquiris.

Guides aligned with the lodge are bird specialists. Tiskita is involved in a Ridley turtle hatchery, and in a program releasing endangered scarlet macaws into the wild. Visitors can participate as volunteers in these programs and are encouraged to help out in

Peter's reforestation projects. Kayaking, snorkeling and all the usual tours can be arranged. Visits to the tide pools include a refreshing dip in a jungle pool at the base of a waterfall.

Getting to Tiskita Jungle Lodge can be either easy or adventurous. The lodge has its own airstrip and flights can be arranged from San José or Golfito. It is about a 10-minute hop from Golfito by five-seater. There is a 25-pound weight restriction on baggage. Driving, however, is a long slog over very poor roads. In the rainy season, the roads turn to chocolate pudding. A few signs point the way as you drive there, but several intersections leave you guessing as to which way to go. As the great Yogi Berra once said, "When you come to a fork in the road, take it." Very few people arrive by car. The website gives a good idea of what the lodge is like, but can leave you puzzled as to where it actually is. On a map, look south of Golfito, just past Pavones to Punta Banco along the peninsula toward Panama.

Vacation Rentals

☆ DRAKE BAY RAINFOREST CHALET
Drake Bay
☎ 506-382-1619, 881-63-142-1536 (sat phone)
www.drakeholiday.com; eyeshine@racsa.co.cr
$1,150 per week

Tracie Stice, The Bug Lady (see *Sunup to Sundown*, page 334), rents a beautifully designed and furnished small house, in the rainforest by a waterfall. It is remote. You have to walk about 45 minutes from Drake Bay up a jungle trail to get there, but the house is situated in the middle of an unspoiled tropical forest.

Osa Peninsula

The cabin is imaginatively built from local hardwoods and is decorated in tropical style. The bathroom and kitchen are tiled and are fully and appointed. The place is small, suitable for a couple who wants privacy amid the forest primeval. There's hot water, electricity, and satellite TV, and the price includes transportation from San José, a day tour to Caño and Corcovado National Park, a night tour, and complimentary guide service on local coastal and inland foot trails, as well as a fully-stocked-with-food kitchen. This would be a unique honeymoon cottage for the adventurous.

CASAS SOMBRERO
Near Matapalo, by Sombrero Beach
☎ 506-735-5062; fax 506-735-5043
www.casassombrero.com
From $600, per week for four people

The manager at Casas Sombrero seemed more interested in surfing than in making our stay comfortable.

Casas Sombrero, offering the Adams Family House and Casa McConnell, is a good example of what to look out for when booking a vacation rental without being able to inspect it beforehand. The houses are interesting but poorly maintained and have only recently been converted to rentals. I rented one of the houses in 2001, and found the website information to be misleading. It neglected to mention there was no hot water, rare electricity, and the "entire" house available was actually to be shared by the Tico caretaker and his family.

When we arrived, we found the three "fully furnished kitchens" included only one broken refrigerator. The manager gave us two ice chests instead and offered to pay for the ice. Of course, we had to go to town to buy the ice every other day since the manager had no car and no way to get to town and back other than hitchhiking. Perhaps by the time this is published the owners will have made substantial price reductions or substantial improvements in the properties and amenities. We made the best of a bad situation and had a great holiday. The Tico family turned out to be charming and fun to have around. We very quickly got used to cold showers and candle-light.

Best Places to Eat

Alive Prices

Prices are given in US $, and are the average price for an entrée or main course, per person, before taxes and service charges are added. Although Costa Rican law says restaurants must show prices on the menu with taxes included, many do not. Menus that include taxes almost always say so.

Drake Bay

Most of the lodges are all-inclusive. The town near Drake Bay has nothing more than a pulpería (basic grocery store). You're pretty much stuck with what the lodges serve up, but that is definitely not a hardship. The lodges all serve great and even memorable food.

Golfito, Zancudo & Pavones

There are no restaurants in Golfito aimed at tourists and few offer anything more than very basic Tico meals. Zancudo and Pavones have a couple of mildly interesting eateries that are more interesting to hang out in than to eat at.

Osa Peninsula

COCONUT CAFE
In Golfito, across from the main dock
☎ 506-775-0518
American and Mexican
$6

The Coconut Café, American-operated, offers the best coffee and fresh juices for miles around. Breakfast and lunch range from burgers to burritos.

MACONDO
Zancudo
☎ 506-776-0157
$10
Italian

A truly Italian restaurant with antipasto, homemade pasta, brick oven bread and seafood. Macondo also sells its own handmade cheeses and sausages.

LA PINA
Pavones
No phone
$10
Italian

Very popular with locals and tourists, La Piña has a pure Italian menu with tortellini, seafood and pizza from their wood-fired oven. They offer a wide variety of sauces over homemade pasta. Great lobster dinners are only $12.

Puerto Jiménez

There are no fancy, or even kind of fancy, places to eat in Puerto Jiménez. Seafood is mostly imported from San José, but can be good. There are not a lot of choices. Most of the lodges serve excellent meals, but it's still nice to hang about in town a bit and check out the restaurants.

RESTAURANT AGUA LUNA
Near the dock in Jiménez
☎ 506-735-5033
$10
Chinese/Costa Rican

This lagoon-side restaurant offers a cross between Chinese and typical Costa Rican dishes, with an emphasis on seafood. The soups are big and the chop suey, although not particularly authentic, is good. Large fried rice dishes with shrimp, chicken, and a variety of other surprising ingredients are economical, and attract both budget and middle class tourists.

The restaurant is huge and is probably never completely full. The best tables are all the way in the back by the lagoon. The sound system makes possible some raucous evenings. You will be able to tell this is going on several blocks before you get there and have a chance to make another dining choice for the evening, if raucous is not your thing. They actually have tablecloths.

BLUE MARLIN
Two blocks off the main drag in Jiménez
No phone
$6
Seafood, Mexican

The Blue Marlin is one of the better places to eat in town. It is clean and friendly, although the meat can be a bit tough and the fish soup rather fishy. Carnitas and the fish specials are good. The music selection is the best in town, although the staff is a bit too enthralled by blaring MTV from the TV hanging over the bar. The young staff speak good English, seems interested in their visitors, and wander around the tables for a chat.

Osa Peninsula

PIZZA ROCK
By the soccer field in Jiménez
☎ 506-735-5295
$6
Pizza

Offering pizzas in the American-style in a funky reggae atmosphere. The owners speak English, Spanish, French and German. They also sell French bread for take-away. The place is a bit rundown but, although pleasant, the whole town is too, so what can you do?

RESTAURANTE CAROLINA
On the main street, just down from the police station
☎ 506-735-5007
$6
Fresh seafood, hamburgers and Costa Rican fare

The chow is okay (certainly not anything to get excited about), and the service is moderately friendly. But, this is the most happening restaurant in town. It's the local hangout for expats and people getting off the bus trying to figure out what to do next. It is a good place for people watching. All the local expats going to seed in the tropics (and all the other ones too) spend time at Carolina's.

If you like to start drinking beer at nine in the morning, Carolina's is the place to do it.

It is open-air and has cheesy plastic table covers. The beer is cold and comes with a glass of ice in the local style. You can throw out the ice and use the glass, or grit your teeth and do what the locals do – pour the beer over the ice and drink it. There is a phone booth right out front and the place next door sells phone cards (*tarjetas telefónicas*). An EcoTrex office is in the restaurant, so you can sort out some adventures while soaking up the atmosphere. I usually get the fish of the day. For breakfast, *gallo pinto* (beans and rice) comes with an omelet, bacon ,or with meat. If you spend any time at all in the Puerto Jiménez area, you'll end up at Carolina's.

JUANITA'S BEER GARDEN
On the main street
$6
Mexican

The burritos and such are interesting, but you certainly won't be writing home about them, at least not in a positive light. What you get sometimes has little resemblance to the descriptions on the menu and the food can be cold when it arrives.

When I was at Juanita's, the "beer garden" served no alcohol and had no plants or trees. No beer and no garden.

"Nachos Borrachos" (drunken nachos) consisted of soggy tortilla chips (cold), with a dab of ground beef (cooked but cold), cheese, and, inexplicably, piles of shredded cabbage. Not very appetizing. The salsa is thin and watery. The enchiladas I ordered came on a small plate all by themselves. My brother ordered the same thing but his came with a huge pile of (cold) rice and (cold) beans for the same price. When we asked what was going on we received a cute shrug. I endured the place two times to be sure I did not simply see it the first time on a bad day. I hate to totally pan a restaurant without being pretty sure of myself. Other travelers I talked to had similar opinions. I won't go back.

☆ BUENA ESPERANZA
15 km (nine miles) from Jiménez on
the road to Matapalo
$6
Eccentric

Also known as Martina's this is a great local, open-air hangout. Martina is a cool-looking German lady who prepares fabulous "mystery" sandwiches, quiche, and, occasionally chicken and rice. She does not always have entire meals ready but you can ar-

Osa Peninsula

range for some of the best ones in the area if you ask in advance. She makes wonderful German bread. Local surfers and other expats hang out here and provide a lively atmosphere. This place is a favorite of mine.

A to Z

Banks

There are few banks in the area other than Bank of Costa Rica in Palmar Norte, Puerto Jiménez and Golfito.

Emergency Medical

There is a small clinic in near Drake Bay in the village of Aguajitas.

Police

911 in all areas.

Post Office

Have your lodging take care of any mail, although beware, the postal service is unreliable and slow.

Tourist Information

There are no impartial tourist information services in the area. Most tours are arranged through lodges and hotels. Since transportation is often difficult, most tour operators will pick you up and drop you off at your hotel. Local lodges and hotels will usually be able to give you good information about tourism opportunities.

Driving information is often contradictory – even asking at the local police station (Fuerza Publica) can get you misleading, or just plain wrong information. Ticos hate to say they don't know, so be sure to ask several people about driving conditions before starting out on a long drive. In Puerto Jiménez, Isabel (☎ 506-232-7883) is the Travelair representative and serves as a focal point for efficiently getting things done, and knows what is going on in the area. Stop by or call her and you may be surprised by how she can help you with your plans and tour logistics.

The **Costa Rican Tourist Board** (ICT) has an office at Avenida 4, Calles 5/7 in downtown San José and one at the airport. They offer some basic tourist maps and books. ☎ 506-223-1733, fax 506-223-5452; In the US, 800-343-6332; www.tourism-costarica. com.

Osa Peninsula

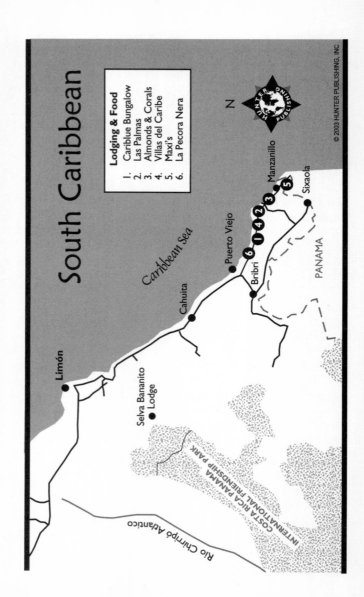

South Caribbean

Lodging & Food

1. Cariblue Bungalow
2. Las Palmas
3. Almonds & Corals
4. Villas del Caribe
5. Maxi's
6. La Pecora Nera

South Caribbean

Overview

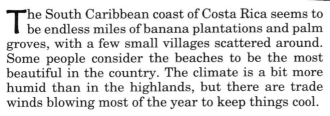

The South Caribbean coast of Costa Rica seems to be endless miles of banana plantations and palm groves, with a few small villages scattered around. Some people consider the beaches to be the most beautiful in the country. The climate is a bit more humid than in the highlands, but there are trade winds blowing most of the year to keep things cool.

A large number of Caribbean people live here and their influence is apparent in the food and dialect. A few indigenous Bribri and other Indians still live in small communities in the forests.

Reports of theft and drugs have hurt tourism in the area over the last few years, but people are realizing the problem was probably exaggerated, and visits are starting to pick up. The area is a slow-moving paradise with some of the best beaches in Costa Rica, dense tropical rainforests, parks, birds, fishing, and wonderful reefs for snorkeling and diving. The area south of Puerto Viejo to Manzanillo is gradually recovering from the bad press and has several comfortable hotels and great restaurants.

The town of **Limón** should be avoided if possible. It is an unpleasant, rundown seaport with little of interest for tourists. A number of cruise ships stop there but passengers are quickly bused off to tours of the nearby parks, rafting trips, jungle walks, etc.

The area around Cahuita and Puerto Viejo has gained a reputation as being a place where European and North American women can come to arrange a romantic holiday liaison with black Costa Rican beach dudes (the women are expected to pay for this service). Perhaps this is the reason many women complain they are often aggressively accosted by young men who seem to think that such a career is just the thing for them. I saw a number of women strolling on the beach with small canisters of Mace clipped on their bikinis – just in case.

> ## ⚡ WARNING
>
> Cannabis and cocaine are a definite part of the South Caribbean scene. Even if you look quite square you may be approached with offers to buy a smoke outside bars in Cahuita and Puerto Viejo. Keep in mind that buying, as well as possessing, even small amounts of drugs is against the law in Costa Rica.

The country is actually quite conservative and, even though you see lots of young guys with dreadlocks hanging about, smoking cannabis is not tolerated by 99% of the locals. If smoking grass is part of your holiday plans, this is the right area, but smoking openly is likely to lead to trouble for you. This is not Amsterdam. Just because you are a well-off tourist doesn't mean the police will cut you any slack. Enjoy the beach and the sun, the beer and the rum, and take your next vacation in Holland or Switzerland.

Most of the tourist action is down south below Cahuita and Puerto Viejo. **Manzanillo** is not much more than a couple of large shacks, and some fishing boats pulled up on the beach, but has a great atmosphere and a wonderful restaurant. (See Maxi's in *Best Places to Eat*, page 404). The **Gandoca-Manzanillo Wildlife Refuge** can be enjoyed easily by going to Manzanillo, leaving your car, and walking the trails along the beach and over the cliffs through the park.

Climate

Hot, muggy and wet is the usual situation, with between 300 and 500 centimeters of rain annually. That's about 15 feet of rain. But that's part of what makes the humid forest region so lush, green and interesting.

There is not really much of a dry season but, if you're lucky, you might get not much more than short, sharp tropical thunderstorms from November through January. Hurricane season runs from September through November but, in the last one hundred years, there has been only one direct hit by a hurricane: Martha in 1969. Average temperatures are 86°F during the day and 70°F at night. A good-quality, lightweight rain jacket is a must. The heaviest rain is from May through August, and there is another period of heavier than usual rain in December and January.

You can usually count on a steady breeze along the coast to keep things cool.

Getting Here

There is an airport in Limón and taxi service is available south to the beach areas. If you look at a map and decide to take what seems to be the shortest route from San José through Cartago and Turrialba to Limón, you will spend an extra couple of hours winding around on small mountain roads through farmland. If you go through

Guapiles on Route 32, your journey will be much quicker and more enjoyable, and you will get to see a bit of Braulio Carrillo National Park.

Several towns have the name Puerto Viejo, so be sure you know which one you are going to before you start out.

If you want to take a sidetrip to Barva volcano, you could take the longer route I just suggested you avoid. The side trip and longer route can add as much as four more hours to what should be a three-to-four hour trip to Cahuita.

Shortly before you get to Guapiles on Route 32, there is a huge sign pointing left to Puerto Viejo. Be sure you keep going straight toward Guacimo, Siquierres and Limón. Realize that turning left at this point would take you to Puerto Viejo de Sarapiquí, which is inland; not to Puerto Viejo de Talamanca, which is on the coast. To make things even more confusing, Puerto Viejo de Talamanca is often referred to as Puerto Viejo de Limón. Many people use the name "Limón" to refer to the whole area – not just the town.

Getting Around

Getting around the southern Caribbean area is easy. There's really only one road, the beautiful **Coconut Highway**, and it is paved for almost its entire length. You don't need a four-wheel-drive; a regular car will do fine. There are a couple of little side roads going to small villages and the main road takes a turn to the right just before Puerto Viejo heading toward Bribri, Sixaola and the border with Panama. The only reason to go down there (besides going to Panama) is to visit the gallery of painter Fran Vazquez just before Bribri, or to get into the Gondoca-Manzanillo Wildlife Refuge from the back side. This is a good area to go extra slow in.

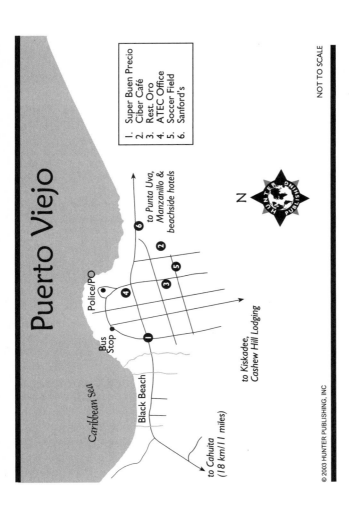

Puerto Viejo

Caribbean Sea

Black Beach

Bus Stop

Police/PO

to Cahuita
(18 km/11 miles)

to Kiskadee,
Cashew Hill Lodging

to Punta Uva,
Manzanillo &
beachside hotels

1. Super Buen Precio
2. Ciber Café
3. Rest. Oro
4. ATEC Office
5. Soccer Field
6. Sanford's

N

NOT TO SCALE

© 2003 HUNTER PUBLISHING, INC

There's not as much traffic here as in other parts of the country. People tend to lollygag about in the middle of the road on bicycles and on foot.

Just because you're blasting along in your car and want to get by doesn't mean people will be in a hurry to get out of the middle of the road. You may find yourself waiting with your foot on the clutch while mere pedestrians leisurely finish a conversation before moving out of the way. Relax. You're not in a hurry, anyway. Wave at them and you'll get a smile in return. Honk at them and you'll get puzzled looks.

Rental Cars

Most people rent a car in San José and drive down. There is little need for four-wheel-drive vehicles in the South Caribbean area. The majority of roads (there are not many) are paved.

 # Sunup to Sundown

Seven-Day Itinerary

The laid-back atmosphere of the South Caribbean means you need to take some time to float down into the scene and get comfortable. Let your hair grow, put your shorts on, and wear your flip-flops. You won't need real shoes here unless you are going for a walk in the forest (in which case I suggest rubber boots). You can drive the whole area in an hour or so, but take your time; go slow; ride a bike; walk on the beach. You don't really need a map or much in the way of directions: there's really only one road.

Days 1 & 2

If you are serious about wildlife or tropical ecology, and can live a night or two without electricity or hot water, you should spend the first two nights in **Selva Bananito Lodge** (see page 394). Drive down from San José and start doing everything slowly.

Day 3

Get up at a leisurely hour and head slowly down the coast to **Cahuita**. Check into the beachside lodge of your choice, put on your bathing suit and take a long, long walk on the beach. Maybe make plans to fish or go scuba diving the next day.

Day 4

Stay in the same place and get up at an even more leisurely hour. If you can't bear to simply veg out on the beach, arrange for a rafting trip on the Pacuare, or bicycle around a bit. Rent a boogie board or surf-board.

Day 5

Get up before the lodge stops serving breakfast, take another walk on the beach, pack up and head south-east to another beachside lodge somewhere near Puerto Viejo. Go to the beach in front of the lodge. Eat lunch at **The Garden** (page 404), and indulge in one of the many tours available in the area. Perhaps try some kayaking, but be sure to go to the beach again. Go to bed early.

Day 6

The surf can be quite rough. Undertows and rip tides claim victims on both the Caribbean and the Pacific coast.

Get up early and go fishing, scuba diving or whichever of the tours or activities you told yourself you would do in the area. You only have one day left and you haven't done much of anything besides lie about on the beach! Eat lunch at **Maxi's** (see page 404) at the end of the road in Manzanillo.

Day 7

Get up early, drive all the way to the end of the road, past Maxi's, and walk on the trail along and above the beach through **Gandoca-Manzanillo Wildlife Refuge**. The views of the headlands and beaches are unforgettable. Maybe have lunch at Maxi's again, and then head back to San José.

Beaches

Beautiful beaches stretch almost uninterrupted all along the southeast Caribbean coast, from the airport outside Limón, all the way to the Panamanian border. Some say the most beautiful beaches in Costa Rica are those on the Caribbean side – especially the ones in the far southeast near Manzanillo.

The beaches on this side are generally a lighter shade than the Pacific beaches, but there are almost black sand beaches in several places, notable just before Puerto Viejo. Coconut palms lean over, heavy surf pounds, and the sun shines down. There is generally lots of driftwood and other junk washed up on shore, but this just adds character. Beaches tend to be separated by rocky points, usually with coral outcrops and snorkeling spots near the points. These coral areas are really the only places in Costa Rica where you can find true coral reefs. Many of the beaches have barrier coral reefs offshore, but they don't really shelter the beaches like they do in the Cayman Islands or the Florida Keys.

Be very careful about where you swim. Surfing is excellent, with the hardcore congregating in Cahuita, Puerto Viejo and Manzanillo.

Diving & Snorkeling

The best diving and snorkeling in Costa Rica is found in the southeast corner of the country on the Caribbean side. **Cocos Island**, about 555 km (350 miles) out in the Pacific, is probably the best-known Costa Rican diving area. The area south of Manzanillo, offshore from the Gandoca-Manzanillo Wildlife Refuge, is not nearly so well known as a dive destination. However, it has hundreds of deep and shallow coral reef dive sites which are rarely visited. There are only three dive operators in the area.

Many visitors expect to be taken on snorkeling trips to the lesser-quality but still good reefs around **Cahuita** and the **Cahuita National Park**. Many reefs are south of Manzanillo, and are hard to get to, so are not frequently dived. There are no ports for small boats so there are no large, well-equipped dive boats.

Many people dismiss diving in the area, explaining that the 1991 earthquake raised the level of the reefs several feet above sea level, and killed most of them by exposing them to air. Runoff from banana plantations is also blamed for ruining reefs in the area.

While both the earthquake and agricultural runoff have certainly damaged some reefs, there are many square miles of thriving reefs and several hundred known diving sites.

Although the earthquake raised some reef areas, others were lowered and are still thriving. Of course, agricultural runoff has not helped the reefs any, but reports of the death of the reefs in the south Caribbean side of Costa Rica have been greatly exaggerated. The reefs are in good shape and the diving is excellent. Visibility, although affected by rainy season runoff and storms, is far superior to the visibility on the Pacific side of the country. The best diving season is August, September, October, but January, February and March can also be good.

There are some snorkelers and glass-bottomed boats visiting Cahuita National Park. Most diving trips organized from Cahuita usually involve a road trip to Manzanillo and the reefs off Gandoca-Manzanillo Wildlife Refuge. The best diving is off Gandoca-Manzanillo Wildlife Refuge and farther south. Call the following operators for trips.

Aquamor Adventures, in Manzanillo (☎ 506-759-0612, aquamor1@racsa.co.cr), run by PADI instructor Greg Larkin, organizes scuba and snorkeling trips to the best sites in southeast Costa Rica. His operation is based as close to the good diving as you can get and he's been here for 10 years. He will arrange shore dives, dives from kayaks and open water dives. PADI certification courses are offered. It's $55 for a two-tank dive with rental equipment.

Los Delfines Watersports, in Punta Cocles (☎ 506-750-0539, www.los-delfines-watersports.com), is run by two Austrians. They offer basic and advanced scuba and snorkeling trips to Cahuita and

Gandoca reefs. The cost is $55 for a two-tank dive with rental equipment.

Reef Runners, (☎ 506-750-0480, arrecife55@hotmail.com) on the Puerto Viejo waterfront near the police station, have PADI-certified instructors and offer certification courses for Discover Scuba (resort course), Open Water Diver, Advanced Open Water Diver, Rescue Diver and Divemaster. They also offer three tank dives. You can call them, or if you're lucky, just show up at 9:30 am for the regular daily dive trip. The cost is $55 for a two-tank dive with rental equipment.

Fishing

Charter fishing is not well developed in the South Caribbean area. There is snook and tarpon fishing, but only a few guides really know how to put you on the fish. There are no harbors in the area. Only very small boats can be dragged across the beach exist.

The **Laguna Gandoca**, in the extreme southeast end of the coast, offers some very interesting possibilities. There are two outlets to the sea from the lagoon with prospects for snook and tarpon. The lagoon gets as deep as 150 feet in some places and, according to fisheries biologists, serves as a spawning area for tarpon and snook. You may be able to talk a local fisherman into going out in his *lancha* and can expect to catch snapper, jack and possibly a dorado or small tuna. An outfit called **Bacalao & Willi**, located in Manzanillo at the very end of the road (☎ 506-759-0714, 506-759-0716), can take you out trolling near shore and on tarpon and snook expeditions to Gondoca Lagoon. The cell phone connections in the area are poor, so keep trying if you don't get an answer right away.

Tennis

Hotel Las Palmas, just north of Manzanillo, has a couple of run-down tennis courts. Other than that, there is no tennis in the area.

Kayaking

Many of the area hotels have kayaks available for guests, but keep in mind that the surf is pretty high most of the time. **Aquamor Adventures**, in Manzanillo (☎ 506-759-0612, aquamor1@racsa.co.cr), offers sea kayaking and trips to Gondoca Lagoon. They can arrange for you to be taken along the coast by launch to the lagoon area. They can also set you up with kayaks for snorkeling trips on the near shore reefs. These guys have been doing kayak outfitting in the area for quite some time, and can handle beginners and the most experienced and ambitious enthusiasts.

Tours

 Most hotels and lodges can arrange for any tours offered in the area. **Costa Rica Expeditions** (☎ 506-257-0766, www.costaricaexpeditions.com) and **Costa Rica Nature Escape** (☎ 506-257-8064, www.crnature.com) can make all arrangements for tours in advance.

Viajes Tropicales (☎ 506-758-2410) offers a variety of tours all over the south Caribbean area, including trips to all the area parks. **Catamaran Tours** (☎ 506-750-0624, www.catamaran-tours.com) runs two tours for viewing dolphins and the reefs.

They provide snorkeling equipment, meals and transportation from your hotel.

The **Botanical Garden**, just outside Puerto Viejo (☎ 506-750-0046), has extensive trails and offers guided walks to see fruit trees, orchids, rainforest ornamentals and has a tree house.

Cacao Tour (☎ 506-750-0075), between Playa Chiquita and Punta Uva, operates its own chocolate factory. They organically grow their own cacao, the plants that have the seeds chocolate is made from, and do fascinating three-hour tours of the whole operation. Call for an appointment, as they don't do the tours on a regular schedule.

Seahorse Stables, in Puerto Viejo (☎ 506-750-0468), offers rides to the jungle and on the beach from $35 per person. You can take longer trips to the area southeast of Manzanillo, or all the way to Gondoca and visit the lagoon. Moat of the area hotels will send you to these guys.

Shop Till You Drop

South of Limón

On the road toward Panama, just before you get to Bribri, the studio of painter **Fran Vazquez** sits by the side of the road. Look for his sign. Expect to see amazing primitive jungle and nature scenes done in oils and acrylics. It's worth the trip down just to visit the studio.

Cahuita

In general, the shopping is pretty poor in Cahuita. There are a few people selling beads and baubles from sidewalk stands and a few small souvenir shops with the usual beachwear and carved toucans.

Check out **Mr. Big J** near the park entrance in Cahuitahas. It has the largest selection in town of T-shirts, bathing suits, wraps, dresses, jewelry made from seeds and shells, postcards and the ubiquitous carved toucans.

Puerto Viejo

You will find the usual small stands on the street selling jewelry made from bits of shells and small pipes. There are only a couple of places to buy souvenirs and crafts.

ARENA Y SOL
Puerto Viejo
☎ 506-750-0526

They have sculptures, pictures, things made out of bamboo and coconut, T-shirts and toucans among the bathing suits and beach wraps.

CASA SISTAR
Puerto Viejo
☎ 506-750-0394

French artist Natasha specializes in ceramic mosaic creations, but also creates mobiles and lamps from things from the sea. She also carries the work of other local artists. No toucans.

SENSEMAYA ART BOUTIQUE
Playa Cocles
☎ 506-750-0151

A better-than-average selection of local arts and crafts, with no toucans.

After Dark

Bars, Discos & Nightclubs

The nightlife in the south Caribbean area tends toward open-air bars and discos. Expect a young crowd doing their thing to tunes played by DJs. There is lots of beer and rum drinking going on.

Cahuita

COCO'S BAR
Cahuita across from Salon Sarafina.

Reggae and surfer dude place.

SALON SARAFINA
Cahuita across from Coco's Bar.

NATIONAL PARK RESTAURANT
Cahuita near the park entrance.
☎ 506-755-0244

Puerto Viejo de Talamanca

EL LOCO NATURAL
In the center of Puerto Viejo
☎ 506-750-0263

Occasional live music with food. Closes at a very early 10 pm.

SODA TAMARA (UPSTAIRS)
Puerto Viejo

☆ JOHNNY'S PLACE
Puerto Viejo near ATEC.

Featuring a DJ mix every night, with a large dance floor and occasional live acts.

STANDFORD'S
Puerto Viejo near Salsa Brava.

Reggae, dub, rap, loud.

Best Places to Stay

Alive Prices

Prices are based on double occupancy during high season, and given in US $. Taxes and meals are not included, unless so noted. Hotels and lodges marked with a ☆ are my personal favorites. "The Best of the Best" choices earn their title by offering top-quality lodging and services.

South of Limón

BEST OF THE BEST

SELVA BANANITO LODGE
Past Bananito Sur. Call for directions.
☎ 506-253-8118; fax 506-280-0820
www.selvabananito.com
$200, inclusive meals, taxes, transportation from Bananito, and some activities

Selva Bananito is one of the most inspiring lodges in Costa Rica as an interesting alternative for responsible nature tourism. It is located at the end of a long, rough logging road at the edge of Parque International La Amistad biosphere, Latin America's largest protected area of virgin forest. For anyone with a more-serious-than-average interest in tropical ecology, Selva Bananito offers a variety of rain forest activities. You get the privilege of experiencing a relatively undisturbed forest and learning about sustainable land use in the lowland tropics. It is uniquely situated for bird watchers. It covers Caribbean lowlands and highlands, and is one of the few places where you can see sun bitterns and great jacamars. Green macaws are occasionally spotted.

Sofia and Jurgen Stein built the lodge on part of the old family farm. They practice low-impact agriculture and cattle management, using approximately a third of 3,500 acres (1,000 hectares). The remaining two-thirds of the land is a forest preserve. It is used by researchers to study one of the few remaining pristine forest areas on the Caribbean side of Central America.

Renowned biologist Barry Hammel discovered two new species while doing research in the preserve. Reforestation projects are tailored for visiting school and special interest groups. Students from Kirkwood College in Iowa and England come to study ecology and biology. Guests have the opportunity to meet and work with students and scientists in an informal setting as they conduct their research.

The hikes and activities are a bit more adventurous than in most Costa Rican nature lodges. Waterfall rappelling, tree climbing, observation from canopy platforms and zip-line tours, are fit into day-long hikes and horseback rides. Although many people don't stray far from the lodge, since they can add significantly to their bird life from the lodge balcony, strenuous walks through the mountains and rivers of primary forest are a primary activity. Birders, orchid and bromeliad enthusiasts find the area to be a dream destination.

One of the goals of the lodge is to earn money for community educational efforts to reduce logging and help local ranchers breed more efficient types of cattle. A portion of their revenue is donated to a non-profit foundation, Cuencas de Limón, established for the protection of local watersheds. To minimize impact on the area, the lodge maintains a low profile, with only 11 rooms. There is no electricity, strenuous recycling programs, solar-heated water and water hyacinth septic systems. Few lights are exposed outside in order to minimize the effect on the original inhabitants of the area: mammals, reptiles, birds and insects.

Cabins are beautifully constructed with Germanic precision from salvaged logs. They are spacious, spotlessly clean and quite comfortable. The meals are excellent with wine, beer and coffee available.

Puerto Viejo de Talamanca

ALMONDS AND CORALS
Just north of Manzanillo
☎ 506-272-2024, 506-272-4175; fax 506-272-2220
www.almondsandcorals.com
$85

The name Almonds and Corals is based on the lodge's location in the rainforest at the edge of a beautiful tropical beach. It is nestled among tall trees. Winding wooden walkways connect the rooms, restaurant and reception area to the beach. The area is flat and low. At high tide, the nearby swamp extending underneath some of the walkways brings the smell of swampy, sulfurous decay. At night, the walkways are lined with small open flame lamps giving a lovely appearance to the canopy overhead, but also giving off smoke, reminding me of San José at rush hour, but without the hustle and bustle. Huge trees are everywhere and the beauty of the forest is intimate. Birds and howler monkeys are so close they seem to be guests as well.

Although advertised as a tent camp, there are really no true tents to be found and the lodge is much more comfortable than a campsite. Each of the 23 guest rooms are situated in what in Costa Rica are known as "ranchos." These are raised wooden platforms with a roof and open (but screened) walls. Inside, metal poles have been set up and draped with canvas to form more or less private bedrooms and bathrooms. Although each room is in its own separate rancho, they are close together, and there is not much privacy. You need to fiddle with the tent walls to feel comfortable about adjacent guests not being able to see you taking a shower. The sinks and showers do not have traps so, when the toilet flushes, smelly gurgles emanate from all the drains. Each "room," or rancho, comes with two single beds, a hammock, fan and futon. There is hot water and electricity but, other than these amenities, the rooms are basic. The restaurant serves simple *tipico* meals with a smile. Breakfast is adequate and is not included in the price.

The beach in front of the lodge is stunning. Although definitely not safe for swimming (you can see the vicious tide rips), walks along the palm tree-lined, almost-white sand are a joy. Punta Uva is a good snorkeling spot about a half-mile away. The hotel rents snorkeling equipment, kayaks and bicycles. The lodge also operates the Crazy Monkey Canopy Ride, a zip-line ride running through the forest around the hotel. The cost is $35 and not really worth it.

CARIBLUE BUNGALOWS HOTEL

Playa Cocles, just southeast of Puerto Viejo
☎ /fax 506-750-0057
www.cariblue.com
$70, breakfast included

Europeans usually fill the Cariblue Bungalows, where Italian owner Sandra Zerneri keeps the rooms and grounds spotless. It is comfortable and friendly. The individual hardwood bungalows have king-size beds, fans, mosaic tile bathrooms and privacy. Cariblue is one of the nicest accommodations on the south Caribbean coast, and is in well-maintained gardens across the street from Playa Cocles.

For some reason, North Americans have not yet discovered Cariblue, although Italians, Germans and Swiss come for special weeklong sessions with instructors in yoga and Tai Chi. Call to find out when special activities are planned. As members of the Charming & Nature Hotels of Costa Rica (www. charminghotels.com) they can assist guests in planning trips to other interesting hotels in the country.

The buffet breakfast (included) is the usual juice, fruit, cereal, gallo pinto and scrambled eggs. The evening meals are not to be missed (see *Best Places to Eat*, page 403). Dinner is vastly superior to the slightly pretentious nearby local favorite, Amimodo.

LAS PALMAS

Just northwest Almonds and Corals before Manzanillo
☎ 506-750-0049; fax 506-750-0079
www.laspalmashotel.com
$65

Trouble-plagued Las Palmas has been through some tough times but may have settled down to a comfortable groove by now. The story is different depending on who tells it, but it runs something like this: Originally built by a Czechoslovakian/Canadian, without permits, too close to the beach and in the Gandoca-Manzanillo Wildlife Refuge, the owners were sued and ordered to demolish the property and return the area to its previous condition. The Costa Rican Supreme Court overturned this ruling, so the local powers that be simply deported the owner because he had overstayed his visa. The project was sold and divided. Eventually, another hotel, the Hotel Suerre Caribe, was built on part of the property.

☆ **VILLAS DEL CARIBE**
Just southeast of Puerto Viejo
☎ 506-750-0202, fax 506-750-0203;
reservations, ☎ 506-233-2200, fax 506-221-2801
www.villascaribe.net
$85

Villas del Caribe, in an area deficient in luxury accommodations, qualifies as one of the most comfortable hotels on the southern Caribbean coast. Although a bit dated and in need of a face-lift, the hotel has wonderful two-story rooms, with kitchens and balconies overlooking the beach. Located in 100 acres (40 hectares) of palm grove right by the ocean, you can visit two sandy beaches, snorkel on coral reefs, surf or soak idly in a tide pool within steps of your room. The rooms are large; upstairs bedrooms have king-size beds and ceiling fans, and kitchens are modestly well-equipped. There are hammocks, couches, lounge chairs and comfortable places to lie about. Volleyball, boogie boards, kayaks and other beach toys are to be had for the asking. A thatched bar and restaurant overlook the grounds.

For the money, you get much more than in most other hotels nearby. The ability to make your own meals and keep drinks in your refrigerator makes Vilas del Caribe the best option in the area.

Vacation Rentals

THE WOOD HOUSE
On the grounds of the Cariblue Bungalows Hotel
Playa Cocles just southeast of Puerto Viejo
☎ /fax 506-750-0057
www.cariblue.com
$1,000/week

The Wood House is just a two-minute walk from the sandy Playa Cocles, a good spot for surfing and snorkeling.

The Wood House is located by itself at the back of gardens of the Cariblue Bungalows Hotel. It is a two bedroom, two full bath rental house, with king-size beds and complete kitchen. Thecompletely furnished rental can sleep up to seven people. A buffet breakfast at the hotel is included in the price, along with daily maid service. It's a beautiful hardwood bungalow with hammocks and fans.

The convenience of having the hotel services is nice, and the house is located privately enough so you don't really feel part of the hotel (which is pretty quiet anyway). There are several good restaurants in the area and plenty of nature-oriented things to do close by.

Best Places to Eat

Alive Prices

Prices are given in US $, and are the average price for an entrée or main course, per person, before taxes and service charges are added. Although Costa Rican law says restaurants must show prices on the menu with taxes included, many do not. Menus that include taxes almost always say so.

South of Limón

There are almost no restaurants of any type before you get to Cahuita. A couple of sodas and a *gasolinera* are all you will find.

Cahuita

Cheapo places on the beach and a couple of goodies grace Cahuita, but the bulk of the interesting places to eat are farther southeast near Puerto Viejo.

CASA CREOLE
Cahuita, Playa Negra Road
☎ 506-755-0104
$20

Creole (as you might expect), with heavy emphasis on fish.

☆ EDITH SODA Y RESTAURANTE
In Cahuita, turn left at the beach
☎ 506-755-0248
$6
Caribbean vegetarian

Edith's is a Caribbean-style restaurant, including the glacial service, but service is not what Edith is all about. Jamaican specialties like jerked chicken and spicy fish are wonderful. The fish comes whole with a very spicy brown sauce. There are plenty of onions and (look out!) habañero peppers covering the fish. The beer is cold and the place is almost always packed with tourists. They speak very strange English and even stranger Spanish. The restaurant is not much more than a shack with tables, but who cares? The ladies in the kitchen know how to cook.

Puerto Viejo de Talamanca

There is an ever-changing assortment of small restaurants in and around Puerto Viejo. Most are past town to the southeast. The Garden, an old standby, is reportedly now open only for a month or two a year because the owner has other things to do.

AMIMODO

Just south of Puerto Viejo
☎ 506-750-0257
$12
Italian

Amimodo (translated as "in my style") does a good job of preparing local seafood in traditional Italian sways. Filete de pargo alla verde is two generous filets of snapper lightly breaded and fried, covered with spinach and cheese sauce, and then broiled to crisp up the cheese. It's delicious! Spaghetti or penne comes with shrimp or lobster. There are usually five or six nightly specials, including unusual tropical desserts. The wine list is heavy on Italian names, but that is to be expected. It's a welcome change from the ever-present Chilean wines found in most restaurants.

The atmosphere is tropical, but the Italian touch is inescapable. Though the dining room is an open-air, typically Costa Rican affair, Mama and Papa walk around shouting out things in Italian, kissing babies, and generally keep things interesting.

Although the food is quite good and I like the place in general, I have to complain about the larcenous bartender. Although he is scrupulous about carefully measuring out the rum for each daiquiri or other blender drink, he is also scrupulous about making sure each drink is a bit too big to fit in the customers' glass. He helps himself to the leftovers and becomes quite happy toward the end of the evening (at the customers' expense). I cannot forgive a weak daiquiri. Lemonade is quite a bit cheaper.

CARIBLUE RESTAURANT
Just southeast of Puerto Viejo,
in the Cariblue Bungalows
☎ 506-750-0035
www.cariblue.com
$16
Italian

The Cariblue is a hidden gem of a place to eat well. It's not particularly cheap unless you stick to basic pasta (not a bad meal, actually). The cook is Italian and, along with the usual penne and spaghetti, he specializes in locally obtained crustaceans: several kinds of crabs, lobster, langostinos and river shrimp. Portions are enormous. The house wine is reasonably priced Chianti and comes chilled in giant glasses. On one visit I asked for a very small salad, a small seafood sampler and fettuccine with shrimp and mushrooms. The salad plate was about 20 inches (½ meter) in diameter and came mounded high with lettuce, palm hearts, peppers, onions, tomatoes, etc. I had made a small dent in the salad when an even larger plate came out that had critters with claws and spines. I ate a variety of weird shrimp and strange lobster-like crustaceans for what seemed like an hour when the fettuccine arrived. This came on a plate even larger than the other two and, although I tried hard, I was defeated. I probably ate less than half my meal, and I hate to leave anything as good as this food on my plate. Oh yes, there was also a side dish of roasted vegetables in olive oil. I probably spent two hours working on the meal and managed two of the giant glasses of chilled Chianti before giving up.

The restaurant is part of the Cariblue Bungalows Hotel and is in a rancho-style building with a traditional thatched roof. It's a bit off the road and set in a quiet garden. The hotel is small (15 rooms), and few outsiders are aware of how good the food is.

THE GARDEN
Near the beach
☎ 506-750-0069
$10

Asian/Caribbean/veggie may best describe the interesting menu. Vera Mabon is the owner/chef, but reportedly opens the restaurant for only at most two months out of the year.

☆ MAXI'S
End of the road in Manzanillo
$8
Caribbean food

Maxi's is certainly nothing fancy, but the food is great. They sell steak, shrimp, lobster and red snapper by the pound, and that's about it. You make your selection, tell the waiter how big you want it to be, wait a bit, and they bring out a big plate loaded down with food.

The whole snapper comes out lightly fried and is completely covered with a pile of sautéed onions and sweet peppers. Side dishes are the normal fried plantain patties, gallo pinto and cabbage salad. The times I've been there the food has been perfectly prepared and delicious. The restaurant is on the upper floor of a typically Costa Rican open-sided building across the street from the beach. A nice breeze blows through. A small bar downstairs is for those who want to hang out. From any of the tables upstairs you can stare hypnotized out to sea and watch the few bathers and sun-worshipers doing their thing.

Maxi's has a bit of a Caribbean feeling to it, which is probably due to the proximity to the beach, the predominately black skin of the people in the area, and the Reggae sounds. The times I have been there it was quiet, with the music kept discreetly low, but I hear it can get "interesting" on Saturday nights.

MISS SAM
You'll have to ask where it is, or just look for the line of locals.
$3

Get fresh johnnycakes in the evenings. It's not fancy at all, but a local specialty not to be missed.

☆ LA PECORA NERA
Just southeast of Puerto Viejo
☎ 506-750-0490
$16
Italian
Open for lunch and dinner. Closed Mondays.

One common sign of a good restaurant is that they are busy. La Pecora Nera fills up fast, especially on the weekends, so be sure to call ahead for reservations. There is a good reason for the crowd: the food is *estupendo*! Although the standard Italian pasta and other dishes are on the menu, the best things are usually the daily specials, which almost always involve seafood. Owners Dario Giannoni and Andrea Biancardi are known to fishermen up and down the coast as buyers of the very best and most interesting items from the sea. One night when I was there, an enormous 31-pound (14-kilo) snapper fell to the forks of diners, along with octopus, crab, lobster, dorado and other seafood delights. The fish for La Pecora Nera is not trucked in from San José; if local fishermen catch something special they know to bring it by La Pecora Nera, where it will be appreciated (and purchased).

All the meals are prepared and presented beautifully, using fresh ingredients. Locally made cheeses top bruschetta. Fresh fruits and vegetables from local gardens become salads and side dishes. Dario makes his own sausage from Mama's recipe. Daily homemade ravioli includes duck, lobster, cheese or other specialties.

When so much great seafood is on offer, it is easy to ignore mundane items like pizza. But the pizzas here are not the usual stiff pieces of cardboard that come frozen in boxes. Yeasty crusts are made individually and have that chewy texture that is a proper base for a magnificent pizza. They are topped with tomato sauce, amazing cheese and your choice of seafood, vegetables or meats. If you can somehow pass up the seafood, the pizzas really should not be missed.

The restaurant is in a tropical garden in an ordinary Costa Rican rancho: a raised wooden floor with roof and no walls. Candles on the tables quickly burn down in the breeze. The service is real Italian: enthusiastic arm-waving, lots of cheek kissing and smiles. The wine list is not extensive, but the house red and white (both served cold) are good, and a real value at $9 a bottle.

If you are staying anywhere on the southern Caribbean coast you should drive down to La Pecora Nera at least once. I ate there repeatedly and declare it to be the very best restaurant on the coast. It's both the first and the last place I visit when I am in the area.

A to Z

Banks

There are banks in Limón and Puerto Viejo.

Emergency Medical

Call 911 in all areas.

Police

Call 911 in all areas.

Post Office

If you must, have your hotel mail things for you. However, the postal service is slow and unreliable. Tiocs usually use faxes and couriers.

Tourist Information

Your best best is to go to to the official tourist office in San José. Hotels can provide you with most of the info you need.

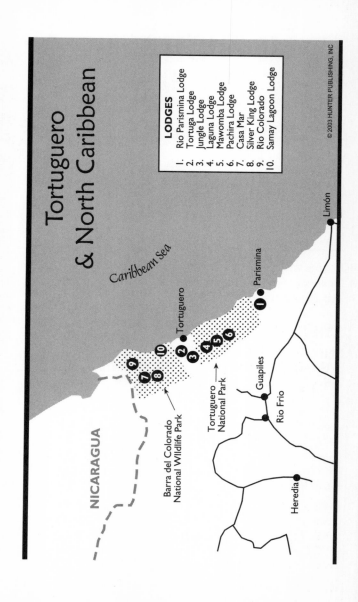

Tortuguero & North Caribbean

LODGES
1. Rio Parismina Lodge
2. Tortuga Lodge
3. Jungle Lodge
4. Laguna Lodge
5. Mawomba Lodge
6. Pachira Lodge
7. Casa Mar
8. Silver King Lodge
9. Rio Colorado
10. Samay Lagoon Lodge

© 2003 HUNTER PUBLISHING, INC

Caribbean Sea

NICARAGUA

Barra del Colorado
National Wildlife Park

Tortuguero
National Park

Tortuguero

Parismina

Limón

Guapiles

Rio Frio

Heredia

Tortuguero &
North Caribbean

Overview

Thick, tropical forests, swamps, lagoons and man-grove wilderness, bordered by over 200 km (120 miles) of deserted beaches, make up the enormous flat plain that is the northeastern corner of the country. This is the least populated part of Costa Rica, and is blessed with **Tortuguero National Park**, as well as **Barra del Colorado National Wildlife Refuge**, two of Costa Rica's largest parks. It's an isolated area with few roads, and is one of Costa Rica's most pristine ecological regions. Although a bit hard to get to, it is probably the best part of the country for bird-watching and wildlife viewing.

Most visitors to the area stay in all-inclusive lodges either in **Parismina**, **Tortuguero** or in **Barra del Colorado**. There are no large cities, and few towns large enough to be considered as 'towns' at all. Wild surf crashes onto the beaches, famous as nesting grounds for loggerhead, green, hawksbill and leatherback turtles. Fishing for snook, tarpon and offshore species is legendary around Parismina, Barra del Colorado and up the Rio Colorado and Rio San Juan.

Tarpon weighing over 75 lbs are a regular catch in this region.

Aside from wilderness and wildlife in the parks and along the canals and rivers, you'll see miles of sugarcane, banana and palm oil plantations as you approach the area by plane or car. The locals are involved in rural pursuits, including agriculture, fishing, poaching, illegal logging and, most recently, providing support for tourism.

Puerto Limón, to the southeast, is the only nearby city of any size. Northeast of Puerto Limón, Costa Rica's Caribbean coast is an almost unbroken, 200-kilometer-long straight line of brown sand beach. It stretches to the Nicaraguan border at Boca de Rio San Juan, the far side of Barra National Wildlife Refuge. Small inlets with vicious riptides occasionally break the long beach. There are no roads along the coast. Navigating the small inlets through the almost continuous wild surf makes offshore travel along the Caribbean difficult. Fortunately, there is a navigable inland waterway, calm and beautiful, running through swamps and canals roughly parallel to the beach all the way along the coast. Small African Queen-style boats carry passengers to and from the lodges, and on wildlife and fishing tours.

A boat tour through on canals and rivers offers one of the best and most comfortable ways to see wildlife in Costa Rica.

Along the west side of the inland waterway are anything from a few feet, to a few miles, of swamp and forest. In back of that, banana plantations, scraggly farms, logging and cattle ranching cut a swath through large areas.

Sportfishermen from Costa Rica are allowed to fish Rio San Juan on the Nicaragua border without clearing Customs. Because it is a border, carry a passport at all times, even on day-trips.

The towns of **Guápiles**, **Guacimo**, **Siquirres** and **Matina** are on Highway 32, between San José and Limón. **Puerto Viejo de Sarapiquí**, on Highway 4, is the only town of any size in the northern part of the region. Rio San Juan borders Nicaragua to the north. Although there have been some border area problems with Nicaragua in the past, there seems to be no current cross-border issues today. Tarpon and snook anglers frequently haul big-uns out of the river, which is the reason most visitors come.

Parismina is a small river-mouth village nestled between swamp and the pounding surf of the Caribbean. Two world-famous fishing and eco-lodges are nearby. As a consequence of haphazard growth and the 1991 earthquake, it seems a cross between run down and hurriedly put together. The village is a couple of miles south of Tortuguero National Park. Tarpon gather in vast surface-feeding schools in the lagoons and just off the beaches January through June. Snook bite well all year, but show a flurry of extra activity between September and December. Turtle worship and nature tours are the other main attractions.

Cheesy tourism-related developments brought by the controversial road to Parismina have contributed to an inevitable trash-strewn, scabby feel that has extinguished any charm the village has ever had. That fate may have been narrowly avoided for Tortuguero. But what can you do? The local population wants development and the park is not staffed well enough to protect itself.

Tortuguero, at the northern edge of Tortuguero National Park, sits on a thin strip of sand at the mouth of the lagoon. The small, plain-looking village feels like something from *The Heart of Darkness*. This is where most people base their explorations of the nearby 19,211-hectare park. The majority of the people in the village work in tourism and the associated businesses that line the edges of the lagoons nearby.

There is a local appreciation of the value and sensitivity of the area and, for the most part, the turtles on the beaches and the animals in the forests are unmolested.

The 119-meter-high (1,700-ft) **Cerro Tortuguero**, a hopefully extinct volcanic crater, is a half-day hike north of the village. It offers a view of the coast and inland lowlands to those who can puff their way up the steep slopes to the top. It is the highest point

412   🌴   Overview

Col Las Lomas de Sierpe, 10 km (six miles) inland from the Tortuguero village, is the highest point in the coastal lowlands.

around except for **Col Las Lomas de Sierpe**, which takes a bit more effort to get to, but is much higher (311 meters/970 feet). Unfortunately, trees obscure the view from the top, but the trip up is worth the effort.

Nearby **Laguna Penitencia** is the route boats take inland to Barra del Colorado. It leads to a nature-lover's dream world of swamp, forest and tiny meandering tea-colored channels through the mangroves. Guides lead you in kayaks, small boats, or even dugout canoes, with quiet, unobtrusive electric motors to see sloths, crocodiles, monkeys, and manatees. Seemingly thousands of rare chestnut-bellied herons and green macaws flit about.

There is a field station and Natural History Visitors Center at the edge of Tortuguero village. There are videos and students on hand to answer questions about the turtle research programs. The center sells books and guides to the area.

Barra del Colorado is a small village at the river mouth near several world-famous fishing lodges. Without even any streets, just sand paths, the word "village" may be a bit too strong. It's in the middle of the much-encroached-upon Barra del Colorado National Wildlife Refuge. The park is the biggest wildlife refuge in Costa Rica (400,000 acres). The size of it, along with the remoteness of the area, means a more pristine environment, with more animals, birds, fish and forest. Few turtles nest here. Although there are times when turtles can be found, most of the nesting occurs farther south in Tortuguero and near Parismina.

Most visitors come for the world-class tarpon and snook fishing, with ecological tourism a distant second. This part of Costa Rica is still not on many tour companies' lists. As in many parks, illegal loggers are stripping the more remote areas. Barra is the end of the line before the border with Nicaragua. Of the three points of focus for exploring the northern Caribbean area, Barra is by far the most remote, the hardest to get to, and has the most wildlife.

Climate

It rains more than one foot every month, so carry the "Costa Rican national flag" (an umbrella).

Hot, muggy and wet is the usual situation with between 300 and 500 centimeters of rain annually; thats's about 15 feet of rain. But this is what makes the humid forest region so lush, green and interesting. You can usually count on a steady breeze along the coast to keep things cool. It is generally pleasant and reasonably comfortable from November through March.

There is not really much of a dry season but, if you're lucky, you might get not much more than short, sharp tropical showers November through March. Hurricane season runs from September through November, but in the last hundred years there has been only one direct hit by a hurricane – Martha in 1969. Average temperatures here are a nice 86°F during the day and 70°F at night. A good-quality, lightweight rain jacket is a must. The heaviest rain is from May through August. There is another period of heavier than usual rain in December and January.

Getting Here

Most visitors fly into Parismina, Tortuguero or Barra del Colorado directly from San José to stay in all-inclusive fishing or eco-lodges. You can also drive from San José to Freeman or Caño Blanco

Tortuguero & North Caribbean

near Parismina, and then transfer to the lodges by boat in less than a day.

Limón is a major Caribbean port with extensive shipping capabilities and a new cruise ship terminal. Visitors to Tortuguero or farther north can arrange transportation along the inland waterway from the nearby town of **Moín**.

There has been some progress rebuilding the famed **Banana Train** running from San José to Puerto Limón. When completed, this should be a popular route for passengers arriving in Limón from cruise ships to access nearby attractions on day-trips. The line was still under construction in mid-2002. In 1991, an earthquake did a serious number on the old rail line. Transportation infrastructure in the area has never fully recovered.

By Car

Driving from San José, after you leave the main highway, the road to Caño Blanco is truly awful. In places the potholes are so big and numerous it looks like some terrible battle has taken place in the middle of the road. There are guarded areas where you can leave a car. It's a half-hour boat trip to Parismina, and an hour or so to Tortuguero. Add another hour or more to get to Barra del Colorado. This is a prime boat trip for wildlife viewing.

It is madness to leave anything at all inside a parked car, even if it's locked.

Highway 32 from San José takes you to Guápiles, and past Siquirres, to Limón. There is no road to the Parismina that is of interest to tourists. There is a village of the same name to the north toward Cairo off Highway 32. Careful! This is not the one you want.

There is currently no road link to Barra del Colorado and the controversial road to Tortuguero was never completed. That road was originally started by loggers and they were encouraged by some local business interests, hoping to stir up tourist traffic to the tiny village and the park. No permission to build the track was sought or given, and it certainly could contribute to deterioration of the park and the surrounding area.

A major earthquake in 1991 destroyed most of the road, phone and electric power infrastructure in this area.

Illegal logging and cattle ranching seriously damaged the western edges of the parks, but has reportedly been stopped.

By Air

There is a small, charter flight-only, airstrip at **Parismina**, and small commercial airports at **Barra** and **Tortuguero**. **Puerto Limón** has the only large airport on the Caribbean coast, with numerous daily flights to San José, and other cities within the country. The flights from San José to Limón, or any of the other airports, are approximately 30 minutes. Most cost $110 round-trip.

By Bus

Express buses run from San José to Puerto Limón hourly. Slower buses (Called *un autobus normal*), stop at towns along the way. It is possible to take a bus to Parismina. Schedules off the main San José-Puerto Limón route can be erratic.

Tortuguero & North Caribbean

Getting Around

Highway 32 is in good condition and runs from San José to Limón. Most other roads in the area are quite limited and all are in poor condition. Canal boats reminiscent of Humphrey Bogart's *African Queen* are the usual way of getting up and down the coast, but there is no scheduled service. Most visitors to the area are flown in to small airports in Parismina, Tortuguero or Barra. Lodges usually pick up their guests at the airports and take them back by boat.

By Car

Highway 32 runs from San José to Limón. Highway 32 and **Highway 4** are the only "good" roads in the area. In Cairo, there is a turnoff to Parismina. As mentioned above, there is an illegally built road from Guápiles heading in the direction of Tortuguero, but construction has been stopped well short of its destination. There are plenty of gas stations along Highway 4 and Highway 32, but it's wise to fill up before venturing off the main roads.

Leisurely nature trips are the main offering of the lodges in Tortuguero.

A trip along the above route (four-wheel-drive only in any season) is a real eye-opener. It is obvious that large areas of the region's forests and lowlands have fallen to illegal loggers and cattle ranchers. There is only a thin veneer of protected forest remaining. Loggers and squatters looking for a few acres to clear or farm are obviously eating into it in a major way.

If you plan to drive to Moín or Parismina to catch a boat, and leave your car, you have a parking problem to consider. While there is guarded parking available at the dock in Moín, certainly nothing left inside the car should be considered safe.

By Boat

The heavy surf and lack of harbors along the coast makes travel offshore in the Caribbean between towns dangerous and impractical. Most transportation is along the inland waterway that parallels the coastline. Although most boats running along the inland waterway are oriented toward taking tourists to and from the all-inclusive lodges, individuals can hire boats and move fairly easily along the inland waterway between Moín, Parismina, Tortuguero and Barra del Colorado.

The trip along the canals and swamps of the inland waterway is not to be missed – it is a prime wildlife-viewing opportunity.

Sunup to Sundown

Seven-Day Itinerary

The best way to enjoy the area is to spend at least three or four days in one of the lodges. This way you have enough to time view wildlife, fish, explore and beachcomb. The fishing lodges around Parismina and Barra del Colorado are aimed directly at hard-core fishermen. They are mad for it and spend upward of 10 hours a day on the water in pursuit of tarpon over 100 pounds and snook over 30 pounds. Many lodges arrange wildlife tours and birding trips by kayak through the lagoons, in addition to the legendary guided fishing expeditions.

Any lodge can help arrange transportation by boat to the other towns on the coast.

The grand tour would be to fly to Parismina and travel by inland waterway from there to Tortuguero and on through Tortuguero National Park, then on to Barra and Barra del Colorado National Wildlife Refuge. You could then take a flight from Barra back to San José, or on to other explorations.

Day 1 & 2

Start in **Parismina**, where guided day-trips for snook or tarpon are an experience not to be missed. Be sure to take your Dramamine if you suffer from seasickness. After spending a couple of days either fishing or exploring the nearby canals, take a boat north to Tortuguero.

Day 3 & 4

Tortuguero offers quite a bit for visitors besides fishing. Most of the lodges cater to eco-tourists and arrange a variety of tours through the nearby **Tortuguero National Park** (page 426). If the season is right, sign up for a nighttime visit to the beaches to observe (discreetly) turtles nesting. This is an experience never to be forgotten. Numbers of visitor to the beaches at night is restricted, so be sure to arrange your trip early.

Guided small boat, kayak or canoe trips through the canals and rivers of the park are one of the highlights of any trip to Costa Rica. The area teems with wildlife. The comfortable boats are an easy way to see it up close. Be sure to go with a guide. Although many of the lodges offer guests the use of canoes and kayaks, you'll see and learn much more if an eagle-eyed guide is on hand to spot and educate.

Take a walk along the beach and through the tiny village. If your lodge is not on the beach side of the lagoon, they will certainly arrange a short ride across. Once again, take a boat through the canals to your next lodge.

Days 5-7

Next visit **Barra del Colorado**. The trip along the canals and rivers between Tortuguero and Barra del Colorado is a spectacular ride. Monkeys, sloths, manatees, river otters and thousands of exotic birds are only a few of the sights. The boat drivers are as fascinated with the wildlife as you are. They spontaneously stop and point out the wonders of their world as you pass by.

> ### ☺ TIP
>
> If you head outside the canals, the sea can be rough. Take Dramamine if you are prone to seasickness.

Barra del Colorado and all the area lodges are set up for one-day or multi-day fishing adventures. In addition to tarpon and snook, there's mojarra, guapote, wahoo, tuna and other tropical fresh and saltwater species.

Wildlife-viewing in the area is even better than in Tortuguero as many less people are out in the canals disturbing things. Manatees can be seen if you are persistent or lucky. The usual sloths, monkeys, tapirs, and even jaguars can be seen in the area. When time runs out, catch a flight back from the airport in Barra to San José.

Tortuguero & North Caribbean

Mosquitoes (Pinga!)

They don't call this the Mosquito Coast for nothing. If you're anywhere outdoors and out of the breeze, you'll quickly realize there are plenty of mosquitoes around day or night. They really come out strong in the early evening when the wind dies down. They congregate in the millions deep in the swamps where you'll want to go for animal and bird viewing. They will welcome you. Mosquito repellent containing around 90% DEET is a must.

In your room at night, you can try burning mosquito coils. They burn like incense and at least give you the feeling you're doing something about the problem, even if they don't work all that well.

There are more than 3,500 different species of mosquitoes in the world, and 20 more are discovered every year. Only a very few carry malaria. Malaria is rare but does occur in the far north and south. It is not considered to be a risk for visitors. If you plan on being outside a lot and staying for a month or more, you should consider a prophylactic like Chloroquine (Aralen). Don't scratch.

Beaches

Between Moín and the Nicaraguan border, there are approximately 200 km (120 miles) of beach. The only interruption is by just a few small inlets, fishing villages and secluded lodges. Leatherback, loggerhead, green and hawksbill turtles apparently feel comfortable in this remote area and thousands come to nest. Long stretches of beach are set aside as protected hatcheries with access restricted at night. Wild surf crashes almost unendingly.

Sharks, riptides and undertows make beaches generally unsafe for swimming.

The beaches are starkly beautiful, wild, hot and salty. Bring plenty of water, sunscreen, bug repellent and a hat. In this corner of the Caribbean, the currents throw up all sorts of interesting things for a sharp-eyed beachcomber to treasure. Taking hikes in the cool of the early morning is a good idea, to avoid the heavy heat of the middle of the day.

Fishing

Both Parismina and Barra del Colorado are famous for tarpon and snook, with line class records held by several visitors, guides and lodge owners. Captain **Eddie Brown** (☎ 506-383-6097, 506-382-3350) holds the IGFA record for a 66-pound snapper caught on 20-pound test. Anglers come from all over the world to pay him and other guides huge sums of money to take them fishing and show them where the big ones are. Tortuguero has plenty of lodges offering fishing as well. The two most famous and best fishing lodges on the Caribbean coast are the **Silver King Lodge** (☎ 506-381-1403) in Barra del Colorado, and the **Rio Parismina Lodge** (☎ 800-338-5688; www.riop.com) in Parismina.

Tip the fishing guides $15-$20 per day, per person.

Tarpon and snook are caught mostly in the lagoons and rivers from January to April, and move off the inlets and beaches in the fall. New offshore fisheries have been discovered around deep-water reefs, canyons and dropoffs. Billfish, dorado, tuna and wahoo are also caught. As larger boats are used, more suited to running to offshore fishing grounds, the

Tortuguero & North Caribbean

mostly unfished waters offshore should produce even more interesting reasons to fish this part of Costa Rica.

Polarized sunglasses are essential for fish spotting. Prescription polarized glasses can be bought from your optician.

The surf along the coast is almost always high. The few inlets in the inland waterway can be very dangerous to navigate due to high incoming surf meeting fast outgoing currents over the shifting sandbars at the river mouths. This limits the number of days suitable for fishing offshore. The best tarpon fishing is done when acres and acres of tarpon school up just outside the passes. They apparently line up and take numbers to gobble flies tossed at them by visiting fishermen. Surf fishing near the inlets is an exciting way to get soaking wet and battle huge tarpon, snook and sharks.

Some of the best tarpon, snook and mojara (small fish like a bluegill) fishing goes on far from the noise and chaos of the surf. Go to the tea-stained backwaters of the canals and lagoons. You need a guide and electric trolling motor to work the mangroves and river mouth swamps with spinning tackle and fly.

When to Go

- ⊚ **Snook:** Come in January, April, May, and December for the big ones off the inlets and beaches.

- ⊚ **Tarpon:** January to May in the canals and lagoons. September and October off the inlets and beaches.

- ⊚ **Sailfish:** March to June.

- ⊚ **Marlin:** Probably best February to June, but the fishery is still being explored, so who knows?

Insect Annoyances

If your ankles are eaten up by invisible little somethings while strolling around in the evening, you've probably been bitten by **no-see-ums**. These extremely tiny bugs live in the sand along the tops of beautiful tropical beaches, bringing just a touch of hell to paradise. They come out in the early evening and generally don't get more than about three feet off the ground. This is why you see so many houses in the area built up off the ground on stilts. The locals want to sleep up in the air away from the no-see-ums and snakes. Sometimes the wind blows them around a bit and they break the three-foot rule. Only very fine mesh screens can keep them out. Mosquito repellent containing a high percentage of DEET doesn't seem to do much against them. Don't scratch.

Chiggers (*coloradillas*) are small critters that lurk in lovely green lawns and tall grass. They deliver one of the itchiest of all insect bites. Eating plenty of garlic may deter them, as may sulphur tablets. This could keep away more than just chiggers, though. The bites can easily get infected in the humid tropics, so wash your itching feet and change your socks often. Don't scratch.

Tortuguero & North Caribbean

Tackle to Bring

The fishing lodges supply all the fishing tackle you need for a satisfactory trip included in the price. Lures and other expendable items are additional.

Popular lures for tarpon include CB14 Rapalas with saltwater hooks and two- to three-ounce Hot Lips jigs.

Lodge tackle shops usually have the lures of the moment on hand, in all the best colors, but the wise fisherman would check with the tour operator, or call the lodge ahead of time. Ask what the hot lures are and stock up on some before leaving for Costa Rica.

I like to have a bit of choice about what to fish with. I bring a medium bait-casting rig light enough to throw plugs on 20-pound test, and heavy enough to troll with. Ultralight rods and spinning reels are used for casting to mojarra and guapote. A number nine fly rod is versatile enough for heavy tarpon and snook or, if you're really a fly-rod enthusiast, sails and other billfish. Some lodges will supply fly-rods, but I suggest you bring your own line and leaders. Rapalas are standard baits.

Pack your rods in a shipping tube and bring your expensive reels separately in your carry-on hand luggage, if you are allowed. Call ahead to your airline and check.

If you are a fly-fisherman, call the lodge before leaving home and check on what type of equipment they have on hand and what you should bring with you.

Captain Eddy Brown Sport Fishing, in Barra del Colorado (☎ 506-383-6097, 506-382-3350, fax 506-252-4426), is owned by the most famous fishing guide on the Caribbean side of Costa Rica. Captain Eddy is the world record holder for snapper on 20-pound test line (66 pounds). He fishes from the *Bull Shark*, a well-equipped 19-foot center console with twin Yamaha four-stroke 80s.

Captain Eddy is very meticulous about releasing game fish to fight again another day.

Eddy works independently with all the lodges from Barra del Colorado to Tortuguero. His English is excellent; his boat spotless and well-organized and, since he has been guiding sport fishermen in the area for over 35 years, he knows where the fish are. Giant tarpon and snook are his specialty, but he may take you to his secret snapper hole if you ask nicely. His boat is the largest and most comfortable in the area with twin fighting chairs and a large casting deck up front for fly fishermen.

National Parks

Barra del Colorado Wildlife Refuge

Barra del Colorado National Wildlife Refuge, at 91,200 hectares, is one of the biggest and most remote national parks in Costa Rica. It runs from about seven km (four miles) north of Tortuguero village to the border with Nicaragua. The northern park boundary follows the Nicaraguan border and the Rio San Juan inland to a point east of Ceiba. The 40 km (25 miles) of beach are the park's eastern boundary.

Although there is some turtle action in Barra, the green turtles pretty much confine themselves a few miles south to Tortuguero. Wildlife includes most of the same species as in Tortuguero. Crocodiles are thick on the banks and the occasional tapir or jaguar might be seen. There is a better chance of seeing manatees here than in almost anyplace else in the Caribbean. Monkeys, pacas, caiman, sloths, and peccaries abound.

Since Barra is harder to get to than Tortuguero there are not nearly so many tourists, and there is much more wildlife. The place is filthy with anglers (myself included). It's a swampy delta with some mangroves near the coast and tropical rainforest inland. There are literally millions of tiny meandering, interlocking waterways through the dense forest. Guided tours by canoe, kayak, *panga* (a small flat-bottomed boat usually with outboard), or catamaran explore this maze to encounter some of the most interesting plant and animal life in the hemisphere.

The western areas of the park are illegally logged and squatted on by cattle ranchers and subsistence farmers. Large agro-business-owned, intense-yield banana and palm oil plantations occupy vast areas around the park. Pesticide and fertilizer runoff from these mostly unregulated agro-industries inevitably pollutes the park and surrounding area.

The park simply does not have the staff to keep the human predators at bay. It's interesting to note that directly across the Rio San Juan, Nicaragua's dense tropical forests seem thick and relatively pristine in comparison to the logging and cattle-ravaged forests on the Costa Rican side.

There is a ranger station near the Silver King lodge where you must stop and pay a 75¢ entry fee.

Tortuguero National Park

The park is 19,211-hectares on land and another 52,000 hectares of marine sanctuary. It runs 22 km (13 miles) along the coast from just north of Parismina to Tortuguero village, 30 km (18 miles) out to sea, and about 15 km (nine miles) inland. The Tortuguero River is roughly the border to the northwest and the Sierpe borders the park to the south. There is a $6 entrance fee.

It is short of personnel and the facilities are very basic. There are two official entrances. To the south near Jalova, there is a small ranger station on the canal.

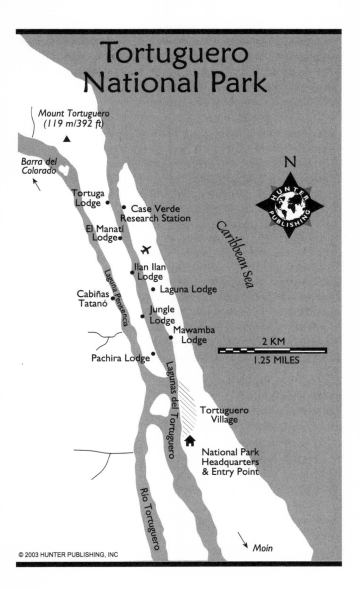

Tortuguero & North Caribbean

Cuatro Esquinas, the north entrance, is park head-quarters. It's on the canal near Tortuguero village. Officially trained and other guides are available near each station for hiking and boat tours. Entrance to the park at night is strictly limited to officially run, small guided tours.

The 22-km (13-mile) beach is the Caribbean's largest and most important green turtle breeding ground. Leatherbacks and hawksbills also nest there, but not in the quantities of the green turtles (estimated at 26,000 in 2000). Tarpon, snook, caiman, crocodiles, otters and manatees are among the stars in the water. Birds you can expect to see include kingfishers, three species of toucans, eight parrot species, hawks, herons, egrets, anhingas, cormorants, aricaris, jacanas, oropendolas, and frigate birds. Agami herons, hummingbirds or a great green macaw are only seen by the exceptionally sharp-eyed. Closer to the ground are sloths, iguanas, howler monkeys, spider monkeys, capuchin monkeys, brown-throated three-toed sloths, Hoffmann's two-toed sloths, anteaters, bats and over 100 species of reptiles. Large and small cats (ocelots, jaguars) and tapirs are there in moderate numbers, but are rarely seen.

The increasing popularity of the park for day-trips from San José means it can feel a bit crowded at times despite its size. The western side of the park is heavily encroached upon and suffers from illegal logging, poaching and cattle ranching. Squatters have cleared large areas. In most areas of the park, there is really only a thin row of jungle seen by tourists separating the canals from the deforested areas in the interior of the park.

Shop Till You Drop

This is not a strong area for shopping, but the dedicated can find hats, T-shirts, and little tops for sale in some of the lodges.

Tortuguero

SOUVENIRS PARAISO TROPICAL
☎ 506-710-0323

You can't miss the enormous, Disney-esque parrot and toucan on the lagoon in Tortuguero that announce the entrance to the Paraíso. This large souvenir store would not be out of place in a large Florida beach town. It has the largest selection of souvenirs and tourist paraphernalia on the entire Caribbean coast, and one of the best selections of clothes in the country. There are plenty of T-shirts, tops, shorts outfits and a few bathing suits and wraps. The carved creatures include the unavoidable toucans smiling broadly, small boxes and jewelry made from flotsam.

If you need to stock up on film, sunscreen, sunglasses or mosquito repellent they have a reasonable selection. There are lots of turtles made from every imaginable material. You can buy plastic blowup turtles, ceramic turtles, turtles made from stone, wood, coconuts or ceramic. They have a nice selection of maps, guidebooks and natural history tomes. You can even top off your shopping expedition with a box of Cuban cigars.

Tortuguero & North Caribbean

Barra del Colorado

There is really only one place in the village that would be of interest to visitors. The lodges all offer a selection of hats and T-shirts with the lodge logo, sunscreen and mosquito repellant.

C & D Souvenirs has a small selection of locally carved bird and animal figures. They also offer phone, fax post office services and tourist information.

After Dark

Most of the entertainment and nightlife scene is confined to individual lodges. This runs from Karaoke happy hours to lying contests about quantities and size of fish caught. For anglers, this is an important part of the total fishing lodge experience. You'll find yourself welcome if you drop in on a neighboring lodge's bar in the evening.

Bars, Discos & Nightclubs

As in most Costa Rican villages there are pulsing, shabby discos where the drinks are cheaper and the clientele perhaps more earthy.

The **Lonestar Cafe** is the bar in the Rio Parismina Lodge. Locals and visiting anglers gather in the evening happy hour to swap tall tales. In Tortuguero, check out **Bar Las Culebras** (Snake Bar), which is loud, boisterous, and fun, with cheap beer and locally brewed firewater (*guaro*).

The **Disco El Bochinche** (slang For "Street Fight")
is loud and drunks can get aggressive later in the
evening. "Disco" means dancing, right?

In Barra del Colorado, there is zilch nightlife outside
the lodges. Visitors to the bar from other lodges are
generally welcome, but be sure you have someone
sober to help you make the boat trip back to your
own place at the end of the night.

Best Places to Stay

All-inclusive fishing amd eco-lodges center in
Parismina, Tortuguero, and in Barra del Colorado. Most visitors stay in one of these places. Although most of the lodges are quite comfortable,
remember they are fishing and jungle camps. None
of the lodges in the area have air conditioning, but
all have ceiling fans, hot water and 24-hour electricity. For the most part, they are very comfortable and
the quality of the service and food can be excellent.

It is difficult to compare the lodges by price since
most, but not all, include services such as guided
fishing trips, three meals a day, and all the rum
drinks you can scarf down, in addition to a room.

All the prices are based on double occupancy during
high season, whenever possible. Taxes and meals
are not included unless so mentioned.

In general, if you go to one of the top lodges for a
week of fishing, with transportation from San José,
you're going to spend over $2,000 per person, double
occupancy. This gets you everything: lodging, meals,
drinks, dedicated guide, and boat for the two of you,
with some offshore fishing included. The inclusive
price covers everything except for any tackle you
lose, break or otherwise render unusable. But we

never lose tackle, do we? Of course, you should tip the guides separately. I find this is in line with similar fishing packages in other parts of the world.

Some guides regularly help clients pull in line-class fish that break world records.

Some of the lodges specialize in fishing or nature tours, but all of them can arrange to provide basically the same tour services. If you're serious about fishing, then choose a lodge aimed at that. Pick one of the others if you're more interested in wildlife and nature tours.

Parismina

Parismina is mainly a fishing destination and the lodges are set up to handle groups of fishermen. Non-fishing companions are well taken care of with jungle and turtle tours, and nature hikes.

RIO PARISMINA LODGE
☎ 800-338-5688 (US); fax 210-824-0151
www.riop.com
$400 per person, per day, all-inclusive fishing packages; weeklong fishing packages from $2,550

The Rio Parismina Lodge, more like a private club than a hotel, is certainly the most famous fishing lodge on the coast. It's set on the bank of the Parismina River in 50 acres (20 hectares) of tropical rainforest, and is well maintained and modern.

The lodge focuses primarily on fishing for tarpon and snook. Almost all of the visitors are mad fishermen who spend hours a day fishing and hours more at night in the bar telling lies about it. These are the guys who buy all those fishing magazines and watch the fishing shows on Saturday morning TV. (I'm one of them.) They have heard about record-breaking tarpon and snook being caught in Costa Rica (owner Judy Heidt recently set the women's 20-pound test snook IGFA world record at 49 pounds). They are willing to spend a substantial amount to fly here and experience the fishing for themselves. Many of them come back year after year.

With 11 skiffs for river fishing, and 12 center console, 21-ft. modified V-hull ocean craft, they are well equipped for comfort and safety. The ocean boats are the nicest on the coast. Tarpon up to 100 pounds and snook up to 25 pounds are caught in the lagoons and river near the lodge. Fishing in the schools just off the river mouths, weather permitting, or casting in surf up to your neck is how the big snook are caught. The biggest are almost always females and are released. Those are usually caught offshore and can run well over 125 pounds. When the big schools are feeding, double and even triple hookups are common. The fishing is simply phenomenal when conditions are right. I have fished the area and swear the stories are all true!

The rooms are the most comfortable of any lodge in the area and the food is excellent. Laundry is picked up from your room in the morning and is washed and dried by lunchtime at no extra charge. The meals, served family-style, are excellent and tend toward American dishes with pork loin, locally caught fish, pasta, chicken, beef and lots of fresh vegetables. The bar is open all day and night. The management encourages guests to feel at home enough to raid the refrigerator if they get hungry during the night. There is a pool, Jacuzzi, and happy hour every night with chips and dip or quesadillas.

Tortuguero National Park is almost next door. Activities include wildlife tours, bird-watching, beach combing, river cruises, jungle walks, and turtle excursions. Howler monkeys hang out by the dock in

Tortuguero & North Caribbean

Parismina is right in the middle of one of the finest wildlife-viewing areas in the Western Hemisphere.

the trees and jeer at the fishermen as they get ready
to set out for the day.

Tortuguero

Tortuguero is one of the best areas in Costa Rica for
wildlife viewing and all of the area lodges are focused on taking guests into the nearby Tortuguero
National Park. Fishing is excellent but not quite up
to the level of Barra del Colorado or Parismina.

TORTUGA LODGE

**BEST OF
THE BEST**

☎ 506-257-0766, 506-222-0333 (San José),
800-948-3770 (US); fax 506-257-1665
www.tortugalodge.com
$116

The lodge is aimed primarily at eco-tourism and
wildlife viewing, with fishing a definite possibility.
It's located on a strip of land along the lagoon with
all of the rooms facing the water. Trogons and monkeys run around undisturbed as they have for thousands of years. The pool is about three feet (one
meter) from the edge of the lagoon. You can lean
your chin on the rim and gaze out at the water flowing by. Herons, egrets, macaws and the occasional
toucan buzz by. The Costa Rican Air Force (brown
pelicans) conduct precision flying aerobatics overhead to the delight of the guests.

The lodge maintains an excellent nature trail, which
is a gentle 30-minute walk where guests regularly
see monkeys, sloths, caimans and dozens of bird species. Howler monkeys conduct early morning sere-
nades to the delight or annoyance of the guests.

The beautiful dining room also overlooks the lagoon
and you can eat on a deck over the water. Food is
served at long tables, family-style, giving guests a

chance to meet each other and swap tales of monkeys seen, snakes screamed about and birds marveled at. The chow is well prepared, based on local recipes, and includes steaks, shrimp, fish, rice and beans and enormous bowls of vegetables cooked in interesting ways. They will cook your snook if you bring them back from river fishing trips. Breakfast is available for a couple hours in the morning. It includes gallo pinto, granola, fruit and eggs cooked to your specifications. Coffee is always on.

The owners pride themselves on an environmentally appropriate approach to the local community. They vigorously practice conservation running the hotel and restaurant. Most of their tour boats use quiet, electric motors when back in the canals and small river tributaries.

Tortuga Lodge is the best place to base yourself in Tortuguero for big-time tarpon and snook fishing. They work mostly with world-famous fishing guide Eddy Brown (see page 424), arranging full-day and half-day packages for fishing in the rivers and lagoons and near shore outside the river mouth.

This is the nicest lodge in the area with large rooms and good service. It is run by Costa Rica Expeditions.

JUNGLE LODGE HOTEL
☎ 506-233-0133; fax 506-233-0778
www.grupopapagayo.com
$150

Jungle Lodge, with 50 modern rooms, is set back from the river. They offer one- to three-day packages, which include wild life tours, jungle tours, fishing, ecological tours, happy hour, and all meals included. There is a swimming pool and game room. The lodge caters mostly to Europeans with an emphasis on birding. The lodge is 21 years old and is in need of maintenance. The rooms are basic and a bit on the small side.

☆ LAGUNA LODGE

☎ 506-225-3740, 506-280-7843; fax 506-283-8031
www.lagunalodgetortuguero.com
$180, inclusive

This lodge feels cozy, with just 52 rooms on 14 acres (5.6 hectares). Activity is aimed at enjoying the nearby Tortuguero National Park. Fishing and nature tours are offered. Somehow escaping the normal jungle lodge architecture, the lodge seems to be entirely made from driftwood. Scavenged beach woods are imaginatively used to made railings, tables, chairs, walls, ceilings, light fixtures. Almost the whole place has been built from beautiful wood that otherwise would have gone to waste. When I was there in mid-2002, a new, surreal reception area was just being completed that seemed like something Gaudi would have dreamed up had he worked in Tortuguero instead of Barcelona.

The restaurant and bar hang over the river. The deck and railings seem to be an extension of the jungle itself with roots sprouting from the bottom of the rail posts and tables weirdly bumpy made from driftwood. The whole lodge has character aplenty. Food, as in the other nearby lodges, is served buffet-style and leans toward typical Costa Rican dishes, featuring fresh vegetables, beef and seafood.

The neat and clean rooms are comfortable, with ceiling fans and hot water, and are steps away from the beachfront. The beach itself seems shallower than in other nearby areas. Although dangerous currents are warned about, guests can enjoy an ocean dip.

MAWAMBA LODGE
☎ 506-223-2421; fax 506-222-5463
www.grupomawamba.com
$295, inclusive

This is a modern lodge aimed at the wildlife-viewing crowd. It's located between the lagoon and the beach on 100 acres (40 hectares), and has 40 rooms, bar, pool, and large conference room. They offer daily lectures on Costa Rica's ecology and wildlife, tours to the canals of the National Park, turtle nesting sojourns, bird-watching and fishing.

The rooms are basic, but comfortable, with ceiling fans and hot water. The grounds front on the beach, but it is littered with logs and other flotsam. The lodge does not allow swimming due to wild waves, dangerous currents and bull sharks, but the pool is delightful. The lodge operates a red-eyed tree frog project. They carefully collect egg sacs deposited during the night on vegetation around the pool, hatch them, raise the tadpoles to maturity, and transfer them into nearby ponds. This does not interfere with enjoyment of the pool. The only way you would know this is going on is from observing the tanks full of frogs in various stages of development arranged by the bar.

The restaurant and game room are large thatched structures near the river. Food is served buffet-style, featuring local recipes of rice and beans, vegetables, and seafood. The lodge maintains a large fleet of boats for bringing guests to and from the lodge, and on ecology tours at the national park.

Grupo Mawamba operates several large boats based at the lodge which bring cruise ship passengers from Limón on day-trips through the park. Turtle viewing is carefully restricted to small groups, with no flashlights and no flash photography to disturb the nesting turtles. Mawamba has the largest fleet of boats in the area which are nicely equipped with electric motors for silent enjoyment of the park.

☆ PACHIRA LODGE
☎ 506-256-7080; fax 506-223-1119
www.pachiralodge.com
$160, inclusive

This new lodge, on 575 acres (230 hectares), has 34 rooms and is set right on the river. It focuses on all-inclusive wildlife viewing packages, with three-day, two-night, all-inclusive specials. Rooms, meals, nature tours and transportation to and from San José are all part of the deal. Pachira Lodge is owned by a Costa Rican woman who has taken great pride in making the lodge and its grounds attractive and comfortable. There are no sidewalks at Pachira. Instead, lily-pad-like stepping-stones wind around the grounds and form patios under the tropical trees by the pool and river.

Most of the area lodges have nice pools but the one at Pachira takes the cake. The pool is very large and is in the shape of a turtle. Turtle eggs form stepping stones through the water at the base of the pool. They also have a Jacuzzi if you feel the need for a soak after a hike up nearby Cerro Tortuguero.

The restaurant is arranged for large buffets. When I was there it had one of the largest cut flower arrangements I've ever seen. The collection of birds of paradise, heliconias and other tropical flowers towered some 15 feet toward the thatched ceiling and spread out at least 12 feet along the back wall. It is renewed every few days. The food is excellent, with emphasis on fresh vegetables.

The rooms are arranged back from the river in small groups and have ceiling fans and hot water. Service is snappy and professional.

Barra del Colorado

Barra del Colorado is mainly a fishing destination and the lodges are set up to handle groups of fishermen. Non-fishing companions are well taken care of with jungle and crocodile tours and nature hikes. Barra del Colorado is one of the very best areas in Central America for wildlife viewing.

☆ CASA MAR
Barra del Colorado
☎ 506-433-9287, 506-433-8834; fax 506-433-9237
www.casamarlodge.com
$1,125 per person for three days and three nights, including meals and fishing

Casa Mar has 12 cabins and a main lodge set in eight tropical acres. It faces the lagoon, and the grounds are filled with fruit, native flowers and wild birds. Each cabin has twin beds with private bathroom and shower. It is really an old-time fishing lodge in the true sense. Casa Mar is very comfortable and well-equipped, but is strictly fishing oriented. Owner Bill Barnes is a delightful person. He'll tell you stories of interesting guests who have stayed at his lodge over the last 40 years, including famous fly-fisherman Lefty Kreh, Hank Williams Junior and Martin Milner (star of television show Adam 12). The place has an outdoorsman flavor provided in part by black-and-tan coonhound Elvis (he comes from Tennessee and sings a lot). Pineapple plants line the sidewalk through the well-kept grounds.

The food is home-cooking, buffet-style, and tends toward American specialties, with a few local dishes. Expect homegrown pineapple, breadfruit, bananas, papaya, mango, oranges, guanabana, coconut and other fruits in season. An open bar is part of the deal.

There is a well-equipped tackle shop. The lodge has 20 17-foot wide-beamed boats with new 25-horsepower motors. The aluminum boats have a casting deck. The guides are some of the best in the area (including the famous Eddie Brown in the Bull Shark center consol, twin outboard. They are knowledgeable in spinning, casting and fly-fishing techniques. The lodge hosts an annual private tarpon tournament to raise funds for the local Barra del Colorado Medical Center. Fly-fishing fundamentals classes are offered. The lodge is home to several world-record catches, including a women's 40-pound jack crevalle on 20-pound test. Hardcore fishermen can spend hours gazing at decades of photos on the walls featuring some of the biggest fish you'll ever hope to catch. This is a nice spot with a good feel about it, but you'd better be in the mood to fish if you come here.

RIO COLORADO LODGE
☎ 506-232-4063, 506-231-5987, fax 506-231-5987
In US, 800-243-9777
www.riocoloradolodge.com
$380, per person, per day, all-inclusive fishing package

Ask about Rio's inclusive summer rate of $280 per person, per day, including tax.

Rió Colorado, founded 30 years ago, is a world-renowned fishing lodge, and almost all the guests come looking for huge tarpon and snook. The lodge has slowly grown from one small building, with guest rooms separated by curtains, and meals prepared by a local woman and handed over the fence, to its present 18 rooms, clubhouse and bar. It is a basic fishing lodge, but comfortable. They have the only air-conditioned rooms in the area and some have TV. There is a large bar lined with the inevitable pictures of guests and celebrities holding up huge fish. A meeting room capable of hosting 30 people lures in small corporate groups and special fishing instruction seminars. The whole complex is built on stilts and the rooms are open to the night breeze from the Caribbean.

Commandante Zero Memorial Jacuzzi is dedicated to the famous guerilla leader who lived at the lodge during the Nicaraguan conflict and used it regularly.

Although there are interesting things for non-fishing companions to do (jungle tour, croc tour), this is really a place for serious fishermen. Many records have been set by guests at the lodge, including the Costa Rica all tackle record for tarpon (207 pounds). The all tackle world record for machaca was caught off the dock using a banana for bait.

Meals are served family-style. The recreation room has game tables and the video room features satellite TV. They have a well-stocked tackle shop and a zoo full of monkeys and tropical birds. Happy hour is from 5 pm to 6:30 pm, when all rum drinks and soft drinks are on the house. That's pretty happy.

SAMAY LAGOON LODGE
☎ 506-284-7047; fax 506-383-6370
www.samay.com
$450, all-inclusive meals, transportation from San José, and one day fishing

German-owned Samay Lagoon Lodge is a bit south from the other Barra del Colorado lodges. It's not strictly a fishing lodge, but can arrange budget fishing trips. Their main activities are riverboat tours, lagoon canoeing and jungle hiking. There are 22 basic rooms with ceiling fans, private baths, local guides for both nature tours and boat excursions. Fiberglass boats and canoes are available. This is the only budget-oriented lodge in the area, but is in need of maintenance.

Tortuguero & North Caribbean

SILVER KING LODGE

BEST OF THE BEST

Barra del Colorado near the airport
☎ 506-381-1403, fax 506-381-0849; In US, ☎ 800-847-3474; beeper, 506-296-3636
www.silverkinglodge.com
$435, per person, per day, inclusive fishing packages. Five-day packages include all lodging and transportation in Costa Rica, fishing, food and drinks.
Closed June 1-Sept. 1, and Dec. 1-Jan. 1.

This is a small 10-room, lagoon-front lodge, and by far the best destination for fishing on the coast. It's very comfortable and the service is among the best I've experienced anywhere in Costa Rica. The food is absolutely wonderful. Fishing packages are all-inclusive, with home-cooked meals and an open bar. They have a large Jacuzzi, pool with waterfall, canoes and ecological tours for non-fishing companions.

Americans Ray and Shawn Feliciano built and run the lodge, which has aquired the reputation over eight years as being the best place to catch gigantic tarpon and enormous snook anywhere in the world.

Shawn's mother Zeta is head chef and lays out a staggering buffet three times a day. It includes items such as biscuits, sausage and gravy, pancakes, chicken cordon-bleu, snook chowder, filet mignon stuffed with langostino, osso bucco, blueberry cobbler, mango pie, homemade ice creams, along with wine and after-dinner drinks. One guest told me the food was "the best I've ever had without going to grandma's house." This is not an exaggeration – the food is absolutely brilliant.

Yvonne, the bartender, greets guests at the dock as they step off the boat with a broad grin and inventive fruit drinks or ice-cold beer. Service here is unusually good. Drinks and snacks are brought to the pool, Jacuzzi or to your room.

Doors are held open for you. Your dirty clothes are picked up off the floor and brought back washed and folded (no extra charge, no need to ask). Every night, a few minutes after I retired to my room, Yvonne showed up with a pitcher of ice water saying, "I thought you might like some cold water. Have a nice night."

The lodge has 10, 23-foot-deep V-hull, unsinkable fiberglass boats, with ship to shore radios and fish finders for coastal fishing. They also have a variety of other boats for fishing offshore or ultralight fishing in the lagoons. They are fully equipped for fly-fishermen and the guides are experienced fly-fishermen themselves. Several enthusiastically tie their own flies. They also have offshore boats with twin motors, radar, fish finder, charter, plotter, GPS, autopilot, outriggers, downriggers, Penn International reels and more.

In four days of fishing in 2002, I battled 12 tarpon and brought four to the boat for a quick photo before releasing them. One was estimated at over 125 pounds. I boated three snook in a morning's fishing. One was 18 pounds. I also caught dozens of jack crevalle in the 20-pound range, and a variety of other tropical, freshwater species, including mojarra and machaca.

When not fishing, guests can go on a variety of guided or unguided tours. You can use the lodge's canoes, or go in launches with sunshades designed for getting back into narrow creeks off the main lagoon channels. Monkeys, sloths, nutrias and iguanas are common sightings. Guides told me they have seen jaguars swimming across the river on several occasions.

Tortuguero & North Caribbean

Best Places to Eat

Most lodges work on the all-inclusive package system, so there really isn't much choice of restaurants. The freshness of the ingredients, especially the seafood, more than makes up for the lack of fancy French sauces. Expect memorable dining, with fresh fish, natural flavors and simplicity of preparation. Fish doesn't get much fresher than in the dining rooms of the fishing lodges. Do not expect linen napkins and crystal wine glasses. The few restaurants outside the lodges are very moderately priced.

You should plan to eat in your lodge, but if you have to eat in Parismina, you can fill your belly at **Bar Y Cabinas Madre De Dios**. The bar gets lively in the evenings with occasional guitar sessions from locals and visitors. It's right in the middle of the village. Food is on offer.

The lodges surrounding Tortuguero are where most visitors eat but there are a couple of other places to eat of interest. Try **Miss Junie's**. You may have to arrange for meals in advance but the place is legendary for special, Costa Rican-style meals.

Panqueque Restaurant is very friendly and has great food. The **Vine Coffee House**, in the middle of the village, serves good coffee, sandwiches and snacks.

Other than eating in one of the lodges, there is really no choice in Barra. There are a couple of pulperías and in Barra del Sur, there is a soda store and a small restaurant.

A to Z

Banks

There are no banks in the area whatsoever. Few of the local establishments will take credit cards. Most of the lodges are all-inclusive deals and are usually paid for in advance. Lodges may take credit cards, or be able to change small amounts of currency, but don't count on it.

Emergency Medical

Call ☎ 911 in all areas.

In **Parismina**, ask at the pulpería for the *medico*.

In **Tortuguero**, there's a small medical center in the middle of town.

Police

Call ☎ 911 in all areas.

There is no police station in **Parismina**. Calls go to Limón, ☎ 911.

In **Tortuguero**, the police station is in the middle of town.

In **Barra del Colorado**, at the small dock by the airport, there is a small police station staffed periodically.

Post Office

If you must, have your hotel mail things for you. However, the postal service is slow and unreliable. Tiocs usually use faxes and couriers.

In **Barra del Colorado**, you can get post office services at **C & D Souvenirs**, ☎ 506-710-6592, in the middle of the village.

Tourist Information

NATURAL HISTORY VISITORS CENTER
Run by the CCC, open Monday-Friday, 10 am-noon and 2 pm-5:30 pm; and 2 pm-5 pm on Sunday.

TORTUGUERO INFORMATION CENTER
Near the Catholic Church

C & D SOUVENIRS
☎ 506-710-6592
Located on the airport side of the estuary.

Appendix

Spanish Vocabulary

Days of the Week

Sunday . . . . domingo
Monday . . . . lunes
Tuesday . . . . martes
Wednesday . . . . miercoles
Thursday . . . . jueves
Friday . . . . viernes
Saturday . . . . sabado

Months of the Year

January . . . . enero
February . . . . febrero
March . . . . marzo
April . . . . abril
May . . . . mayo
June . . . . junio
July . . . . julio
August . . . . agosto
September . . . . septiembre
October . . . . octubre
November . . . . noviembre
December . . . . diciembre

Numbers

one . . . . uno
two . . . . dos
three . . . . tres
four . . . . cuatro
five . . . . cinco
six . . . . seis
seven . . . . siete
eight . . . . ocho

nine .... nueve
ten .... diez
eleven .... once
twelve .... doce
thirteen .... trece
fourteen .... catorce
fifteen .... quince
sixteen .... dieciséis
seventeen .... diecisiete
eighteen .... dieciocho
nineteen .... diecinueve
twenty .... veinte
twenty-one .... vientiuno
twenty-two .... vientidos
thirty..................................... treinta
forty...................................... cuarenta
fifty....................................... cincuenta
sixty...................................... sesenta
seventy................................... setenta
eighty .... ochenta
ninety .... noventa
one hundred .... ciento
one hundred and one...................... ciento uno
five hundred .... quinientos
one thousand .... mil
one thousand and one .... mil uno
two thousand .... dos mil
one million .... un millón
one billion .... mil millones
first .... primero
second.................................... segundo
third .... tercero
last....................................... último

Conversation

How are you? .... ¿Como esta usted?
Well, thanks. And you? .... Bien, gracias. ¿Y usted?
Good morning. .... Buenas dias.
Good afternoon.. .... Buenas tardas.
Good evening/night.................. Buenas noches.
Goodbye. .... Adios.
Glad to meet you............. Mucho gusto de conocerle.

Thank you. . . . . Gracias.
Please. . . . . Por favor.
You're welcome.. . . . . De nada/con mucho gusto.
Pardon me. . . . . Perdoneme.
I'm sorry. . . . . Lo siento.
What is your name? . . . . ¿Como se llama usted?
My name is... . . . . Me llamo...
I don't know. . . . . No se.
I'm thirsty. . . . . Tengo sed.
I'm hungry. . . . . Tengo hambre.
I'm an American.. . . . . Soy norteamericano/a.
Where can I find...? . . . . ¿Donde puedo encontar...?
What is this?. . . . . ¿Que es esto?
Do you speak English?. . . . . ¿Habla usted ingles?
I speak/understand . . . . Hablo/entiendo un poco
... a little Spanish. . . . . Español.
Is there anyone . . . . ¿Hay alguien aqui que
here who speaks English?   habla ingles?
I don't understand. No entiendo.
Please repeat. . . . . Repita por favor.

Telling Time

What time is it? . . . . ¿Que hora es?
It's.... . . . . Son las...
... five o'clock . . . .cinco.
... ten past eight . . . . ocho y diez.
... quarter past six . . . . seis y cuarto.
... half past five . . . . cinco y media.
Last night. . . . . Anoche.
This morning. . . . . Esta mañana.
At noon.. . . . . A mediodia.
In the evening. . . . . En la noche.
At night. . . . . De noche.
At midnight . . . . A medianoche.
Tomorrow . . . . Mañana.

Directions

Which way is...? . . . . ¿En que direccíon queda...?
Take me to... please. . . . . Lleveme a... por favor.
Turn right. . . . . De vuelta a la derecha.
Turn left. . . . . De vuelta a la isquierda.

How far is it to...? . . . . ¿A que distancia estamos de...?
Is this the road to...? . . . . ¿Es este el camino a...?
Is it... . . . . ¿Es...
... near? . . . . cerca?
... far? . . . . lejos?
... north? . . . . norte?
... south? . . . . sur?
... east? . . . . este?
... west? . . . . oeste?
Please point. . . . . Indiqueme por favor.
Please direct me to... . . . . Hagame favor de decirme
donde esta...
... a telephone . . . . el telephono.
... a bathroom. . . . . el excusado.
... a post office . . . . el correo.
... a bank . . . . el banco.
... a police station . . . . la comisaria.

Accommodations

Where is a hotel, pension? . . . . ¿Donde hay hotel/pensión?
I'm looking for a hotel that's... . Estoy buscando un hotel...
... good. . . . . bueno.
... cheap. . . . . barato.
... nearby. . . . . cercano.
... clean.. . . . . limpio.
Do you have available rooms? . . . ¿Hay habitaciones libres?
Where are the bathrooms? . . . . . . ¿Donde están los baños?
I would like a.... . . . . Quisiera un...
... single room. . . . . cuarto sencillo.
... room with a bath. . . . . cuarto con baño.
... double room. . . . . cuarto doble.
May I see it?. . . . . ¿Puedo verlo?
What's the cost?. . . . . ¿Cuanto cuesta?
It's too expensive! . . . . ¡Es demasiado caro!

Ticoisms, Slang (dicharachos) & Useful Localisms

Águila . . . . slang name for the local beer
(It actually means eagle – the bottle has an eagle on it.)

Aguacero . . . . small, intense rainstorm
Alcoholemia . . . . breathalyzer test
Apartotel . . . . Apartment-type hotel
(usually furnished with kitchen facilities)
Beneficio . . . . coffee factory
Boca . . . . appetizer or bar snack
Bomba . . . . gas station
Boyero . . . . oxcart driver
Buena nota . . . . OK, great
Cacuyo . . . . dugout canoe
Carreta . . . . traditional wooden, ox-drawn carts
Cedula . . . . national identity card
Chapulines . . . . youth gangs
Chepe . . . . San José (local slang)
Chorizo . . . . bribe
¡Que chuso! . . . . How cool!
¿Cómo amaneció? . . . . How did you wake up?
(used as "How are you?")
Dando cuerva . . . . making eyes, flirting
¿Diay? . . . . oh well, what can you do?
Duendes . . . . Legendary elf-like men who
live in the forest and cut off the thumbs of the unwary
(they have no thumbs themselves but want them).
Fauna silvestre . . . . wildlife
Gringo . . . . North American (not derogatory)
Guaro . . . . local cane liquor
Hora Americana . . . . punctual
Hora tica . . . . not punctual
Indígena . . . . native inhabitant
Mae . . . . Man, dude (Man! What a bad trip that was!)
Maje . . . . buddy, pal, close friend (literally, dummy)
Marías . . . . taxi meter
Mota . . . . marijuana, cannabis
¡Porta mí! . . . . I don't care!
Precarista . . . . squatter
Prenda la maría por favor . . . . Start the meter, please
Pulpería . . . . grocery store or local shop
Pura vida . . . . . . cool, far out, also used to greet someone
Quedar bien . . . . to leave a good impression
Rojo, un . . . . 1,000 colónes
Sabanero . . . . cowboy
Salado . . . . too bad, tough luck
Sendero . . . . nature trail

Soda . . . . restaurant or café (does not serve alcohol)
Tico(a). . . . . Costa Rican
(this is what they call themselves and is perfectly polite to
use).
Tuanis . . . . cool, far out
Tucán, un . . . . 5,000 colónes
Turgio . . . . slum
¿Upe! . . . . Is anyone home? (rural use)

Recipes: Tico Specialties

GALLO PINTO (Spotted Rooster)

Breakfast is not breakfast in Costa Rica without gallo pinto. Basically, it's a dirty rice liberally sprinkled with black beans.

To prepare it you need three cups of cooked white rice left over from last night's dinner and one cup of cooked black beans from the same source.

Heat corn oil in a frying pan and sauté just a few onions and some garlic. Add cilantro and a little salt and pepper, then throw in the rice and beans. Include a small portion of juice from the bean pot. Stir for just a few minutes until the whole mixture is hot. Serve with Tabasco or Lizano sauce, if you have any.

BARRA DEL COLORADO MANGO PIE

This is prepared like an apple pie, but without so much sugar. Mangoes are naturally a little sweeter than pie apples. It is best made with green, just starting to get ripe, mangos. Peel and slice enough mangos to fill a large piecrust, just as you would apples.

Mix two tablespoons of flour and a half-cup of sugar into the sliced mangos and pour everything into an unbaked piecrust. There should be a bit of juicy slurry. Squeeze lime juice over the pie. Dot the pie with butter and, if you want to get fancy, sprinkle just a touch of nutmeg, cinnamon, or ginger over the pie before placing the top crust on.

Bake at 350° for about 30 minutes but, while baking, keep an eye on the crust for browning. Take the pie out quickly if it looks like it might be getting over-done. Garnish with mint when serving.

SILVER KING MANGO SOUFFLÉ

This is a side dish – not a dessert.

2½ cups crushed mango
3 eggs, beaten
¼ cup sugar
1½ tablespoons butter, melted
3 tablespoons flour
4 teaspoons lemon juice
Pinch of salt

Place all ingredients in a bowl and mix well. Spoon into a greased soufflé dish and bake at 350°F for 45 minutes to one hour, or until it has the consistency of soft pudding. You can also use pineapple or a combination of mango and pineapple.

Information Sources

Publications

Hunter Publishing's **Adventure Guide to Costa Rica, 4th Edition**, by Bruce and June Conord (recently revised) is another up-to-date, complete, thick and meaty travel guide.

An Annotated Checklist of the Birds of Monteverde and Peñas Blancas, Michael Fogden, 1993.

Costa Rica: A Traveler's Literary Companion, Barbara Ras, Consortium Book Sales, 1994.

Costa Rica: Land of Volcanoes, Guillermo Alvarado

Costa Rican Natural History, Daniel Janzen, University of Chicago, 1983.

The Geography of Costa Rica, Miguel Obregón

A Guide to the Birds of Costa Rica, Gary Stiles and Alexander Skutch, Cornell University Press, 1990.

La Loca de Grandoca, Ana Cristina Rossi

The National Parks of Costa Rica, Mario Boza

Neo Tropical Companion, Turtle Bogue, Harry LeFever, Susquehanna University Press.

The Windward Road: Adventures of a Naturalist on Remote Caribbean Shores, Archie Carr, University Press of Florida, 1979.

The Sea Turtle: So Excellent a Fishe, by Archie Carr, Scribner, 1984.

Websites

The Web has a wealth of sites with tourist and research information about traveling in Costa Rica. Here are some recommendations:

Costa Rica Tourism Board (ICT): provides general background information, www.tourism-costa-rica.com; e-mail tourism@tourissm.co.cr

La Nacion: the countrty's leading newspaper, with an English section. www.nacion.co.cr.

Tico Times: Costa Rica's English newspaper, www.ticotimes.net

Costa Rica Discover: travel service from hotel and car reservations to customized tours. www.costaricadiscover.com; e-mail office@latindiscover.com.

Costa Rica Chamber of Tourism: www.costarica.tourism.co.cr; e-mail info@tourism.co.cr.

Others to try:

www.info.costarica.com
www.costaricaweb.com
www.costarica.com
www.costaricatravelfishing.com
www.costaricadiscovery.com
www.costaricasportfishing.com
www.tortuguero.com
www.costaricaoutdoors.com

Online in Costa Rica

Dial-up Services

RADIOGRAFICA COSTARRICENSE (RACSA)
Calle 1, Avenida 5, San José
☎ 506-287-0087, 506-287-0515
mercadeo@sol.racsa.co.cr
$20/month

Dial-up services, hosting, email.

TICONET
ICE building in San Pedro
☎ 506-280-0932
mercadeo@tr.ticonet.co.cr

Dial-up services, hosting, e-mail.

Internet Cafés

Most medium-size towns sport one or two Internet cafés. I found friendly, reasonably modern facilities in some surprisingly funky areas. Connections are usually fast (not dial-up), and rates around $5/hour.

BROWSERS
Plaza Colonial Shopping Center in Escazú
Open Monday-Saturday, 9am-8 pm.

CYBER CAFÉ LAS ARCADAS
In the Las Arcadas Building, near the National Theater, San José
Open Monday-Friday, 7 am-11 pm; weekends 7-7.

Y2K NET CAFE COSTA RICA
Just east of Universidad Latina in San Pedro, San José
☎ 506-283-4829

Index

Index